A Shtetl under the Sun

Jeannette van Ditzhuijzen

A SHTETL UNDER THE SUN The Ashkenazic Community of Curaçao

KIT Publishers – Amsterdam

Contents

Foreword	7
Prologue	11
Part I: How it all started	13
1 The Sephardic and Ashkenazic Jews of Curaçao	14
2 Flight from the Eastern European Shtetl	20
Part II: The Pioneering Years of the 1920s and 1930s	37
3 Arrival on an Unknown Island	38
4 Working Hard to Earn a Living	53
5 The Newcomers – Better Off Without Them	68
6 Living Like a Jew as Much as Possible	75
Part III – The Second World War	85
7 Jewish Refugees Interned on the Islands	86
8 Daily Life During the War Years	93
Part IV – The Second Half of the 20th Century	103
9 The Ashkenazic Community Expands	104
10 The Rise and Fall of Social Life	116
11 Their Own Shiel and the Old Traditions	130
12 A Jewish School and Other Jewish Education	145
13 Doing Business in Good and Bad Times	157
14 The Community Becomes Smaller and More Orthodox	174
Part V – Relations Outside the Jewish Community	189
15 Contacts with the Jews on Other Islands	190
16 The Relationship with the Sephardim and Mikvé Israel-Emanuel	198
17 From *Polakos* to Curaçao Islanders?	210
Epilogue	228
Notes	231
Jewish definitions	236
Sources	238
Bibliography	239
Index	241

Foreword

Much is known about the Jews of Curaçao. That is to say, much is known about the Sephardic Jews that came to Curaçao from Spain and Portugal via the Netherlands in the 17th century. But Curaçao is also home to a second group of Jews, the Ashkenazim or Eastern European Jews. They emigrated to Curaçao starting in 1926 and, in a short span of time, created a thriving community for themselves on the island. Little information can be found about this latter-day group. And that is a pity, because, even though only a little more than one hundred Ashkenazim live on the island today, they are a substantial part of Curaçao's history.

Due to the lack of written information about the Ashkenazim, the memories and stories of the immigrants themselves have become crucial. The task of writing these memories and stories down has had a particular urgency because many of the first and second generation Ashkenazim have died or are very old. In order to learn about this history, I began in 2008 to interview the older members of the Ashkenazic community with the support of the *Joods Historisch Museum* (Jewish Historical Museum) in Amsterdam and the *Fonds voor Bijzondere Journalistieke Projecten* (Fund for Special Journalistic Projects). These people had come to Curaçao as children and often could still recall certain details about that time: what was it like to travel from Eastern Europe to Curaçao; with whom did they and their parents associate; where did they live at first and how did their parents make a living?

Next I talked to a large number of Ashkenazic Jews from the subsequent generations (sometimes by telephone or via e-mail). They were often able to provide very detailed information about the lives of their parents, who had been born in Eastern Europe. They also talked about their own memories. I spoke to other inhabitants of Curaçao as well, including Sephardic Jews, and to Ashkenazic Jews who had lived on Curaçao temporarily. For a complete list of the people interviewed, please consult the list of sources at the end of this book.

Each person interviewed provided at least one, but usually many pieces of the puzzle that were necessary to create a picture of the history of the Curaçao Ashkenazim. I was able to flesh these out with snippets of information gathered from archives and various books. The collection of bulletins distributed by the Jewish congregations on the island I found in the Mongui Maduro Library on Curaçao were particularly helpful for placing the oral information I gathered in a chronological and more factual context.

The result is a book from, for and about the Curaçao Ashkenazic Jews. Without their cooperation, their memories and the time they took to dig up details, without the searches they made for old photographs and documents, this stirring history would never have been recorded for future generations.

JEANNETTE VAN DITZHUIJZEN
Almelo, 11 September 2009

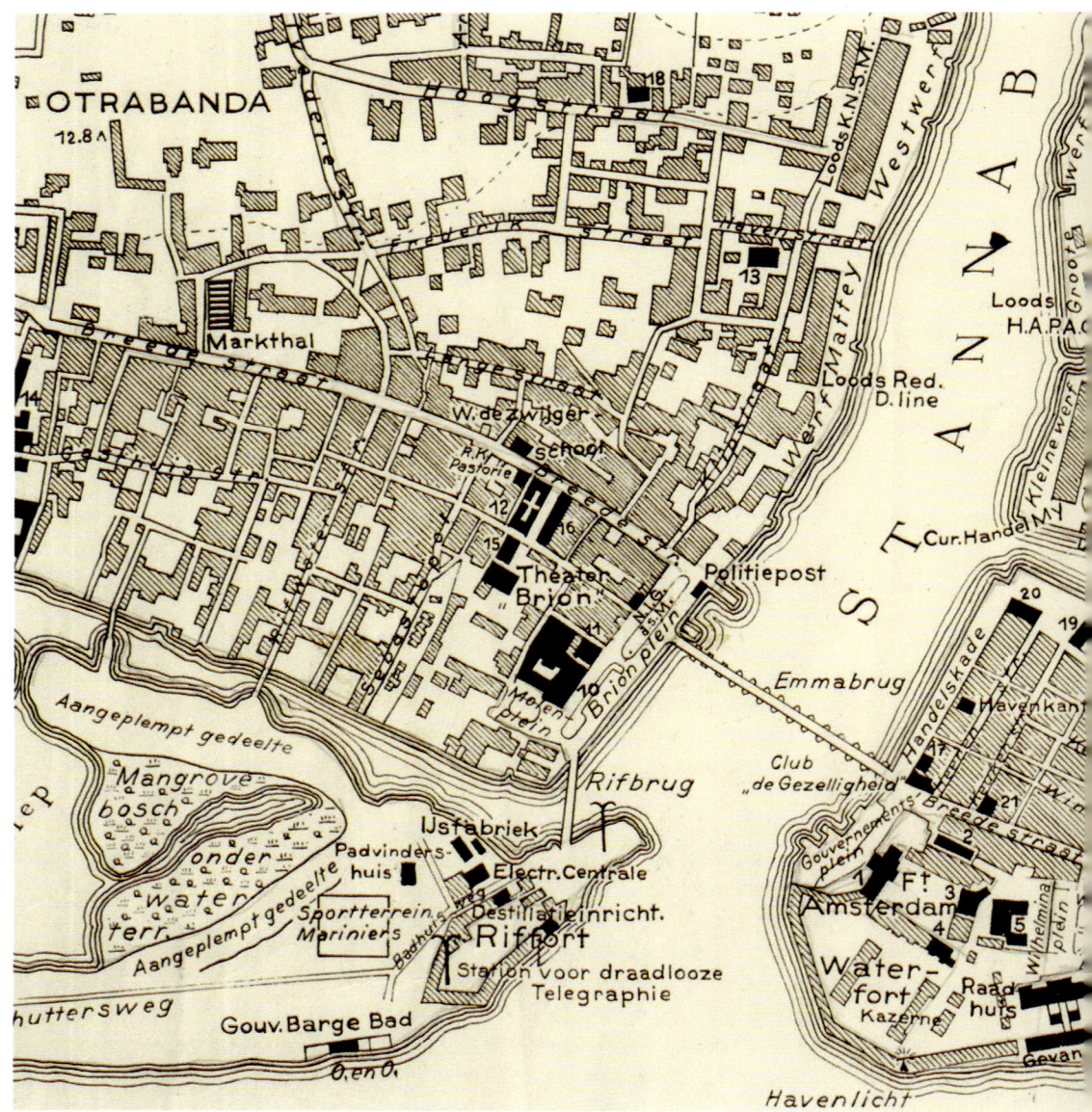

Map of Willemstad from 1934, published by R.K. Boekhandel St. Augustinus. The scale of the original map is 1:4.000, the size 35 by 52 cm. (Source: Koninklijk Instituut voor de Tropen [Royal Institute for the Tropics] Library number: KK 109-04-09)

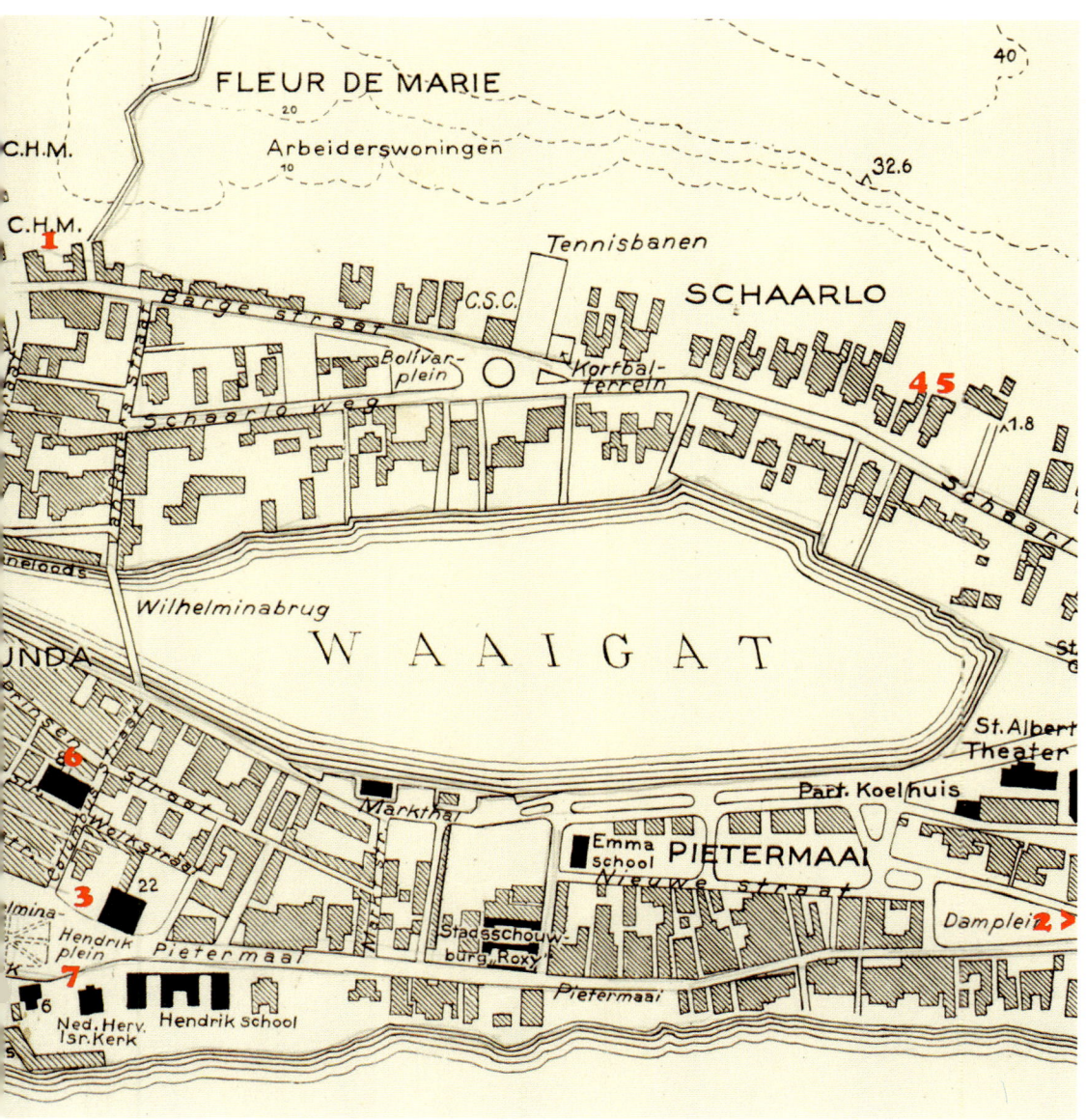

Legend:
1. Synagogue on the Bargestraat (1930-1949)
2. Club Union on the Penstraat (1934)
3. Club Union at Hendrikplein 3 (1940-1949)
4. Synagogue at Scharlooweg 39 (ca. 1955-1986)
5. Club Union at Scharlooweg 41 (1949-1982)
6. Mikvé Israel Synagogue (snoa, since 1732)
7. Temple Emanu-El (1867-1964)

Prologue

America. That is where Eastern European Jews wanted to go. Not only for a better economic life and to escape widespread poverty after the First World War, but also to get away from the restrictive measures that made the lives of Jews in Eastern Europe increasingly unpleasant. They were no longer allowed to practice certain professions and their children faced restrictions on being admitted to schools and universities. So they wanted to go to America, the land of freedom. North or South America, it didn't really matter, many of them did not even know the difference between the two continents.

So they embarked on a journey to the Americas, getting off their ship at Curaçao, Trinidad, Venezuela or Colombia. Due to the 1924 quota restrictions admittance to the United States was out of the question. Under these restrictions, only a limited number of immigrants from each European country could enter the United States.[1]

In 1926 Moishe Seibald, from the Polish city of Sniatyn, became the very first Eastern European Jew to arrive on Curaçao. Other Jews from Sniatyn and the surrounding area soon followed in his wake. In the years to follow, countless Jews left Eastern Europe hoping to earn a lot of money very quickly. Hersch Leizer Cheis, for example, left the Romanian city of Herța after his uncles wrote from America that one could become rich there in just a couple of years. He left Europe in 1930 with some ten other men from Herța and discovered soon after his arrival that he had not landed in North, but in South America, i.e. on Curaçao. His daughter Dora Suchar-Cheis: "They thought they were going to New York. When they landed, they didn't know where they were."

Other Eastern European Jews also accidentally ended up on Curaçao. As early as the 1920s, increasing numbers of ships stopped to refuel on Curaçao, where the Shell oil refinery[2] – officially opened in 1918 – was undergoing further expansion. Such was the case with the ship on which Isaac Gerstenbluth traveled. He was a grain merchant from the Polish city of Chorostków. In 1930 he was returning from Costa Rica after trying to sell soya there, but the cargo had spoiled due to lack of refrigeration. When his ship refueled on Curaçao, Gerstenbluth walked into the center of Punda. There he saw various Jewish inscriptions and even ran into a Polish friend he had not seen in years: Moses Leib Altnaj, who had come to Curaçao via Cuba. He persuaded Gerstenbluth to stay on the island and set up a store.

Leib Zonenschain from Romania settled on Curaçao in a similar manner. He and his brother-in-law had set foot on the island back in 1927 when their ship had stopped to refuel. Once on land, Leib ran into Jewish friends from his home city of Noua Suliță and decided to remain on the island.[3] He was able to find work at Shell and there were fellow countrymen, Jews no less, to welcome him. What more could he ask for?

This scenario played out for many others. Those that had remained in the old country, in far-off Poland or Romania, became aware of the good fortunes of a certain family that received goods and money from Curaçao. This convinced the next family to leave the homeland and try their luck in the New World. This is why most Eastern European Jews on Curaçao come from the same region: Bukovina, especially from Czernowitz, and Bessarabia, especially from Noua Suliță, in what was Romania at the time, and then Polish Galicia, especially Sniatyn (see Chapter 2).

On arriving in Curaçao, the new immigrants trod their individual paths, often starting out as peddlers. With their families by their side, they worked so hard that they succeeded in becoming reputable merchants and storekeepers in a short span of time. The poverty of their early years on the island soon disappeared completely.

Part 1

How it all started

1   The Sephardic and Ashkenazic Jews of Curaçao

Curaçao is home to both Sephardic and Ashkenazic Jews. The Sephardic Jews originally came from Spain and Portugal and have lived on the island for more than three centuries. The Ashkenazic Jews came to Curaçao less than a hundred years ago from Eastern Europe.

The Origin of the Sephardic Jews

Moishe Seibald, Leib Zonenschain, Moses Altnaj and all the other Jews that came to Curaçao from what was then Poland and Romania were Ashkenazic Jews. When they arrived on the island, they found two synagogues. Both synagogues were founded and attended by Sephardic Jews. The term 'Sephardic' comes from *Sefarad,* which is the Hebrew word for Spain, but it is also used for the entire Iberian Peninsula. So the Sephardic Jews of Curaçao originated from Spain and Portugal. On Curaçao they are often referred to as Portuguese Jews.

Jews had lived on the Iberian Peninsula since Roman times. Under the Moors, they enjoyed relative freedom and Spain became a center for Jewish arts and sciences. With the reconquest of Spain by the Christians starting in the 11th century, this freedom came to an end. Christian anti-Semitism flared up, the Inquisition began and countless Jews were burned at the stake. In 1492, the Spanish monarchs King Ferdinand and Queen Isabella expelled all Jews from their realm who refused to be baptized. Many Jews left for Portugal. In vain, because four years later they were expelled from that country too. Of course, the Jews were offered a way out, just as in Spain – conversion to Roman Catholicism – but many of them preferred to flee, particularly in 1536 when the Inquisition spread to Portugal.

Some of them journeyed north to the Netherlands. From there, a group of Jews traveled to northeastern Brazil, where the Dutch West India Company (WIC) had settled in 1624. The Sephardim financed the sugar industry there and exported sugar. Some of them even had sugar mills. They were also involved in the slave trade.

In 1654, the Dutch adventures of the WIC in Brazil ended and the Portuguese resumed the position of lord and master. A number of Sephardic Jews then journeyed to Curaçao via Amsterdam. Others before them had sailed to the

The newest cemetery at Berg Altena. (photo: Jeannette van Ditzhuijzen)

island directly from Brazil.[4] As planters, the Sephardic Jews initially settled outside the city limits, establishing their congregation *Mikvé Israel* – the Hope of Israel. There, northwest of the *Schottegat,* an enormous inland waterway, now lies the Jewish cemetery of *Beth Haim,* House of the Living. Officially, the cemetery is named *Beth Haim Blenheim,* but many people simply refer to it as *Beth Haim*.

Life on a plantation was not a prosperous existence in the dry climate of Curaçao. Soon the Jews turned their efforts to both domestic and overseas shipping and trade. Later they would also become involved in financing the slave trade. The Jewish tradesmen moved to 'the city', Punda, where in 1732 they built the impressive synagogue of *Mikvé Israel*, the third one at that location. This synagogue, also called *snoa,* is famous for being the oldest synagogue in the New World continuously in use until the present day.

Over the years, the Sephardic Jews have increased their wealth and prestige. After acquiring the same civil rights as white Protestants in 1825, they were able to hold public office.[5] From the middle of the 19th century, especially, Curaçao's Jews met with success. They operated commercial businesses, owned ships and shipyards and in 1917 they opened the first commercial bank, now the Maduro & Curiel's Bank.

Liberal and Orthodox Sephardic Jews

In the middle of the 19th century, religious problems arose within the Sephardic congregation. In 1864, a group of Jews split off from *Mikvé Israel*, which was too orthodox in their eyes. They founded the *Nederlandsch Hervormd Israëlitische Gemeente Emanu-El* (Dutch Jewish Reform Congregation 'Emanu-El' or 'God is with us') and had their own house of prayer built at Pietermaai. This Temple was consecrated on 12 September 1867.[6] After that, for nearly a century the island had two Sephardic congregations: the orthodox *Mikvé Israel* and the reformed congregation of *Emanu-El*. On *Berg Altena* the reformed congregation even established their own cemetery; later *Mikvé Israel* purchased the adjoining land for the burial of orthodox Jews.[7]

By the mid 20th century, the differences between the congregations had become smaller and there were too few members to justify two synagogues and two rabbis. The liberal rabbi Simeon Maslin brought the two groups together in 1964 and, as a compromise, this 'new' congregation joined the liberal Jewish Reconstructionist Federation. The wall that separated the orthodox part of the cemetery on *Berg Altena* from the liberal section had been pulled down earlier in 1958.[8]

The Origins of the Ashkenazic Jews

It is commonly assumed that the Ashkenazic Jews emigrated en masse to Eastern Europe during the middle ages from countries such as Germany (the Germany theory). But there is another theory that says that the Ashkenazim came to Eastern Europe from Khazaria, situated much further to the east. Khazaria, a medieval empire, was located in the northern Caucasus region between the Black Sea and the Caspian Sea.

Do the Ashkenazim Come from Germany?

Around the year 1000 AD, a large number of Jews were living in German cities such as Cologne, Mainz, Worms and Spiers and they gradually became known as the Ashkenazim. This term could be related to the Biblical name *Ashkenaz*, a medieval Hebrew name for Germany.

During the middle ages, in Catholic Europe, the Jews were not taken seriously. They were not allowed to be members of guilds and were supposed to stay far away from government offices. Marriages with Christians were absolutely forbidden.

Because Christians were not allowed to charge interest on money they lent, whereas Jews were, at least from non-Jews, many Jews gradually specialized in banking. They soon gained a reputation for being extortionists because the interest they charged was quite high. In their defense, they were forced to charge high rates because of the exorbitant taxes imposed on them.

Differences in lifestyle and appearance combined with their high interest loans resulted in Jews being isolated from society. These facts, coupled with the allegation that they had nailed Christ to the cross, were reasons enough for the superstitious medieval Christians to view the Jews as scapegoats for everything under the sun. In the 14th century, for instance, the Jews were blamed for the plague. This disease cropped up regularly and it was generally believed at the time that it had been caused by the Jews poisoning the water. For this reason, the Jews were brutally murdered on a large scale, especially in Germany and France.

According to the Germany theory, those Jews who escaped with their lives moved eastwards. Poland and Lithuania, as well as other Eastern European countries, were favorite places to settle. The kings in these countries welcomed the Jewish traders and moneylenders with open arms in order to promote the development of trade and of their cities. The Jews were allowed to practice their religion and were not restricted in their choice of profession. Over time, some kings even became dependent on the Jews for financing their wars.

Or Do the Ashkenazim Come from Khazaria?

According to the Khazaria theory, a large number of Khazars converted to Judaism during the 9th century.[9] They were a powerful people, until the Russians attacked their empire at the end of the 10th century. From that moment on, the Khazar Jews moved westward in the direction of Hungary and Poland.[10]

In his book *De herkomst van de Asjkenazische joden: de controverse opgelost* (The Origin of Ashkenazic Jews: The Controversy Solved), Jits van Straten is a passionate advocate of this theory. According to him, the Ashkenazic Jews could simply not be descendants of the Jews that had left Germany and moved eastward. He holds this view not only because data from the *Judaica Germanica* make it clear that nothing is known about a mass migration of German Jews to Poland and Lithuania during the pogroms in the middle ages.[11] Numerically a migration from Germany was simply not credible. According to Van Straten's calculations, around the year 1500 between 460,000 and 860,000 Jews were living in Eastern Europe. Because Germany was home to far fewer Jews during the middle ages, all of these Eastern European Jews simply could not, in his view, have come from Germany.[12]

According to the Khazaria theory, Yiddish arose through the Khazar Jews' contact with German-speaking Polish city dwellers.[13]

Centuries of Discrimination

Whether they originally came from the west or from the east, the fact is that, toward the end of the middle ages life became much more difficult for the Ashkenazic Jews in Poland and Lithuania. The relative freedom they had come to enjoy in religious and economic life came to an end in 1648 when Cossacks and

The old Jewish cemetery at Blenheim. (photo: Jeannette van Ditzhuijzen)

Crimean Tartars revolted against the Polish landowners and the Jewish traders that worked for them. A bloodbath followed. Many survivors escaped to the west, for instance to Germany and the Netherlands.

After the Partitions of Poland at the end of the 18th century, Poland and Lithuania came into the hands of the neighboring countries of Russia, Austria and Prussia. The new situation was not an improvement for the Jews. In Prussia, for example, various discriminatory laws were in effect. Though the Jews gained full civil rights at the start of the 19th century, after 1814 these rights were taken away again.

Russians had never tolerated the Jews. After the Partitions of Poland, the Jews were allowed to settle only in the western border areas. They were oppressed and they had no free choice of profession. Czar Nicholas I (1825-1855) would have preferred the Jews to assimilate. He tried to accomplish this, among other ways, by imposing a mandatory 25-year period of military service on Jewish boys from the age of 12, thereby brutally separating them from their Jewish communities. Under his successor, Alexander II, this conscription was abolished though, while other anti-Jewish measures were softened somewhat.

Because the murder of Alexander II in 1881 involved a Jewish woman, a wave of pogroms ensued – raids that were accompanied by plundering and murder. To escape this nightmare, the Jews began emigrating en masse to the United States.[14]

Numbers of Ashkenazim on Curaçao

The Ashkenazic Jews that settled on Curaçao starting in 1926 were not the very first Ashkenazic Jews to land there. Over the centuries, Ashkenazic Jews had come to the island occasionally for short or long periods as soldiers, doctors or merchants. Some of them remained on the island and are now buried in one of the Jewish cemeteries. The German merchant Moses Mikal, for example, found his last resting place in 1740 at *Beth Haim*.[15] Amsterdam-born Levi Heijman Snoek traveled to Curaçao as a soldier in 1858 simply because he really wanted to. He liked the island, got married and, after his death in 1882, was buried in the Jewish cemetery at *Berg Altena*.[16]

Undoubtedly, these transients were welcome in the orthodox synagogue in Punda or in the liberal Temple at Pietermaai. But the Ashkenazim who came to the island from 1926 on certainly did not feel welcome. So they soon rented a space where they could hold their own services. Over time this resulted in the creation of a third Jewish congregation, *Shaarei Tsedek*, Gates of Righteousness.

As shown in table 1, the number of Ashkenazim that lived on the island increased considerably in the first forty years. After that their numbers declined. This was caused by their departure to other countries after the riots of May 1969 and the fall of the Venezuelan bolivar in 1983 (see Chapter 13).

The Sephardic Jews had already decreased in numbers before then. When the English, with a short interruption, controlled Curaçao from 1800 to 1816, trade moved to other Caribbean islands, particularly St. Thomas. Curaçao Jews, who were very active in trade, followed the trading activities and emigrated.

Both the Ashkenazic and the Sephardic Jews have declined in numbers since the 1960s, due in part to the departure of young people to countries abroad in order to study. Not everyone returned and, because the size of families decreased over the same period, there were fewer Jews left on the island. Another factor contributing to the decline of Sephardim was the increasing number of mixed marriages.

Table 1 Numbers of Jews on Curaçao compared to total population 1789-2009[17]

	1789	1902	1926	1950	1968	2009
population of Curaçao	20,988 (of whom 12,864 were slaves)	31,547	38,781	102,206	141,393	141,756
number of Jews	1,095 (among a total of 3,564 whites)	839	548	600	± 740	± 225
Mikvé Israel-Emanuel	—		—	420	300	134
Shaarei Tsedek	—		—	180	450	103

2 Flight from the Eastern European Shtetl

In the period between the two world wars, poverty in Eastern Europe was widespread. Anti-Semitism gradually increased there during the same period. For the Jews, these were important reasons to leave their native soil and seek refuge elsewhere.

Life in a Shtetl at the Start of the 20th Century

In the 1920s and '30s, the Polish border city of Chorostków was home to some 2,000 Jews out of 6,000 inhabitants. Janina Katz used to live there, as did Jacob Gabriel Gerstenbluth, or Bill for short. Chorostków is an example of a *shtetl*[18], a small Eastern European city where many Jews, and sometimes only Jews, lived. The Jewish children went to the public school in the morning. After having lunch at home, they went to the *cheder*, a private school run by a rabbi, where they received instruction in religion, Jewish history and the Hebrew language until 8 in the evening.[19] After that, they had homework to do.

Many Jewish children were also members of one of the Jewish youth organizations. Jacob 'Bill' Gerstenbluth – 13 years old when he left Chorostków – was a member of the Zionist organization *Hanoar Hatzioni*, meant for young people aged 12 to 24. He remembered that lectures were given and plays were performed. He could also borrow books there, have discussions with others and play ping-pong. Other organizations included *Gordonia*, *Young Pioneer*, *Frayheyt*, the left-wing *Ha-Shomer Ha-Tsair* (the Young Guard) and *Betar*, an extreme-right movement.[20]

Like in many shtetls, Jews in Chorostków were primarily storekeepers, (grain) merchants and peddlers. The last group took their wares to the villages in the neighboring countryside, where they would buy vegetables and fruit using the proceeds they had earned by selling their goods.[21] The weekly market was important. In Chorostków it was always held on Monday. Farmers and traders came from the surrounding villages to buy and sell. On that day, the Jews kept their morning prayers short and the children left the *cheder* earlier so that they could help their family at the market. The teachers at the *cheder* were not always present on Monday because they also had businesses to attend to at the market or their own family to help out.

On some of the gravestones, the deceased's Romanian or Polish place of birth is mentioned. (photos: Jeannette van Ditzhuijzen)

Generally speaking, the Jews were very religious. According to the author Sam Halpern, Chorostków had some eight synagogues[22] and on Friday afternoon the Jewish stores closed early so that everyone could go to the synagogue or prepare for the Sabbath meal.[23] No one worked on the Sabbath, all stores were closed. Gerstenbluth: "My family was religious to the core. On Friday evening the candles were lit and the lights were turned on and off by a *Shabbes goy,* a gentile that performed work that Jews were not allowed to do on the Sabbath. On Yom Kippur, I sat in the synagogue all day long with my grandfather because that's what he wanted. We attended the large synagogue, almost as big as the *snoa* here in Punda. My memory of it was that the ceiling inside was more beautiful than the ceiling of the Sistine Chapel in Rome."

The Katz family was also very religious. Like nearly all inhabitants of Chorostków, Janina's grandmother had a stove with a wooden divider in the middle to keep the dairy and meat products separated, one of the requirements of a kosher kitchen. And they had an oven in which they not only baked bread, it was also used to keep the pre-cooked meal hot on the Sabbath, because cooking on the Sabbath was not allowed. "Not everyone had an oven like this. So the neighbors came over to our house to put their meals in the oven. This really annoyed my mother because, as soon as we sat down for our Friday evening meal, the neighbors invariably showed up to get their food out of the oven."

Janina Katz was born in 1932 and did not come to Curaçao until after the war. She remembered her grandparents' house very well. At the front was a fabric store, behind it a living room and a dining room, and then at the back an open space where the family usually sat. "My grandmother had two cows. She made kosher butter from the milk, which she sold so she had money to help out other people. Someone always needed a new roof or someone else had to give a daughter away in marriage. As a child, I always found it remarkable to see how hard she worked and how she helped others. I remember that on Fridays many poor people waited outside the house for the bread and soup that my grandmother gave them."

Fleeing from Poverty, Discrimination and Conscription

The preceding paragraphs paint a rather 'romantic' picture of life in an Eastern European shtetl. But the Jews did not leave for the West without reason. At primary school, Gerstenbluth sat separated from his non-Jewish classmates because Jews and non-Jews were not allowed to sit in the same row; the cheerful Monday market in Chorostków often ended with anti-Semitic outbursts,[24] and, as a child, Dora Suchar-Cheis, born in the then Romanian city of Herța, was scared stiff of Alexander Cuza. This extreme anti-Jewish professor and politician wanted to ban the Jews entirely from public life.[25] As a child, she heard stories about women who were molested and about the destruction of stores. The Jewish school in Herța even closed down regularly 'due to the fear of Alexander Cuza'. For this reason, Dora's brother and sister did not attend a Jewish school like she did, but went to a Romanian school instead.

The Spritzer family on the evening before Wolf Spritzer left for Venezuela in December 1926. Later he moved to Curaçao, his family followed in 1929. (photo: private collection of Ralph Spritzer)

Still, anti-Semitism was not the main reason that many Jews left their native soil. It was primarily down to their poor economic situation, which was a direct consequence of the anti-Semitism. Jewish stores were boycotted, for example, so their income decreased. And they could not apply for jobs with the government. Jews were second-class citizens who often lived in dire poverty due to the anti-Jewish measures.

Ralph Spritzer's father, who was born in Budapest, lived in Berlin with his parents and little sister before his departure to Curaçao. Ralph heard from him that in Berlin he sometimes could not go to school because his shoes had to be polished for that. The Spritzer family simply did not have enough money to buy shoe polish at the time.

Another reason to leave was compulsory military service. In the armies of both Poland and Romania, anti-Semitism was rife and many Jewish boys left their country in order to escape being conscripted into the army. This was the case for Abraham Wiznitzer and his brothers, who left the Romanian city of Czernowitz. Joske Faerman lived in Mogilev Podolski, part of Russia at the time. In 1928 he was given not only the rabbi's advice, but even his blessing to leave the country, he told his daughter. "Had he stayed, he probably would not have survived the Russian army."

A drawing by Ernö Spritzer showing the room where he lived with his parents and sister in Berlin. The watchmakers worked at the table in the middle (see the portrait included in this chapter). (drawing: private collection of Ralph Spritzer)

Men that planned to leave but who were supposed to serve in the army sometimes changed their date of birth before their departure. For example, Elias Linder from Sniatyn altered his date of birth so as to appear older than he actually was. Apparently this could be done without much problem in pre-war Eastern Europe; even in a passport or another official document.

The History of the Ashkenazim from Galicia[26]

The 'Curaçao Jews' primarily came from Galicia, in what was southeast Poland at the time, and from Bukovina and Bessarabia, in what was then Romania. After the Polish Partitions at the end of the 18th century, Polish Galicia fell into the hands of Austria, later the Austro-Hungarian dual monarchy of the Habsburgs. It was only after the First World War that it was reunited with Poland, which as a result had a larger number of Jews than any other European country: over three million.

In 1931, 9.3 per cent of the Galician population was Jewish, orthodox or otherwise. Three-quarters of them lived in cities, one-quarter in the villages in the countryside. The percentage of Jews gradually declined in the 1930s for varying reasons, including emigration to America, Palestine and other areas.

The Jews were not the only minority in Galicia. In fact, after the First World War, one-third of the total population of Poland consisted of non-Polish

Husband and wife Rachmiel and Mina Geiger-Zuckerman were married in Sniatyn, Poland, according to Jewish rites. In 1932 they married in Curaçao according to civil law at the registry office. (photo: private collection of Marcia Linder-Geiger)

nationalities. Galicia, for example, was also home to Ukrainians and White Russians. In Eastern Galicia, from which many Curaçao Jews originated, the Jews were primarily surrounded by Ukrainians and Poles.

Among themselves, the Galician Jews spoke mainly Yiddish[27], which the 'Polish Jews' of Curaçao confirmed: "The Polish language was acquired", said Leon Seibald, who was around the age of four when he left the Polish city of Czernelica. "At home we always spoke Yiddish. You cannot sweep the Yiddish away, it is a part of you." Janina Katz occasionally spoke Polish, but her grandmother didn't approve. "Stop with the Polish and speak Yiddish", she was told.

Jewish culture flourished in Poland. There was a selection of Yiddish newspapers, Yiddish theater plays were performed and the country was the centre for Yiddish literature. The author Isaac Bashevis Singer, born in 1904, grew up in this Jewish cultural milieu before he left for America in 1935.

There were also several Jewish schools. The *tarbut*, for example (*tarbut* means 'culture' in Hebrew), where instruction in Hebrew was given. This officially recognized school prepared the students for emigration to Palestine (present-day Israel). There was no discrimination encountered there, as was the case in most of the public schools. According to Jacob 'Bill' Gerstenbluth, who attended a Polish gymnasium for a year, the *tarbut* schools were well-reputed, better than the Polish gymnasia. "Where the students played a lot, were against Jews, and went out on the town on occasion."[28]

On leaving Sniatyn, 16-year-old Moishe Seibald took a certificate of good conduct with him, in case he might need it. (from the private collection of Benny Seibald)

Polish Minority Treaty, Yet No Equal Rights

The recognition of Jewish schools came about as a result of the Paris Peace Conference in 1919. There the Polish government signed a so-called Polish Minority Treaty, which established, among other things, freedom of religion and education for the minorities in the new country, including the Jews. Subsequently, all national citizens were given equal rights in the Polish Constitution of 1921. At least officially, because neither the Minority Treaty nor the Constitution had much positive effect on the anti-Jewish sentiments. On the contrary, after the

First World War, Polish nationalism ran rampant; the new Poland belonged to the Polish and minorities had to adapt.

Besides, a 'real' Pole was Roman Catholic and not Jewish. The left-wing parties were of the opinion that the Jews should secularize and become Polish; the right wing considered the Jews to be enemies of the state and considered the assimilation of this group impossible.[29] Despite the Minority Treaty, neither wing supported the funding of Jewish schools.

Anti-Jewish Violence

Due to this nationalism, immediately after the creation of the Polish nation the Jews encountered outbreaks of anti-Semitism, sometimes coupled with violence. The Habsburg Empire had only just fallen when the Jews in the Galician city of Lwów (now Lviv) became victims of a violent pogrom. In battles between the Polish and the Ukrainians in November 1918, the Jews were rumored to have sided with the Ukrainians, though they had actually taken a neutral stance in the conflict. Dozens of Jews were murdered and hundreds wounded as a result of the ensuing pogrom, which drew international attention. In the months to follow, Poland experienced even more outbreaks of violence against Jews.

In 1920, after the war with Russia, the Jews were also accused of collaborating with the enemy, the Bolsheviks in this case. Violence followed, as did people's tribunals with executions of Jews who were suspected of conspiracy. In reality, many Jews had signed up as volunteers and fought against the Russians.[30]

Nachman Grynsztein heard from his parents, who lived in Wysokie Mazowieckie (between Warsaw and Bialystok), that they regularly stayed indoors because pogroms were underway in the vicinity. "Not the real large pogroms, which were in Russia. But life for the Jews was very difficult in Poland."

After Józef Piłsudski assumed power in 1926 via a coup, anti-Semitism decreased somewhat. He pretty much left the Jews in peace and even protected them against attacks and pogroms. But the anti-Jewish sentiment never disappeared and after Piłsudski's death in 1935 it resumed with full force. The new government made a visible effort to rid the country of the Jews by promoting emigration, among other things.

There was also an attempt in 1936 to get an official ban passed on the ritual slaughtering of animals, which the Jews saw as a restriction on their right to religious freedom. The admission of Jews to universities was also limited and often they were forced to attend lectures while sitting on separate benches[31], separated from the other students.

Economic Boycott of the Jews

The most serious measure was the economic boycott. The Polish Jews primarily earned a living in trade. In 1921 this affected 62.6 per cent of all Jews. In Galicia, the percentage came to 74.1. Many Jews owned their own businesses, stores or market stalls, which allowed them to decide for themselves to close on the Sabbath. Some were grain merchants, such as Bill Gerstenbluth's father. The father of

In 1930, Salomon Seibald traveled from the Italian port of Genoa to Curaçao. (from the private collection of Benny Seibald)

Janina Katz had a farm. Her grandfather sold fabrics in Chorostków. And Leon Seibald's grandfather once owned six watermills where he milled grain. They were all small independent business people of which Galicia had a lot at that time.

But, with the support of the government and the Catholic Church, Christians were persuaded to avoid doing business with the Jews and only buy from the 'real' Poles. Groups of activists entered towns and cities to make it very clear to people not to do any business with the Jews, whether they liked it or not. These visits were often accompanied by violence against Jewish stores, such as the breaking of store windows. A law passed in 1936 requiring stores and businesses to have a name, only simplified the economic boycott[32], since Jewish names were easily recognizable. Renting houses to Jews was included in this boycott as well.

As early as 1919, a ban was issued on working on Sunday. Although this ban was not directed towards the Jews, it was perceived to be: in addition to the Sabbath, the Jews now had another day on which they were not allowed to work. Sometimes they had to choose between working on Saturday or being fired. And anyone looking for work outside commerce or industry had to deal with the government's anti-Jewish policy: in Galicia, for example, Jews were not allowed to hold government jobs.

The economic boycott and all other measures against the Jews came down hard on a community that was already living in dire poverty.[33] Like all Poles, the Jews had emerged from the First World War impoverished, and the international stock exchange crash of 1929 did not improve their situation. Countless Jewish businesses were peering over the edge of an abyss and the boycott simply pushed them over it.

Ezra Mendelsohn reveals in his book[34] that the number of Jewish stores throughout Poland drastically declined between 1932 and 1937. For instance, in the small city where Grynsztein's parents lived, Wysokie Mazowieckie, 91 per cent of the stores in 1932 were owned by Jews. In 1937 this percentage fell to 69. In other cities, the decline was sometimes greater.

Little could be done to counter the boycott. The Jews had no political power despite the fact that there were a number of Jewish political parties. Some of them were Zionist in outlook, others expressly not, but the discord among the Jewish parties was large. Supporters of Zionism, by the way, were most numerous in Galicia.

One way to escape the difficulties and poverty in Poland was to emigrate. Many Jews had already left for America, but after 1924, it was virtually impossible to enter the United States. Consequently, more than 32,000 Polish Jews emigrated to Palestine. It was probably around that time that the Polish Jew Ezra Lerner arrived on Curaçao. He never settled there, but he was the pioneer who inaugurated an influx of Polish Jews who ventured to make the long journey to this island.

The History of the Jews from Bukovina and Bessarabia[35]

On the map (see p. 25) one can see that Bukovina, Bessarabia and Galicia border on one another. From the end of the 18th century to the middle of the 19th century, Bukovina was even a part of Galicia. And up to 1918, both regions were a part of the Austro-Hungarian Empire. The more easterly lying Bessarabia was held by the Russians from 1812 to 1918.

Bessarabia, Bukovina and several other regions were added to Romania after the First World War, causing the country to almost double in size. For the Jews, this new country spelled an end to a relatively peaceful era. Romanian troops in Bukovina soon resorted to using sheer violence, even in the case of minor 'offences' Jews were subjected to looting and, in an official declaration made by the future minister of Bukovina, Jancu Flondor, they were told that they should submit to the majority – the Romanians.[36] This submission meant, for example, that Romanian became the official language, which was a foreign language for most of the Jews in the new areas.

Second-class Citizens in Romania

Jews had lived in the area of what would later become known as Romania since the time of the Romans. In the middle ages, other Jews joined them from the Khazar Empire and/or from Germany and France (see Chapter 1), as well as from countries such as Poland. The rulers of Moldavia and Wallachia (from which Romania would later emerge) welcomed them because they helped to develop the country and its economy. But the Greek Orthodox Church held a different view. In 1640 it officially declared the Jews to be the equivalent of heretics. Contacts between Christians and Jews were therefore absolutely forbidden.

This anti-Jewish attitude grew over time, particularly in the 19th century. Jews were increasingly viewed as being foreigners and not considered to be Romanians. They were treated as second-class citizens or, worse, 'enemies of Romania'.[37] This nationalism and resulting xenophobia was due, in part, to the fact that the common Romanian came from the countryside, while many landowners were descended from foreigners. In pre-war Romania, Jews were seldom landowners, because in the 19th century, only Romanians were allowed to own land, and to become Romanian you had to be Christian.[38] The Jews did, however, often act as mediators for large landowners.

In Bukovina the situation was different. There, in 1867, the Habsburg Empire had granted the Jews equal rights and many Jews owned land which they farmed. In Bessarabia, too, a relatively large number of Jews were farmers.

The Deteriorating Situation after 1918

Nationalism, xenophobia and anti-Semitism were inflamed by the enormous number of non-Romanians that populated the new territories after 1918: Hungarians, Germans, Russians, Ukrainians and Jews. Bukovina and Bessarabia in particular had many Jewish inhabitants. In 1930, Jews made up 4.2 per cent of the total population of Romania, in Bukovina that was 10.9 per cent, and in Bessarabia 7.2 per cent.[39] The Jews lived primarily in the cities, where they often formed the majority.[40]

Of course, just as in Poland, economic motives also played a role in this hatred of foreigners. In the eyes of the Romanians, the Jews occupied positions that they themselves wanted to take over. The belief was nurtured that the Jews controlled the economy and the Romanians came off second best. Despite the Paris Peace Treaties, in which Romania had, under heavy pressure, promised its minorities equal rights, the Jews were excluded from a range of government jobs after the war.

On their journey to the Western Hemisphere, some Ashkenazim took along their Shabbat candle sticks. These candle sticks come from Chorostków, Poland. (photo: Jeannette van Ditzhuijzen)

In other respects, too, the equal rights granted were short-lived. Although the Jews had been promised in 1919 that they would be considered as Romanian citizens in the new areas, a law adopted in 1924 stipulated something different. Jews could not become Romanian if they had come to live in Bukovina after 1908 (for Bessarabia: after 1918). The same ruling applied to the Jews that had settled there before 1908 or 1918, respectively, but had not yet come of age. Jewish children of a mother who was married only according to the Jewish rites and who hailed from another part of the former Austro-Hungarian Empire were also not eligible for Romanian citizenship.[41] Thus many Jews had become 'foreigners'.

The law from 1924 was partly the result of violent student protests in 1922 led by, among others, the anti-Semitic professor Alexander Cuza, whom Dora Suchar-Cheis from Curaçao remembered as a type of bogeyman. The students feared the Jews gaining full civil rights because that would only increase competition on the future job market. In the years to follow, Romanian students regularly took an anti-Semitic stance and did not refrain from using violence against Jews.

The Romanians did not hesitate to express their anti-Semitism openly. A sign hung in a park in Bucharest made it clear Jews were not wanted. The text read: "No dogs and kikes".[42] Clara Faerman-Libman remembered that in the early 1930s, her mother in Bessarabia was expressly told that all Jews should move to Palestine.

The anti-Semitic feeling went from bad to worse. In 1934, a law was adopted that stipulated that 80 per cent of the employees at any company had to be Romanian. In view of the fact that Jews were not considered to be Romanian, this meant that many Jews lost their jobs. They had no safety net because Romanian Jews were anything but rich. The Jews were helped, however, by the

Shura Vorona (center) shortly before his departure to Trinidad at the end of 1938. To his right is Gitta Fruchter, to his left the small daughter of his uncle and aunt, Zelik and Tauba Sztam-Faerman. The girl died from an illness contracted during the war. (photo: private collection of Frieda Pais-Fruchter)

American Jewish Joint Distribution Committee, an international Jewish aid organization.

In 1937 Cuza and another anti-Semitic politician, Octavian Goga, entered the Government for a short time. In their view, Jews had to be vanquished from the economy and the universities. Jewish newspapers and libraries also had to take the blame. After two months, their Government disappeared from the scene, but not their ideas.

Jewish Culture: Yiddish-speaking and Orthodox

Like the Jews from Galicia, the majority of the Jews from Bukovina and Bessarabia were orthodox and used Yiddish to communicate with each other.[43] Mendelsohn called this the Eastern European type. Jews of the Eastern European type[44] formed their own communities and seldom married anyone from outside. According to Mendelsohn, the Jewish communities of the Western European type had distanced themselves more from orthodoxy and the Yiddish language.

There was a difference between Bukovina and Bessarabia, though. As mentioned before, the Jews in Bukovina gained equal rights under the Habsburgs (1867). In the capital Czernowitz, especially, Jewish culture flourished. Interestingly enough, here a majority of the Jews also spoke German in addition to Yiddish.

Frieda Fruchter, who in 1947 left Czernowitz as a child and moved to Curaçao, remembered that the very first children's songs she learned were in German. "It was actually the language everyone used to communicate." Her older sister Gitta remembered that the Jews on Curaçao could not understand why the Fruchters still spoke German after everything they had experienced during the war. "After that we switched to speaking Yiddish at home, since we could speak it as well." In the family of Marie Brandes, who was born in Czernowitz in 1926 and who arrived on Curaçao in 1930, German was always spoken. It was only after the outbreak of the Second World War that the family refused to continue speaking German and that Yiddish became the language of communication. The transition was not difficult: "You heard Yiddish everywhere on Curaçao and it was very similar to German."

The Czernowitz Jews read German newspapers, attended the German-language theater productions and, in remarkably large numbers, attended the German-language University of Czernowitz, which had been founded in 1875. In 1914, 38.5 per cent of the students were Jewish and the faculty held many Jews.[45]

Bessarabia Jews in Dire Straits

While there was some acculturation in Galicia and Bukovina[46], in Bessarabia there was much less trace of it. Even prior to the First World War, the Jews there were not afforded the relative freedom experienced by the Jews in Galicia and Bukovina. Instead they faced Russian oppression. At the end of the 19th century, the Jews in Bessarabia were regularly driven from their villages and many still remembered, after the First World War, the horrors of the pogrom of Chisinau (Bessarabia's capital) in 1903, when nearly 50 Jews met their deaths. The reason for the pogrom was an allegation of ritual murder. Like elsewhere in Europe, the Jews in Romania were regularly accused of murdering small children. It was rumored that they used their victims' blood for the preparation of matzos, the unleavened bread the Jews eat at Passover.

Initially, the many Yiddish and Hebrew schools in Bessarabia were allowed to stay open[47], but gradually pressure was put on them to provide education in the official language of the country – Romanian. Beginning in 1925, diplomas from Jewish schools were recognized only if Romanian was the language used for instruction. This meant the end of many Yiddish schools. A number of private *tarbut* schools that provided education in Hebrew were still able to survive, though it became increasingly difficult for the impoverished population to keep them going. Noua Suliță, for example, had a primary and secondary *tarbut* school between the two world wars. Romanian and Hebrew were taught at both of them.

Although the Bessarabia Jews had no pleasant memories of the Russians, the Romanians considered them to be pro-Russian. The Jews were all thought to be Bolsheviks and striving for reunification with Russia. This was more than enough reason for the Romanians to hate the Jews. In this new province, anti-Semitism was synonymous with anti-Communism.

Rosita Zonenschain remembered that her own family and her husband's family left Noua Suliţă mainly because of anti-Semitism and the pogroms, and because "they sensed that the war was coming". An understandable sentiment, because as early as 1927 the Iron Guard, an extreme anti-Semitic, fascist organization, was active in Romania. It was led by Corneliu Codreanu, who broke with the party founded by Cuza.

Flight from Bitter Poverty

Apart from the anti-Semitism, the Jewish population in Bukovina and especially in Bessarabia suffered dire poverty. In Bessarabia, Jewish traders also had to cope with the loss of the Russian market. In fact, all of Romania was an economically poor region. The government measures targeting the Jews did not help any. On the contrary, Jews were no longer allowed to practice certain functions, including in government, and their merchant's or peddler's licenses were withdrawn. Civil servants that could not master the Romanian language within a prescribed period were sacked. Doctors and lawyers also encountered professional obstacles.

So the Jews fell on hard times financially. One escape from poverty was to study at the university, at least for those who had the abilities to do so. But starting from the 1920s this route was also cut off, because then the universities began to admit only limited numbers of Jews. Those Jews that did attend university were regularly harassed and barred from Romanian dormitories.

The general poverty caused by the war and the crash of 1929, combined with the anti-Semitic measures, prompted the Jews to leave. Dora Suchar-Cheis remembered that her father left Romania in 1930 because of his poor financial situation. He left on his own, because there was not enough money to take his wife and children with him. Besides, he thought he would be away only a couple of years: after he had acquired wealth in 'America', he would return to Romania. On Curaçao, too, where he arrived in 1930, he initially had debts. But in 1934 he was able to have his family join him there.

One of the first Romanian Jews to set foot on Curaçao soil was Wilu Weisinger from Czernowitz. He thought he was bound for America and had no idea where the ship had let him off. That was around 1927. Leib Zonenschain arrived a year later from Bessarabia. Abram Ackerman, also from Bessarabia, and Samuel Brandes from Czernowitz arrived in 1929, the same year in which the wife and children of Zonenschain set foot on Curaçao soil.

▶ **Ernö Spritzer (Budapest, 1919-1997)**

"I was born at a chaotic time, shortly after the collapse of the Austro-Hungarian Empire. Under the leadership of Béla Kun, a communist government was formed. Several months later it was overthrown by Admiral Miklós Horthy. My family had already suffered under the red terror of Béla

Ernö Spritzer in 1933. (photo: private collection of Ralph Spritzer)

Kun, but things got even worse for the Jews when, after he took power, Horthy started encouraging people to persecute Jews."

"My father lost his business in watches, clocks and jewelry during the First World War. Now his life was being threatened. So at the end of 1919 he fled Hungary. My mother remained behind with my four-year-old sister and me, not yet a year old. In Berlin, my father tried everything to find a job, but it took him three years before he finally got one. So it was 1923 before the rest of us arrived in Berlin, where inflation was running rampant and things were difficult for foreigners. With great difficulty he was able to sublet a room in one of the large, gray tenement houses in north Berlin. We lived there for many years and I remember that room very clearly: it served not only as a living room, dining room and bedroom for the four of us, it was also my father's workroom. He was a watchmaker and an eight-hour day was unheard of in this type of cottage industry. I remember sometimes waking up in the middle of the night and there he would be with three other watchmakers working at his workbench and chatting away with his colleagues. It made me feel very safe."

"At school in Berlin, I was the only Jewish boy and therefore was an easy target for teasing and ridicule. On Saturday and on Jewish holidays I did not go to school because our family was orthodox. I could not trade sandwiches with other children because I had to observe the kosher dietary rules. Furthermore, I attended Jewish classes twice a week."

"My father's brother had already left Europe; he lived in Maracaibo, the oil-producing city of Venezuela. Because my father could see no opportunity to improve his financial situation in Berlin and to care for us, he decided to go to Maracaibo as well. He considered this to be a hazardous undertaking and could not pay the passage for the entire family. So, in 1927, he set off alone and traveled to Maracaibo, where he set up a business as a watchmaker. At the time, Venezuela was ruled by the dictator Juan Gómez and a small disagreement with a government official was enough to have my father expelled from the country within 24 hours. All travel connections with Maracaibo ran via Curaçao in those days. This beautiful and friendly island appealed to him and so he decided to try his luck again there."

"In the meantime, my mother and we children had remained behind in Berlin. She had to work to make a living for us, so we children were more or less left to our own devices during the day. The two years we spent in Berlin without a father were, in hindsight, probably the most difficult years our family experienced. It took months to receive an answer to letters. Finally, at the end of 1929, the big day arrived: one morning I shall never forget, the mailman delivered a letter from father containing our boat tickets."

"The trip took three weeks and made an enormous impression on me, a ten-year-old boy from a very poor neighborhood. It was a wonderful adventure and, although we naturally traveled third class, I found life very luxurious aboard ship. My enthusiasm waned, however, towards the end of the trip. The Venezuelan port cities of La Guaira and Puerto Cabello, with their shabbily dressed people, made a dirty and grimy impression and the air stank. But once we reached Curaçao everything changed immediately. Willemstad was clean and the people were well-dressed and friendly. Only later did I become aware that this was due to the influence of the Dutch."

"Father took us to our new home on the Penstraat, which he had rented and furnished. You can imagine our reaction when we entered this six-room house. Everything was spacious and new. Coming from the drab row houses of Berlin, as we had, the difference with what we had left behind was striking."

"As a Jewish boy in Germany, I was the odd man out in our neighborhood. On Curaçao, my friends were the children of Portuguese Jews. As a European that did not speak their language well, I was again the outsider. But this time I was accepted into their circle with smiles all around."[48] ◄

Part II

The Pioneering Years of the 1920s and 1930s

3   Arriving on an Unknown Island

After a long journey, the Eastern European Jews arrived on an island that was completely unknown to them. Curaçao was often not a deliberate choice as a place to settle. Chance often played a role in them ending up on the island. Once they had settled, a few of the men returned temporarily to Europe in order, for example, to find a wife from their own community.

The Men Traveled Ahead

As far as can be ascertained, the vast majority of Eastern European Jews arrived on Curaçao in the period 1926-1935. After the Second World War, a small second wave of family members followed who had survived the Holocaust. When arriving on the island this group stepped into an existing community: there was an Ashkenazic synagogue, a social club (Club Union) and the Ashkenazic Jews owned various stores and businesses where the new immigrants could find work.

For the pioneers things were very different. For the first Jews, the journey to the Western Hemisphere alone was an enormous undertaking. They traveled by train to one of the European ports and then continued on by ship. Third class. Often they traveled on a KNSM ship (*Koninklijke Nederlandsche Stoomboot Maatschappij* / Royal Dutch Steamboot Company) from Amsterdam. Some of them, such as Shloime Seibald, traveled via Genoa where the *Navigazione Generale Italiana* began its journey to North and South America. Those interviewed also mentioned the French ship *Colombie* of the *Compagnie Générale Transatlantique*. It sailed from Le Havre to the Western Hemisphere and brought the Cheis family, among many others, to Curaçao. Finally, the home port of the *Orinoco*, owned by the Hamburg-America Line, was the German city of Hamburg. Among others, it brought the Zonenschain family to Curaçao's shores in September 1929.

Not all Eastern European Jews had chosen Curaçao as their final destination. Abram Ackerman from Bessarabia, for example, was headed for Colombia in February 1929 to meet up with an uncle who lived there. Back home, he had cared for his mother, but there were few opportunities to earn a living in pre-war Romania. Upon arriving on Curaçao, where the ship refueled, the passengers heard that an uprising had just begun in Colombia.[49] The ship would not be able

Immigrants on the German ship Orinoco, which arrived in Curaçao on 25 September 1929. Among them were Miriam Zonenschain and her children Sloima and Sonia, and Haica Meit-Alexandrouich with her sons Pinhos and Isuhar. (photo: private collection of Rosita Zonenschain-Linker)

to continue and so he stayed on the island, where he found work at Shell. Later he started a store selling men's clothing, shoes, sewing supplies and similar wares – the business was eventually to become the large fabric store of Ackerman in Punda. But sometimes Eastern European Jews first worked in Colombia or Venezuela before finally ending up on Curaçao.

It is likely that when Ackerman disembarked from the ship he was met by members of the Ashkenazic community. That was the way in which the Jews sought contact with fellow countrymen and perhaps people from their home region. They enquired into which of the passengers spoke Yiddish and called out the name of their country of origin in the hope of finding someone from their village who could give them some news from home. Anyone that wanted to remain on the island was welcome. The Ashkenazic Jews took the new immigrants in and made sure they soon felt at home on this tropical island where the sun almost always shines and the temperatures can rise up to 34°C. Only the trade wind, which blows virtually the entire year from the east, brought them some respite from the heat.

Wife and Children Follow

In the early 1930s Leon Seibald was about four years old when he sailed to Curaçao on the *Colombia*. This KNSM ship had been sailing between Amsterdam and the West Indies on biweekly journeys since 1930. Seibald remembered the

Dunia Acherman (above in the center) did not come to Curaçao until 1938. Traveling with Greta Pimsler (left), she sailed on the Colombia. (photo: private collection of Isaac and Lily Kisilevich-Bonaparte)

black personnel in particular ("It was the first time I had ever met dark-skinned people"), who taught him Dutch words. He also remembered that other Jewish families were on board who, like his family, disembarked at Curaçao.

With his mother and little brother, the small Leon traveled to Curaçao following the path of his father Selig, who had already been living on the island for more than three years. That's how it was done in those days – married men usually made the journey alone to scout out the situation, and it was only a year or more later, once they had earned enough money, that they sent for their wife and children.

Thus, mother Altnaj and her two daughters left the Polish city of Chorostków in 1930. Together with a nephew[50], the three traveled to Genoa to take a ship that would bring them to her husband and the children's father. In Genoa they stayed in a house for immigrants. After the nephew had left for the synagogue in order to form a minyan (a quorum of ten Jewish men over thirteen years of age required for certain prayers or worship at the synagogue), his aunt had him fetched back because she needed his help. He had just returned when the apparently poorly built house collapsed. Only the 15-year-old daughter Tonia survived the disaster. She returned to Poland and in 1937 finally made the journey to Curaçao, where she was reunited with her father, Moses Altnaj.[51]

When mother Linder followed her husband Elias in 1933, she took the 14-year-old neighbor, Herman Tauber, with her, who in turn was following the path of his brother Leon. Tauber: "My father persuaded her to take me with her on the journey so that I wouldn't have to travel alone."

The Sephardic Snoa as Enticement

Those Jews that remained in the homeland weren't always happy to follow their spouses to the Western Hemisphere. Berta Becher-Bialostocky had already received money from her husband Gershon three times to pay for her passage to Venezuela, where he was still living at the time. But Berta had absolutely no desire to leave the Polish city of Grodno. She lived there comfortably with her parents and married sisters on a large estate. She asked herself what she and her three small children would do in the 'jungle' of an unknown land.

During the same period, her husband met the Ashkenazic Jew Max Bruder from Curaçao, who traveled regularly to Venezuela for business. Bruder advised him to come to Curaçao, where the Jews at least had a good reputation and were not persecuted. He also suggested that father Becher have a photograph of the synagogue made, which would make a favorable impression on his wife. The fact that the synagogue was Sephardic did not matter. Becher took the advice. He moved to Curaçao, sent a photograph of the *snoa* to his wife and the beautiful building did the trick. In 1930 his family arrived on the island.

In 1936, mother Libman also had no desire to move to the Western Hemisphere. She thought it would be better for her husband to return to Romania. Finally, she asked the rabbi of the city where she lived, Noua Suliță, to advise her on the issue. His advice was clear: take the children and depart, because things were not looking very rosy in the world they lived in. The family home was sold to the family of Saul Ghitman, who lived across the street from the Libmans. Ghitman himself would later come to Curaçao as well and become director of the wholesale business Peicher & Kardonski.

The Unknown Curaçao

Curaçao is an island that is approximately 60 kilometers long. Its width varies between 5 and 14 kilometers. It lies some 70 kilometers north of Venezuela and at the end of the 1920s had a population of approximately 43,000. Most of the island's people still lived in 'the city', which referred to the Willemstad districts of Punda, Otrobanda, Pietermaai and Scharloo. The Sephardic Jews lived primarily in Pietermaai and Scharloo, where prominent residences had been built since the end of the 19th century. Starting in the late 1930s, the prosperous residents of the four old city districts gradually moved out of the city. This development accelerated with the introduction of the car. New districts such as Van Engelen and Mahaai sprang up.

Punda was the commercial center. That is where most of the stores were located, often operating as import firms as well, and frequently owned by Sephardic Jews. The phenomenon of store windows was not yet known. The stores had large wooden doors that stood open during the day. In those days the floors above the stores still partially served as living quarters. Several Eastern European Jews, for example, found a place to live there.

Between Punda and Scharloo lies the *Waaigat*, an inland bay that was later partially filled in. Anna Bay separates Punda from Otrobanda, the oldest city district of Curaçao after Punda. This bay is a narrow passageway leading to the natural harbor of Willemstad, which is called the *Schottegat*. At the time, the Queen Emma Bridge, a floating swing bridge, was the only connection between Punda and Otrobanda.

Together with the white Protestants, who often had lived on Curaçao for generations, and a small group of lightly colored and white Catholics, the Sephardic Jews formed the elite of Curaçao. In addition to this elite, the island had a very large group of mixed-race and black people, who had converted to Roman Catholicism during the slave era. In 1929, approximately 85 per cent of the people on Curaçao were Roman Catholic.[52]

When the Eastern European Jews arrived on Curaçao in the 1920s and '30s, the island was still a Dutch colony, so Dutch was the official language, although the vast majority of the population predominantly spoke Papiamento.

Simple Accommodations

The first places several Ashkenazic Jews went to live are still known: on the Prinsenstraat (*straat* means street) and on the Bakkerstraat in Punda, for example. They also found living quarters in Pietermaai, with its alleyways that ran down to the sea, and on the Penstraat. The Werfstraat and the Bargestraat in Scharloo were also places where the newly arrived men could find rooms, sometimes in a board-

Wolf and Rachel Spritzer in their home on the Bargestraat in 1935. (photo: private collection of Ralph Spritzer)

Ida, Lucien and Victoire Hirschberg in Brussels, where the children stayed with Roman Catholic nuns until their parents had settled on Curaçao. See also the portrait of Ida Hirschberg in Chapter 8. (photo: private collection of Ida Aminoff-Hirschberg)

ing house. In Otrobanda they lived on the Breedestraat and the Langestraat. These early accommodations were mostly quite simple, bordering on dingy.

According to Frieda Geller-Faerman, her father Joske Faerman initially lived with a group of men together in a house in Saliña, while the five members of the Hirschberg family started out living in a single room in Pietermaai. The landladies were two Sephardic women.

It wasn't until the wife and children arrived that the families moved into an entire floor or a simple house. The Hirschbergs quickly found an apartment with more space for the whole family. Apparently they prospered, because seven years after their arrival the family had their own house built on the Abraham de Veerstraat.

When the Eastern Europeans set up their own stores in the 1930s, they often lived above or next to the store. This was the case for Gershon Becher, who began a laundry. His daughter Fanya: "When we arrived in 1930, my father had the ground floor in a large house in Pietermaai. On the second floor lived the Sephardic Robles family. At the back, which looked out on the sea, was the laundry. Later on he had three laundries at different locations. He was also keen on buying and selling real estate for a profit. This enabled him to build a large building in Saliña, where we lived for a year. The laundry was on the ground floor. In 1936 we moved to Van Engelen because my father loved the outdoors. He couldn't afford to buy a real plantation house, so instead he built his own small plantation house."

The emigrants took along as many documents from their country of origin as possible. From this document it seems that there is no extant birth certificate for Miny Zuckerman. (from the private collection of the late Chaim Geiger Jacob)

A New Beginning: Adapted Names and Ages

Once the immigrants reached Curaçao, many altered their surnames. The Romanians with a *ch* in their name soon changed it to a *k*. The Romanian *ch* is pronounced like a *k* and thus, on Curaçao, Acherman became Ackerman, Chisilevici became Kisilevich (the last *ch* pronounced like a *ch* in English) and, to make things simple, the Cheis family called their store Casa Keis. The Josub's original name was Aron Josub, but they were initially called Aranowitz as well. Both names were also used in Romania. The Polish Jew Moses Leib Altnaj left Curaçao for the United States. There in 1942, when he was naturalized as an American citizen, he had his name officially changed to Altman. Moses became Morris.

Besides, many names were written in different ways. To the Curaçao authorities it must sometimes have been a real challenge to decipher handwritten names such as Grynsztein, Walfenzao and Sylbersztejn in passports and other documents. Thus, the latter surname was easily transformed into Silberstein.

Ages were also often incorrect. As mentioned in Chapter 2, men who were eligible for military service sometimes changed their date of birth. If they knew their date of birth, that is, because the Jews in Eastern Europe did not use the Christian calendar. They recalled the day their child was born often as something

```
                    BURGERLIJKE STAND
                BIJ DE JOODSE GEMEENTE IN GRODNO         No. 2542.

        ZEGEL: 1 ZLOTU

        STEMPEL: DE JOODSE GEMEENTE
                 IN GRODNO
                    G E B O O R T E - A K T E
        Hierbij wordt verklaard, dat in het geboortenregister der
        Joodse Bevolking van de stad Grodno in het jaar negentien
        honderd twee en twintig (-1922-) onder het nummer 306 p.m.
        is aangetekend dat uit het huwelijk voltrokken tussen:
                           Gerzon
                Zoon van: Arji Becher

                             en

                           Berta
                Dochter van: Aron Bialostocky
        is geboren te Grodno den 21sten November in het jaar
        negentien honderd twee en twintig (-1922-), een zoon
        aan wien de naam gegeven is "FAJWEL".

               Datum van inschrijving 28 November 1922.

               Het geboorte-bewijs wordt afgegeven met het
        doel tot het verkrijgen van een paspoort.

                    Grodno, den 16den December 1929.

                    De ambtenaar van de Burgerlijke Stand D. Rozowski
                         Rabbijn van de stad Grodno
                    De handtekening v.d. ambtenaar v.d. Burgerlijke
                         Stand van den Heer D. Rozowski

                    Het Bureau van de Joodse Gemeente te Grodno bevestigt.
                         Secretaris A. Senesky.
                    Joodse Gemeente te Grodno (stempel)

                           Voor getrouwe vertaling


                           David Adlerstein.
                           Bij Gouvernements-Beschikking van 31 October
                           1947 no. 9703 aangewezen om deze geboorte-akte
        Curaca, 6 October 1949.  te vertalen in het Nederlands.
```

Birth certificate of Fajwel Becher, translated by David Adlerstein. (from the private collection of Ivan Becher)

like 'three weeks before Yom Kippur' or 'a week after Purim'. Some of those interviewed said that their parents never celebrated birthdays. That was not the custom. Documents show that the immigrants made an effort to take their birth certificates with them, though they were not always successful. The official Polish-language papers of Mina Zuckerman and Moishe Seibald (born in 1907 and

1910 respectively) state that their birth certificates were destroyed by the Russians or could not be found due to the Russian invasion.

Countries of Origin

How many Jews arrived on Curaçao, when and from which country can no longer be ascertained. The fact is that the locals soon referred to them by the Papiamento name *Polakos*[53], meaning Poles. The fact that they were not called 'Romanians' is probably because, in the very beginning, more Polish Jews came to the island. They were soon to be followed by the Romanian Jews and in 1930, 25 Poles and 63 Romanians officially lived on the island[54], which had a total population of 50,000. Whether they were all Jews cannot be ascertained exactly. It is striking that more Eastern European men than women lived on the island (21 Polish and 47 Romanian men), the women often immigrating later.

Based on the nationality of the Ashkenazim that are buried at the *Berg Altena* cemetery and on oral statements, one can justifiably conclude that up to the Second World War roughly equal numbers of Ashkenazim came from Poland and from Romania. A fairly small group came from other Eastern European countries such as Russia and Hungary.

The mail traffic also reveals something about the origins of the Eastern Europeans. Of course the postal traffic was not only between Ashkenazic Jews, but in the accompanying table[55] there is a striking increase in the number of postal items moving to and from Poland and Romania. Such a substantial increase is not evident for other countries, such as Russia or Czechoslovakia. The increase in the postal traffic is particularly noticeable in the period 1928-1930, the years in which a number of men were alone on the island and sent letters to the families they had left behind. Later, when their wives and children had joined them, fewer letters were sent back and forth, but still considerably more than in 1925 and 1926.

Table 2
Number of postal items moving to and from Poland and Romania, 1926-1934

	1925	1926	1927	1928	1929	1930	1931	1932	1933	1934
Mail to Poland	26	182	221	390	1,963	2,795	1,183	923	871	637
Mail from Poland	65	117	143	663	1,001	3,668	1,493	1,625	1,092	793
Mail to Romania	26	91	416	1,430	3,042	3,601	1,469	858	598	507
Mail from Romania	92	78	533	1,131	3,887	4,498	1,716	1,352	1,027	1,157

Getting Rich Quickly and then Returning Home?

The arrival of European Jews on Curaçao did not always mean a definite break with Europe. Many Jews had left their homeland with the idea that their stay on the island would be temporary. They wanted to get rich and then go back. That was also the reason that so many men came to the island alone and only at a later stage – when they realized that they would be staying permanently – sent for their families.

Moishe Geiger from Sniatyn, who was attracted to Curaçao through the stories he had heard from his townsman Ezra Lerner, had earned enough money to return to Poland at a certain moment. Once back, he married and was blessed with a son. But as time passed, the money he had earned on Curaçao ran out and he decided to go to the island for the second time; alone. Again, things went well for him on Curaçao and again he wanted to return to Poland. This time he was stranded in England because the war broke out during his journey back. After the war, he traveled to Curaçao for the third time; now with his English wife. His family in Poland had not survived the war.

Not everyone succeeded in earning enough money in a short time. Dora Suchar-Cheis remembered her father, Hersch Cheis, arriving on the island in 1930 with a group of Jewish men, but the majority returned to Europe disillusioned after a year and a half. They no longer thought they could make a go of it on the island.

Her father also wanted to leave. He made a living as a peddler and could not get used to collecting the weekly installment payments. "I did not have the heart to ask people for money when I could see that they were so poor that they simply could not pay", he had said. This meant that he was unable to get rich quickly, as he had hoped. In 1933 he had had enough and decided to return to Europe once and for all.

Casa Keis, founded in 1933 by Hersch Cheis, still exists. (photo: Jeannette van Ditzhuijzen)

A friend of his, the Sephardic merchant Atilio de Marchena, called him crazy. In Europe Hitler had come to power and he thought it unwise to return to Romania at that time. But De Marchena saw that Cheis was thoroughly miserable without his family. So he lent him money with which to start a store – a store with fixed prices and no payment in installments. In 1934 Cheis' family came to the island.

The store, *Casa Keis* on the De Ruyterkade[56], still exists. As does *Casa Marco*, the store that Cheis opened for his 15-year-old son Marco on the same wharf around 1935.

Temporary Return to Look for a Wife

Several Ashkenazic Jews returned to Europe in the 1930s to visit family or to look for a wife in their home community. Zalman Aron Josub went back to Romania to visit his parents. His friend Joske Faerman had asked him to drop in on his family while there and to give them his love. During his visit to the Faerman family, Zalman fell in love with Joske's sister Manea. He and Joske made sure that Manea would be able to come to Curaçao in 1937, where they married. Because

In order to visit family in Romania, Zalman Aron Josub had to apply for a new passport at the Romanian consulate in New York. (from the private collection of Willy Aron Josub)

Manea was not yet 20, she was not allowed to travel alone. So she simply added two years to her age.

In 1936, Herman Tauber combined a family visit with a business trip. He purchased goods in various European countries and visited his parents. But he made quite sure that he left Poland by the end of the year. In 1937 he would turn 18 and, because he was still a Polish citizen[57], he would be required to serve in the military. So he returned to Curaçao, never to see his parents again.

Fridel Ashendorf had been on Curaçao for only a couple of months when he went back to Europe to look for a wife. In a photo studio in Sniatyn, on the border with his native country Romania, he saw a photo of a friendly-looking and beautiful girl called Klara. He knew at first sight that this was the girl he wanted to marry. He asked for her address and went to visit the family. To his great surprise, they treated his unexpected visit as quite normal and he was received most affectionately. Later, Fridel learned that another Jew from Curaçao had announced to this same family in a letter delivered by a friend that he (the other Jew who had written the letter) would be visiting them. He had heard that they had an eligible daughter and he wanted to marry her. But no name was given in the letter sent from Curaçao. So when Fridel appeared at the door and said that he had come from Curaçao, the girl's parents assumed that he was the man who

While visiting family in Romania, Zalman Aron Josub met Manea Faerman. She came to Curaçao in 1937 to marry Zalman. (from the private collection of Willy Aron Josub)

hoped to marry their daughter. According to the letter, he was very wealthy. This might have been the reason that they showed him such hospitality.

Klara's granddaughter, Esty da Costa-Frankel, said that Fridel and Klara left for Curaçao together eight days after that initial visit to the family. "My grandmother always said that, at the time, she was head over heels in love with someone else. But nothing came of it. My grandparents, though, had the happiest marriage I have ever seen. They were crazy about each other."

Sometimes the men did not travel to Europe, but had a prospective bride come to Curaçao instead. This is what Abram Ackerman, mentioned earlier, did. He had just turned 18 when a friend on Curaçao showed him a photo of his pretty cousin, who had lost her mother at a very young age. Abram became interested, arranged for her to come to Curaçao via the friend and finally married her. As often happened, first there was a religious wedding and only later was a civil marriage concluded.[58] In the case of the Ackermans, more than ten years elapsed before they married under civil law.

Temporary Return for the Children

Single men were not the only ones to return to Europe temporarily. Sometimes parents undertook the long trip so that their children could get to know the family that had stayed behind or to let their child be born in the home country. Chaim Jacob Geiger's mother, for example, really wanted to be with her mother when she was pregnant with him. She journeyed back with her daughter Marcia, gave birth to her son in Poland and stayed away from Curaçao for two years.

Nettie Brandes wanted her children to attend school in Europe. First she traveled alone to Prague to see her sister. Then – in 1937 – she went there again with her two daughters aged 9 and 11. One of them: "She wanted us to have a good education and she had already found a school for us. But the non-Jewish headmistress warned her that, with Hitler in power, it would be better for her and the children to return to Curaçao."

A year and a half after his arrival in 1929, Ernö Spritzer returned to Europe. In those days, the highest education one could receive on Curaçao was advanced elementary education and his father Wolf hoped that his son could study further in Europe and perhaps even enter higher education. So, at age 11, Ernö returned to Berlin where he moved in with a distinctly German family. He was convinced that this family would have made him "a dyed-in-the-wool German boy" had Hitler not come to power in 1933. When this happened, his father let him come back to Curaçao.

Ernö left late enough to experience the boycott of Jewish stores in Germany on 1 April 1933: "Someone at our school decided on that day to exclude all Jewish boys from the lessons. In hindsight, this action was trivial teasing compared with what many were to experience later."

After 'two wonderful months on Curaçao with my parents and friends' Ernö's father Wolf insisted that his son would complete his education in Europe. This time he was sent to the Netherlands, where he attended high school in Arnhem. But the young Ernö kept an eye on events in Germany and finally – in 1937 – he convinced his father that it would be better for him to leave Europe.

Yiddish, English, Dutch and Papiamento

Of course, most of the Ashkenazic children remained on the island. After arriving, almost all of them attended the public Hendrik School (for boys) or Wilhelmina School (for girls). These schools provided a nine-year and later a ten-year program for advanced elementary education. Sometimes the children were placed a couple of years lower than they would normally be for their age until their mastery of the Dutch language was good enough to keep up in class. In most cases that happened fairly quickly. From their friends they also learned to speak Papiamento, while some of them (later) spoke English with staff members from the Windward Islands or other islands. Even today, many Ashkenazic Jews speak different languages interchangeably. They speak Yiddish with one person, Dutch, English or Papiamento with others. Even members of one family make an easy transition from speaking Yiddish to speaking English or Papiamento.

The use of Yiddish is clearly declining. The older generation grew up with it and many older Jews spoke only Yiddish with their parents. But the young children do not speak it or only a few words.

The Yiddish that is spoken is not spoken or pronounced the same by everyone. The Jews that generally come from Lithuania, northern Poland and White Russia speak Litvish Yiddish. The others speak Galician Yiddish and talk about *shiel* when referring to the synagogue; in Litvish Yiddish it is called *shul*.

Although the former residents of Czernowitz also speak Galician Yiddish, the Ashkenazim hear a clear difference between the Yiddish spoken by the Poles and the Yiddish spoken by people from Czernowitz. Because many Czernowitz Jews originally used the High German of the Habsburg Empire, according to the Polish Jews they spoke a 'Germanized Yiddish'. The Romanian Jews, on the other hand, asserted that they spoke the only true Yiddish.

▶ **Lily Kisilevich-Bonaparte (New York, 1940)**

"My father lived in Darabani, in Moldavia (Romania). He had three sisters and his father died when he was very young. So he had to work and study in the cheder to help his family. What he really wanted to do was to attend the gymnasium (advanced college preparatory high school), but that was not possible due to the numerus clausus. This meant that only one or two Jews were admitted per class or per school. Because of this discrimination, he departed for Venezuela with a cousin. But he didn't like it at all there, so he moved on to Curaçao. That would have been in the early 1930s."
"On Curaçao my father became a 'klopper', which is Yiddish for peddler. With a rucksack full of goods, he would set out. In this way, he earned enough money to start up a business in Otrobanda: La Violetta at Breedestraat 76."

Isaac and Lily Kisilevich-Bonaparte. (photo: Jeannette van Ditzhuijzen)

"My mother, Dunia Acherman, didn't come to Curaçao until 1938. She still remembered the pogroms in Noua Suliță; that the Cossacks had stolen all the copper pots, and that her mother sent the girls away so that the soldiers would not abuse them. Financially, they didn't have it so bad there; they had a small grocery."

"In Noua Suliță my mother fought as a communist for the rights of the workers. Because the police were looking for her, her sister, Lea Meit-Acherman, sent her a ticket for the passage to Curaçao. In those days it was inappropriate for a woman to live alone. That is why they found a husband for her on the island. So it was an arranged marriage, like many others at the time. Even as late as in the 1950s."

"She went to New York to give birth to me and, later, to my brother Mark. She had several brothers and sisters living there. Thus my brother and I acquired the 'golden passport'. That still happens. People arrange to give birth to children in America for the passport."

"As a child, I always spoke Yiddish with my parents. I also learned to read it and read the Forwarts, a Yiddish language newspaper. My father taught me Romanian as well." ◀

4 Working Hard to Earn a Living

It is often suggested that all Ashkenazic Jews started working as peddlers immediately after arriving on Curaçao. But some of them found jobs at the Shell refinery, while others set up small businesses. Women and even children worked very hard alongside the men. In this way, many of them were able to develop into successful storekeepers and businessmen in a short time.

Earning Money in the Far-off Americas

Just how the first Eastern European Jews found their way on the tropical island of Curaçao we will never really know. It must have been a strange transition for them to make. After enduring a sea journey of several weeks, they often arrived destitute on an island that many of them had never heard of. But based on the stories told, it is possible to reconstruct a few things.

The first one to explore the island, though not to make it his home was the Pole Ezra Lerner. His journey to the Western Hemisphere in the 1920s was an escape, according to a nephew. In those days, the new border between Poland and Russia was not yet established precisely and Lerner apparently had an altercation with a Russian officer. The officer had maltreated a Jewish friend of his and according to family stories, the officer was wounded during the incident and probably even killed. So under the circumstances, it was best for Lerner to leave Poland. He headed west with his wife Basea Seibald from Sniatyn, and visited Curaçao, among other ports of call.

It is thought that Lerner returned to Poland in 1925. Once there, he undoubtedly told his wife's family stories about the opportunities he had seen overseas. The Seibald family thought it would be a good idea for the youngest son, the nearly 16-year-old Moishe, to see whether a good life could be earned in far-off 'America'. So Moishe left for Venezuela, where Ezra Lerner was living at the time. According to Moishe's daughter, her father was not allowed to enter Venezuela. That is why he left for Curaçao (probably by hitching a ride on a fishing boat), an island Lerner was familiar with.

According to historian Johan Hartog, Moishe arrived on Curaçao in July of 1926. That seems likely, because in April of that year he collected a certificate of good conduct in his hometown Sniatyn, and a statement from the office of Jewish birth certificates. The first weeks and months were probably not easy for such a youngster. We do know that Herman Tauber, who as a 14-year-old arrived on Curaçao in 1933 to join his brother, cried incessantly for the first few days. He was terribly homesick. Whether or not Moishe also felt homesick, we do not know. But as time went on, things went so well for him that his brothers Selig and Salomon decided in 1930 to follow him to Curaçao[59].

Selig's son Leon related what his father then did. Ezra Lerner, who regularly traveled to Curaçao from Venezuela, supposedly gave him a suitcase filled with fabrics. "He had to sell them door-to-door, on credit. The sales were written down on the tab and at the end of the week you had to go back for the payments due."

Selig's brother Salomon also soon started peddling. He arrived at the end of May 1930 and his official peddling permit dates from three months later. He was allowed to sell furniture, dry goods and kitchenware in the 1st and 2nd districts until 9 in the evening.[60]

Shell Offers New Opportunities

The fact that things went so well on Curaçao for Moishe and many others that followed surely had to do with the enormous zest for work the immigrants had. They also had the good fortune to arrive at a time when the economy was prospering, i.e. shortly after the establishment of Shell's oil refinery, which was popularly referred to as the *Isla*. It brought great change to the island in the 1920s.

At the end of the 19th and the start of the 20th century, there was widespread poverty on Curaçao. After the extraction of phosphate came to an end at the Tafelberg in East Curaçao in 1895, hundreds of disillusioned unemployed people were left behind. Farming, always a marginal activity on the island, could not make up for this economic downturn due to a persistent drought. Women tried to earn a few meager pennies by weaving straw hats, but that could not alter the fact that poverty on the island was rampant.

With the arrival of Shell, employment increased quickly starting in the 1920s. The demand for labor was so great that Shell started to look for employees beyond the island. The result was a substantial increase in the population: from 34,893 inhabitants in 1920 to 50,165 in 1930.[61] At the end of 1930, approximately one-third (28 per cent) of the population was not a Curaçao native. By contrast, only 6 per cent of the population had been non-native in 1925.[62]

Curaçaoans that used to expend considerable effort scraping together a living in farming or fishing could now find work fairly easily at Shell. For the straw hat weavers, better-paid jobs opened up as housemaids and laundresses for the Shell employees that had come over from the Netherlands.

In those years, there was both a larger market and increased buying power. The Ashkenazic Jews who peddled their wares from door to door took advantage of this boom. The Curaçao natives who lived outside Punda and Otrobanda suddenly had more money to spend. And thanks to the Jewish peddlers, they did not have to go to the city to shop – still a long journey in those days. From the peddlers they would purchase things such as fabric, sewing supplies, furniture, pots and pans; usually on an installment plan, a possibility that they had seldom or never had in the city.

The peddlers called themselves '*kloppers*', which literally means 'knockers' in English. It is most likely derived from the Yiddish word '*kloppen*': when the peddlers came by to sell their wares or to collect money, they knocked on the doors.[63]

A *Klopper* Going from Door to Door

One of the Jewish peddlers was Josif (Joske) Faerman. Starting in 1928, he walked to 'Post V', where the refinery was located, in order to show his goods from door to door. But he also walked all the way to Westpunt with a sack full of textile goods on his back. He said that the distance of some forty kilometers took him three days.[64] Around 1935, he started his own store, called The New Store. According to one of his daughters, this store employed some one hundred staff in the end. By then it was named 'José Faerman'.

Joske became friends with Zalman Aron Josub, who arrived on Curaçao from Romania around 1930. Aron Josub also became a *klopper*. His son Willy: "He purchased fabrics and small costumes for children, walked from door to door and sold on credit. Each week he returned to his customers to collect the two or three guilders that they were due. By 1934 he had his own store, so he wasn't a peddler for a long time."

Initially, most of the *kloppers* traveled on foot. But some of them, such as Mozes Meit Jr., had a donkey. Others were able to buy a horse and wagon or bicycle over time, such as Haim Gandelman and Joske Faerman.

According to Marcia Linder-Geiger, her uncle Moishe told her that he bought goods at *Casa Cohen*, owned by the Sephardic Jew William Cohen, and sold them door-to-door in Otrobanda. He wasn't always welcome. Sometimes only a crack in the door would appear. In those cases, he was quick to stick his foot in the doorway and this strategy helped him sell things after all.

An old resident of Baraltwijk (Otrobanda) remembered how the *kloppers* lugged around enormous suitcases. She said they carried them on their backs using ropes. "I remember that one of them regularly called on my grandmother, with whom I lived. He would open the suitcase so that all the neighbors could see what he was selling: sheets, towels, kitchen towels, etc. My grandmother would then make a cup of coffee for him and he would take out his sandwiches and sit down, while the neighbors looked at the contents of the suitcase and eventually bought something."

By maintaining direct contact with Curaçao residents, the *kloppers* knew exactly what the needs of their customers were. This knowledge served them well when they later opened their own stores in Punda and Otrobanda. Because they didn't spend their entire lives going door-to-door selling goods on credit. The last *klopper* probably gave up his rounds at the end of the 1930s.

Selling on Credit

Only in the furniture trade, selling products on an installment plan was practiced until long after the Second World War.[65] Although at that time the Lebanese (originating from Syria and Lebanon, see Chapter 14) appeared to have a monopoly in the furniture trade, one Ashkenazic family was also involved in the sector: the Seibalds. Evidenced by his peddler's license, Salomon sold furniture as early as 1930. The other brothers probably did so as well. It is certain that the three brothers (Selig, Salomon and Moishe) all finally ended up in the 'furniture business selling on credit'.

The peddler's license issued to Salomon Seibald in 1930. (from the private collection of Benny Seibald)

Because Shell paid wages on Saturday, the Jewish traders went by customers' houses on Sunday to collect the debts. Moishe's children remembered clearly how their father left home early in the 1960s and 1970s on this collection day. The customers did not always have cash on hand at home. In this case, the *klopper* would be told by a child: "My mother says that she is not home."

They also remembered Moishe's 'address book', which seldom contained real addresses, since streets did not always have names. The book did have cryptic notes in it, such as "Maria, the sister of so-and-so, who lives in the blue house with a tree, two houses down from the corner". With notes like these, Moishe knew exactly where he had to be. But not his children, who inherited the address book after his death. Frieda Geller-Faerman also remembered that in the 1930s her father recognized the addresses by the color and the shape of the houses.

The Tauber brothers never sold on credit. Leon, who arrived in 1929, began his small clothing store on the Breedestraat in Otrobanda back in 1930. In contrast to his fellow countrymen, Leon bought and sold items purely on a cash-up-front basis. According to his brother, he did not want to be helped by anyone, so he did not provide credit plans.

Peddlers and Other Professions

Between 1926 and 1929, the number of 'traders' (salesmen without a store, including both peddlers and wholesalers) on the island more than doubled (see table 3).[66]

Table 3 Number of traders in the urban districts of Curaçao, 1926-1929

	1926	1927	1928	1929
traders in 1st district	423	464	493	786
traders in other districts	39	55	207	223
total	462	519	700	1,009

This increase very probably was caused by the arrival of the Eastern European Jews who, just as the Lebanese, started out as peddlers.

The large number of traders in 1929 does not mean that all Eastern European immigrants began as peddlers, though that impression is occasionally created. The assumption that over half of these immigrants did in fact start off as peddlers is probably justified, but the remainder found other ways to earn a living. Some of them worked for Shell or were employed elsewhere before they began their own businesses. The self-owned stores usually focused on textiles, since the peddlers principally traded in textiles.

Chaim Kisilevich from Noua Suliță first worked for a Sephardic Jew. With the money that he earned, he bought a simple kiosk on the Handelskade, where he sold cigarettes and soft drinks. He then started a soda fountain. It was only later that he entered the men's clothing business.

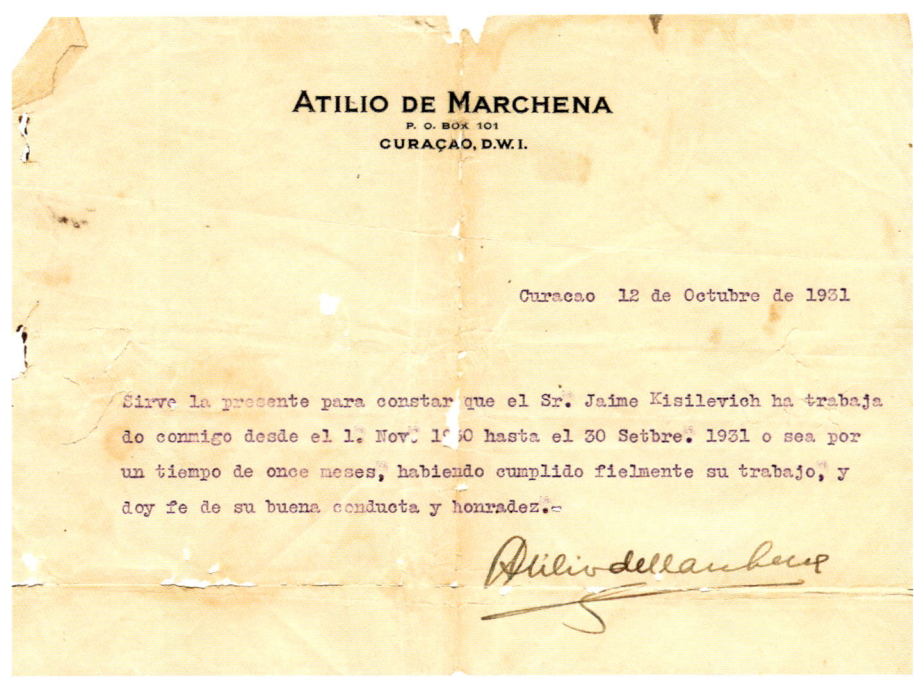

A testimonial for Chaim Kisilevich written in Spanish by the Sephardic merchant Atilio de Marchena. (from the private collection of Isaac Kisilevich)

Rachmiel Geiger from Sniatyn had his comb and scissors with him when he stepped off the boat at the end of the 1920s. Curaçao appealed to him very much and he started earning a living as a barber. Later, his wife also opened a barbershop. Following a period working at Shell, Gershon Becher began a laundry and also earned money by buying and selling land and houses. And, of course, there were Wolf Spritzer and Charles Fuhrmann, who began making a living simply by repairing watches. They were later to run the largest jewelry business in the Caribbean region (see the portrait in Chapter 13).

The Lure of Success

The immigrants worked extremely hard and lived frugally. They sent some of the money they saved home to the family they had left behind and who often lived in poverty. But that was not always possible. Wolf Spritzer initially struggled on Curaçao so much that he could hardly send any money to his wife and children in Berlin. The family primarily had to rely on the little bit of money that mother Spritzer could earn through needlework and mending.

Later, after Spritzer and Fuhrmann began working together, they still followed the rule that they would only spend nine out of every ten guilders they earned. That is, if they did earn ten guilders, said Charles Fuhrmann in 1977 at the 50th anniversary of Spritzer+Fuhrmann.

Chaim Kisilevich in his kiosk on the Handelskade, circa 1932. (photo: private collection of Isaac Kisilevich)

Lily Kisilevich-Bonaparte's father regularly received letters from his mother in which she asked for money. But he did not have much money and did not like doing business. As opposed to his wife. "My mother liked doing business. She worked hard and secretly sent a package of clothing to her mother-in-law, who she did not even know."

Neighbors and friends of successful immigrants' families that did receive money, noticed their good fortune. In this way, news of the success the Seibalds were having, for example, spread around the Polish town of Sniatyn, from where they originated. The Taubers knew the Seibalds and, because Leon Tauber did not want to be conscripted into the Polish army, around 1929 he decided to journey to Curaçao, just as the Seibalds had. Elias Linder, a neighbor of the Taubers in Sniatyn, made the same journey in 1929. His son Bruno remembered another Sniatyn neighbor who had already been to Curaçao and had returned with money. It was the start of a chain of migration from the town to Curaçao.

Wolf and Rosa Spritzer in front of their first store, still called Relojeria Alemana at the time. (photo: collection of the National Archives of Curaçao)

A Tightly-Knit Community

More and more, people started to come to Curaçao because they knew someone there. And those that didn't know anyone but ended up on the island by chance, were almost immediately welcomed into the ever increasing family of Ashkenazim. For that stands out above all else: it was a tightly-knit community that took care of its own like family. One of the people interviewed: "If one family was having a difficult time, the others would help even financially."

Charles Fuhrmann in front of his first store on the Handelskade. (photo: collection of the National Archives of Curaçao)

A good example of this is the help the community offered to Yitzak Grynsztein. After arriving on the island in 1927, the Polish Grynsztein worked as a road worker – until the day that the foreman, who was also Jewish, heard him speak Yiddish. He was surprised and asked Grynsztein why he did not go from door to door as a peddler like the others. Grynsztein gave it a try, but not for long. Not much later he could be seen selling food from his boat moored adjacent to the current post office in Punda.

He did this until, one ill-fated day, the boat sank. Everything was lost, but the Ashkenazic Jewish community stepped into the breach immediately to help out a fellow Jew. Everyone donated a little money, which was used to rent a business for Grynsztein on the De Ruyterkade.

As it happened, just at that time one of his fellow Jews was about to leave for New York. On arriving there he made contact with an exporter of kosher foods, and from that moment on, Grynsztein supplied the Jewish community with kosher food from his new store. His son Nachman: "Everyone was happy, because now they could buy kosher sausage or cheese."

The Ashkenazic Traders Become Competitors

Trade on Curaçao had, to a large degree, been in the hands of the Sephardic Jews. Not only the wholesale businesses, but also the stores in the city were often run by Sephardic merchants. It has often been suggested that they immediately saw the newcomers from Eastern Europe as competitors. In truth, things may have been different: after the arrival of the Ashkenazim, the Sephardim sold goods on credit to the peddlers, who used the goods to tap a new market, i.e. the outlying districts of Curaçao. They purchased goods, for example, from the Sephardic merchant Atilio de Marchena, who imported dry goods, fancy articles and perfumes.[67] His office was located on the Breedestraat 9/13 (Punda).[68]

Herman Tauber said that his brother once worked as a *klopper* for *Casa Cohen*, a large Sephardic Jewish store that sold virtually everything. He wasn't the only one. That meant that he and others went door-to-door in the outlying districts as sales representatives with goods from *Casa Cohen* only. A letter of recommendation from the aforementioned De Marchena reveals that Chaim Kisilevich worked for him for the first eleven months of his stay on the island. Did he perhaps work as a *klopper*? The letter says nothing about it, but it is most likely.

Ironically, the depression of 1929 provided the *Polakos* with new opportunities. The very same depression that had prompted many of them to flee Europe. On Curaçao, the consequences of the depression did not begin to hit until 1930. Oil production decreased and the refining of oil went down with it. The prosperity of the 1920s made way for a period of layoffs at the refinery and related businesses. Due to the increasing unemployment, many foreign employees left the island. The large traders in Punda were stuck with their stocks as a result and their turnover fell.

At this point, the Polish and Romanian immigrants suddenly became competitors of the established merchants. They lived simple lives and had little or no stocks hanging around their necks like millstones. Since they bought and sold goods on a small scale, they could easily save the profits. And because they did not have any expensive store properties, they could hold out easier than the established merchants, who owned stores and residential properties and were used to a high standard of living.

In these economically difficult years for trade on Curaçao, the Ashkenazic traders grabbed their opportunity. Some of them had saved just enough money to buy up the surplus stocks of the Sephardic Jews for next to nothing. They sold these goods either door-to-door or in the small stores that a few of them had been able to open on the edges of Punda and Otrobanda.

Due to the recession, a few of them even saw their way clear to start up stores on the very chic Heerenstraat in Punda. They moved into buildings, for example, that the Sephardic Jews had been forced to shut down. Or a storekeeper would rent a part of his store to an Ashkenazic trader because the costs of the building as a whole were too much to be borne by his budget. This is probably how, in 1933, Max and Jacobo Fruchter from Sniatyn began their store *El Continental* in a part of the department store owned by the Henriquez brothers at Heerenstraat 24. In addition to the Fruchters, four other Eastern European Jews opened businesses on the Heerenstraat at the end of the 1930s: Samuel Pimsler opened *La Estrella,* Jan Groisman *El Chic Americano,* Moishe Altnaj began his *Oriental Store* and Adolf Haber started *The New York Store.*[69]

By Curaçao standards, this expansion of the Ashkenazic Jews must have seemed like a drastic change. Even the *Curaçaosch Verslag* of 1934 mentions it: "Small storekeepers from foreign nations who have limited needs and can easily adapt to local circumstances started their businesses small, outside the center of Curaçao's commercial class. They worked their way up and saw an opportunity to expand their businesses gradually. With this rise in success, they are approaching, step by step, the old commercial center, thereby driving former, native Curaçao merchants from their once seemingly unassailable position."[70]

Haim Gandelman with his apparently newly acquired bicycle in 1933. (photo: private collection of Basia Bitterman-Gandelman)

Importing from America and Japan

Once it had begun, the advance seemed unstoppable. Particularly when the recession came to an end in 1934. Not only did increasing numbers of Eastern European Jews acquire their own stores, they also began to import fabrics and other goods themselves.

By importing their own goods, the Ashkenazim were no longer dependent on the Sephardic merchants and were able to purchase their wares at lower prices. This appealed very much to the price-conscious Curaçaons and they ignored the established stores with their more expensive articles. Furthermore, the Ashkenazic importers brought ready-to-wear clothing to the island. That was new. Up to then, women had purchased fabric by the meter. From this they would have clothing made or they sewed garments themselves.

Some Ashkenazic traders, such as Leon Tauber, traveled to New York to

Salomon (left) and Abraham Wiznitzer in their store, circa 1935. (photo: private collection of Leo Wiznitzer)

purchase merchandise. Others imported cheap textiles from Japan, following the example of the East Indians who brought in embroidery and silk fabrics from Japan and China.[71]

As a result, imports from Japan increased considerably. In 1929, the Japanese share of total imports to Curaçao expressed in guilders amounted to less than 0.5 per cent. In 1936, this share rose to over 2.2 per cent. If we consider only textiles and clothing, we see that in 1929 2.5 per cent came from Japan and in 1936 this rose to 76.5 per cent (this concerns the imports to all of the Netherlands Antilles).[72] Well-known importers were the Sterental brothers (from *La Fama* on the De Ruyterkade) and the Wiznitzer Brothers (later *La Confianza*).

Wives and Children Help Out

The rapid commercial rise of the Ashkenazim can be attributed in part to the women and children. There was no money to hire staff and so the women rolled up their sleeves. Just like the American mom and pop store, Curaçao had its '*mama ku papa* store' with mother working behind the counter. This was a new phenomenon for (commercial) Curaçao, where people were used to seeing men run the businesses.

Helping out in the stores was an urgent necessity. Official store closing times were not established until the mid 1930s. Before then, many stores were open until 11 in the evening. According to Dora Suchar-Cheis, *Casa Keis* was often open as late as 1 in the morning; and Bruno Linder remembered that their *refreskeria* next to Brión Square was initially open until midnight.

He and his brother Felix always had to help out on the Queen's Birthday. They could never take part in the festivities because their parents had their biggest turnover in the *refreskeria* on that day. So they had to make themselves useful. They often had to help out after school too.

As a child, Dora also assisted regularly in the store. When school let out at 12 noon, instead of going home she went to her parents' store. This allowed her parents to go home for lunch while she looked after the store. A little later, her eldest sister would take over so that Dora could get something to eat at home. When her father attended the synagogue on Saturday, the children had to help out in the store as well. "We were very small, but we knew things were difficult and that we had to help in order for the family to move forward." Paul Ackerman also remembered the Saturdays that he was required to spend in the store. And like Dora and Bruno, he also helped out after school.

Furthermore, many Ashkenazic women tried to earn a little extra money outside the store. Bruno's mother and several other women cooked initially for single Eastern European men. Nettie Brandes, Ana Gandelman, Sonia Kisilevich and Beila Libman even opened small restaurants. After a long day of peddling in the burning sun, the unmarried Jewish men liked to receive a familiar meal served by fellow countrywomen. Wolf Spritzer ate at Kisilevich in his first years on the island; apparently he occasionally did not have any money to pay for it. According to Charles Gomes Casseres, Ana Gandelman even had a kosher restaurant on the Columbusstraat. There was also a small library with Yiddish books[73] that, according to daughter-in-law Fanya Gandelman-Becher, belonged to her father-in-law. "People would come to him to borrow these books."

Women earned a living in other ways, too. Frieda Hirschberg, for example, was a beautician and made the fact known immediately after arriving on the island in 1930. Very soon thereafter, the well-to-do Sephardic ladies would send their chauffeur-driven car to pick Frieda up so that they could enjoy her services in the comfort of their homes. Later on she opened a salon in her own house and became known as 'Madame Frieda'. And the mother of Fanny Sprung-Weisinger earned extra money by sewing clothes for the neighbors and the wealthy Sephardic Jews in Scharloo.

Credit from the Sephardic Maduro & Curiel's Bank

Due to these small-scale activities, the Eastern Europeans needed very little capital shortly after their arrival. The single men lived in rented rooms and otherwise had few expenditures. They also bought small amounts of merchandise and from the money they earned they could buy new goods and perhaps a better knapsack or a horse.

It wasn't until they acquired their own stores over the course of the 1930s and started to import merchandise themselves that they began to need more money. To fill this need, the newcomers approached the Sephardic Jewish Maduro & Curiel's Bank (MCB). The Ashkenazic Jews unanimously agree that the MCB placed enormous trust in them and gave them excellent assistance. They could borrow money easily and any one of them that wanted to start a store, first went and talked to the MCB.

The bank's director at the time, Sha Capriles, had a 'good business sense' according to his son Lio. "With a single handshake, he knew whether he could trust someone. This group of people had come to Curaçao without funds, but they did have an enormous drive to work and the will to make it a success. That is why they could borrow money from the bank so easily."

So business-wise relations were still good between the Ashkenazic and the Sephardic Jews, despite the increasing competition. That is apparent from the fact that many a Sephardic Jew sold goods to Ashkenazic Jews on credit and even lent them money. Atilio de Marchena, mentioned earlier, helped not only Hersch Cheis financially (see Chapter 3), Elias Linder from Sniatyn was also able to borrow money from him. With this loan and with money he won in the *Jamaica Sweepstake,* he was able to pay the passage for his wife and four children in 1933.

By the way, Atilio was the brother-in-law of bank director Sha Capriles. Through his contacts with the Ashkenazim, he brought many customers to the MCB. The good business contacts between the two groups of fellow Jews stand in sharp contrast to the social contacts between them. These were virtually non-existent.

▶ Marie Brandes (Czernowitz, 1926)

"My father had a business in Czernowitz. But the stores were boycotted and then came the 1929 crash. We knew that America had closed its doors, but my mother had a cousin who lived on Curaçao – Saul Crivosei. He had written to my father encouraging him to come there. He then traveled to Curaçao, where he arrived without any money, like everyone else. Initially, they were all poor. I don't know what my father did after he arrived. He was certainly not a klopper, that simply wasn't a part of his nature."

"My mother, my sister Margit and I arrived on the island in 1930. My mother opened a restaurant in the house where we lived on the De Ruyterkade. The few Jews that lived in the neighborhood came to eat at her restaurant. Joske Faerman and Zalman Aron Josub, for instance. My father then opened his own business – the Casa Brandes, also on the De Ruyterkade."

"As a child I attended the Wilhelmina School in Punda. I did not receive religious instruction from the Sephardic rabbi. That was still only available to boys at the time. At school I came in contact with the Sephardic Jews, but I was never invited into their homes. Later on that became more normal. Until the end of the 1960s, we had no social contacts with them, only business contacts."

"My family was not extremely religious. On Saturday we simply worked, but we did light candles on Friday evening. My father went to the synagogue, my mother did not. And we didn't eat kosher. Kosher food had to be imported and that was very expensive. The chickens we ate were slaughtered at home. The Jewish ritual slaughterer Gersz Szmukler was the first one to slaughter chickens."

"The Ashkenazic Jews did not live separately from the local population. We took part in everything – in the Dutch public holidays, for example. There was no animosity towards us. They did call us Polakos, but it had nothing to do with our religion. We were considered different because we came from Europe, that's why we were called *Polakos*."

"I have lived in America for 40 years now, but I still maintain contact with the Jews of Curaçao. When they come to Miami, they call me up or they come by. You see, we were a small and very tightly-knit group of people." ◀

5 The Newcomers – Better Off Without Them

From a social viewpoint, the Ashkenazic Jews were not given a warm welcome by their Sephardic fellow Jews. The differences in their origin and social status were simply too great. Initially, the Ashkenazim did receive business assistance from the Sephardic merchants. Yet, once they developed into formidable competitors, relations cooled significantly.

The Old and New Jews of Curaçao

On the face of it, one would expect the Sephardic Jews already living on Curaçao to have embraced the newly arrived Eastern Europeans. What could be more obvious than to help their fellow Jews settle on the island? In one or two cases they did, judging by Atilio de Marchena's account (see Chapter 3). But as a general rule, the Sephardic and Ashkenazic Jews did not interact. Moreover, the Ashkenazic Jews clearly felt that the Sephardic merchants – fellow Jews! – looked down on them. A sentiment some still remember only too well.

According to Herman Tauber, there was a distinct division between the two groups. "We were not smart enough and not good enough. That was obvious. That is why we wanted to do better than them. Although we came to the island later, we did want to be the best."

It is easy to understand why the Sephardim kept their distance. How were they supposed to relate to this group of poor and often poorly educated Jews that had unexpectedly entered their world? Selig Seibald, for instance, never went to school because, from a young age, he had to provide for his family after his father was killed in the First World War. Furthermore, their traditions were different: the Eastern European Jews brought their own history with them and they spoke a different language. When they first arrived wearing their Eastern European clothing, the Ashkenazim must have formed a distinctly foreign element in Curaçao society.

Even the local population made a distinction between the Sephardim and the 'new' Jews. The Sephardic Jews were always referred to as *Hudiunan* (Jews). For the people of Curaçao, this term was manifestly unsuitable for the new

Jewish group, which had none of the sophisticated elegance of the Sephardim. Hence they gave the Eastern European Jews another name: *Polakos*.

The difference between the newcomers and the well-educated and, to a large extent, prosperous Sephardic Jews was indeed great. After barely three centuries in Curaçao, the latter had developed into '*a Latin-Caribbean cultural aristocracy*'.[74] Not that all Sephardic Jews were rich, but in view of the large number of bankers and merchants among them, they were generally seen as such. The Ashkenazic Jews could do no more than look up to these well-to-do citizens in their magnificent houses in Scharloo who generally moved in the island's highest social echelons. By the way, the Ashkenazim did not think it out of the ordinary that they occupied an isolated position in Curaçao society. In Poland and Romania, it had been no different. There too their everyday language, Yiddish, had set them apart.

The children did, however, meet at school in Punda. Here again, it appeared that the two distinct Jewish groups had as little in common as their parents. Socially they lived in different worlds. Sometimes an Ashkenazic child would be invited to a Sephardic friend's birthday party. And Marjorie da Costa Gomez-Brandao, a Sephardic Jew, remembered that as a child she played with Tila Cheis, an Ashkenazi, and they did their homework together. As she recalled, it was usually the older generation that kept their distance from the Eastern

In 1938, Rabbi Isaac Emmanuel of Mikvé Israel organized a commemoration evening on the occasion of the 500th birthday of the Portuguese scholar and rabbi Don Isaac Abravanel. Although the Ashkenazic and Sephardic Jews at the time operated in complete segregation from one another, several Ashkenazic Jews took part nonetheless, as seen by this program item. Seven of the twelve prophets were depicted by Ashkenazim. (from the collection of the Mongui Maduro Library, Curaçao)

European Jews. Still, the difference in backgrounds was generally too great for close and lasting friendships to be established. "That's just the way it was", a few interviewees acknowledged.

It is remarkable that some Ashkenazim now say, so many decades later, that the attitude of the Sephardic Jews was not all that bad. This is probably because relations are much better today. And perhaps too because they are well aware that they themselves were a very close-knit group that formed a united front against the outside world. Just as they had in their homeland. So perhaps on their part too, there was initially little attempt at rapprochement.

A few Ashkenazim, particularly the younger ones, even show a measure of understanding for the attitude of the Sephardic Jews in those days. As a member of the post-war generation said, "When I watch old movies, I can understand to some extent the reaction of the Sephardic Jews. So I can't really blame them. I would probably have done the same. There was just such a big cultural gap." Yet that does not alter the fact that a few Ashkenazim, young and old, still hold some resentment for the rejection showed by their Sephardic fellow Jews.

For that matter, the Sephardic Jews led a similarly isolated existence after their arrival on Curaçao in the middle of the 17th century.[75] Then, too, they stuck together when differences in language, religion and culture between the Jews and the white Protestants were irreconcilably great. That isolation continued for a long time. Until the 1940s, the different sections of Curaçao's population – the Catholics, the Protestants and the Sephardic Jews – led separate lives, not only in religious terms, but also in social and cultural terms. In the segregated Netherlands of those years, the situation was actually not dissimilar.

The Established Merchants Rebel

Despite the rift between the two groups of Jews, business relations between them were generally good during the first few years (see Chapter 4). As long as the Eastern European peddlers and small retailers bought their merchandise from the Sephardic Jews, there was nothing to fear. That changed when the Ashkenazic Jews opened more and larger stores and became stronger competitors – even competing among each other, for that matter.

As early as June 1932, when the financial crisis in Curaçao could still be felt, more than fifty Curaçao merchants – Jewish and non-Jewish – sent a letter to the Governor in which they complained of "unfair competition from the unwelcome immigrants [...] who have unbelievably low standards and tend not to employ any staff". Immigration restrictions by the government had not helped, they reported. The Curaçao business community had hoped the immigrants themselves would understand that they should halt their 'unfair competition'. But this did not happen. It soon appeared that "these merchants are conducting their trade practices even more vigorously than before, if possible, from the crack of dawn till late at night".

The merchants advised the governor that "these disastrous business practices by people with the lowest standards of living, who perform all the work themselves, allowing no one else to earn a livelihood and contributing next to nothing in taxes, threaten to lead to the bankruptcy of several old and fragile establishments and to the layoff of hundreds of office and store employees".

The employees and clerks also sent a letter to the governor. They wholeheartedly supported their bosses' complaint. Some were already without work, or receiving lower salaries. They wrote that if the government did not do something soon, then in the not too distant future they would suffer 'dire hardships'.

In their petition, the Curaçao merchants offered an immediate solution to the problem: enforced closing times for stores and a legal prohibition on foreigners 'of the type mentioned above' practicing a trade on the island. To 'temper the severity of the measure' they proposed that the ban should be applicable only to foreigners who had arrived on Curaçao after 1 June 1926. Furthermore, they should be given a reasonable period of time in which to liquidate their businesses.[76] Since the first Eastern European Jew had arrived on the island in July 1926, there is no doubt that the proposed measure was directed against the Ashkenazic Jews. The Ashkenazim would certainly have seen it in this light. This also explains the resentment that some still feel towards their fellow Jews' unfriendly reception.

Proposals against Ashkenazic Competition

The ordinance concerning closing times requested by the merchants was introduced that same year (1932), although it did not actually come into force until 1935. Then the curtain fell and stores were no longer permitted to stay open until late in the evening. A letter of protest was written by a number of retailers, mostly Ashkenazi, but to no avail. They thought the law should be more flexible, arguing that, on occasion, ships arrived late in the harbor and crew members were known to make 'significant purchases'.[77]

A second response to the above-mentioned appeal for help from the established Curaçao business community was the 'Ordinance containing some provisions for traders', submitted in October 1932. In the explanatory memorandum, Governor Bartholomeus van Slobbe noted that new merchants must provide a bank guarantee "such that persons, as referred to by the petitioners, are deterred from starting an enterprise and prevented from joining the business community to which, through their conduct and lifestyle, they do more harm than good".[78]

The ordinance, however, remained in the draft phase. The Dutch Minister for the Colonies, Simon de Graaff, did not like the idea of a prohibition on establishing a business. In a secret letter dated November 1932, the governor tried to convince Minister De Graaff that the local business community needed to be protected against Ashkenazic competition. He wrote that 'some of these traders had already left the area with unsettled debts'.[79] But according to the Dutch Minister, competition was a universal phenomenon, even when that competition originated from 'foreigners with very low standards of living'.

Competition became even fiercer when, starting in 1934, Ashkenazic traders began to import cheap goods directly from Japan (see Chapter 4). This provided the well-established businessmen with a reason to lobby strongly again for the introduction of a business license. The lobby was led by Julius Penha[80], a Sephardic Jew who imported dry goods, luxury goods, perfumes and cigars. He served as president of the Curaçao Chamber of Commerce from 1916 to1933.

In a letter sent at the end of 1934 to the *Koloniale Raad* (Colonial Council), A.J.C. Henriquez and others once again urged for speed to be taken regarding the draft ordinance of 1932. Not only did Eastern Europeans and Asians cause 'ruinous competition' to established trade, "only a small proportion of the profits [is] put into circulation because the lion's share is saved to be taken back to the homeland, or is transferred to the families who stayed behind for their support or capitalization".[81]

It would take until 1937 for a business-establishment ordinance to come into effect.[82] The Chamber of Commerce, for which Sephardic merchant Haim Cohen Henriquez served as president at the time, had advised the government in this respect.[83] The new national ordinance determined that from then on foreigners not only needed an entry permit, but once on Curaçao they would also have to submit an application for a business license to start a company or store. A license was only issued by the governor after a recommendation had been obtained from the Chamber of Commerce, which was dominated by the established merchants.

Boycott of German Goods Brings Matters into Focus

The licensing regulation and the efforts of the established Curaçao merchants to get it imposed did not enhance relations between the Ashkenazic and Sephardic Jews. Much less so since, at that time, there was another issue which undoubtedly drove a wedge between the two groups of Jews. It concerned the boycott of German goods and products after Adolf Hitler seized power in Germany in 1933.

In a secret letter written in 1933 from the Dutch Central Intelligence Service to the Dutch Ministers of the Colonies and Justice[84], it appears that on Hitler's assumption of power all Curaçao Jews boycotted German products. Whereas the Sephardic Jews normally traveled to Europe on HAPAG or the Horn Line, now they refused to sail on German ships. By the same token, they only used non-German ships to transport their merchandise.

At least in theory. Sometimes finances took priority over principles. For instance, the Sephardi Elias Curiel carried on quietly importing Holsten beer from Germany; to the indignation of the Ashkenazic Jews.

In view of their background, this outrage was understandable. The Sephardim of Curaçao – who around 1500 fled the Inquisition on the Iberian Peninsula – never again suffered persecution. Unlike the Eastern European Jews, who had so recently experienced anti-Semitism. To them, the persecution of the Jews in Germany was far more personal and threatening, which is why the import of German beer by a fellow Jew was particularly painful to this group. Because Curiel was a member of the Board of Directors at the Maduro &

Curiel's Bank, the Ashkenazic Jews, according to the Central Intelligence Service, threatened to transfer their financial affairs to a competitor, the *Hollandsche Bank van West-Indië*.

The Ashkenazim then also founded an association for 'the boycott of German goods and steamship companies'. Each member paid a 75 guilder deposit plus a monthly membership fee. Those who did decide to import German products lost their money. The odds were low that one of the Ashkenazic businessmen from this small community would have violated such a commitment.

▶ ### Nachman Grijnsztein (Curaçao, 1937)

> "My parents came from Wysokie Mazowieckie in Poland. Theirs was an arranged marriage that took place before they left Poland. My father was an accountant in a flour factory. He was extremely well-informed in all things Jewish. Many people came to his home to hear his opinion and to ask him whether he thought they were doing things correctly. Yet he was not a very pious Jew himself."
>
> "His elder brother ended up in America and it seems he suggested that my father should join him there. He had heard the economy in Poland was not doing well. My father took the boat – in 1927 I believe – but disem-

Nachman Grynsztein. (photo: Jeannette van Ditzhuijzen)

barked here. The boat was not allowed to dock in America. Curaçao was one of the few places that permitted ships with foreigners to enter. My mother and two elder brothers did not come until 1935, as my father first had to earn enough money to pay for their passages."

"In Poland my brothers attended a *cheder,* because, in those years, Jews in villages like ours could not go to a regular school. So they received instruction together with other Jewish boys from the village. But here on Curaçao, they were quick to adapt. At home we spoke Yiddish, at school Dutch."

"Although my parents were not very religious, we always lit candles on Fridays. Of course we knew it was the Sabbath, but we did not have a Sabbath meal every Friday. My father's store always closed late. Meanwhile, we were dying of hunger waiting for him, so we usually just went ahead and ate."

"We lived in Punda and I walked to the Hendrik School every day. There were Sephardic Jews there too, but we had nothing in common; nothing to talk about. They lived comfortably in Scharloo, while we and our parents had a simple, small house in Punda. But I never resented them. My sons did much better. At the Hebrew School [which both Ashkenazic and Sephardic children attended, *jvd*] they had something in common: their religion. In this way, a gradual rapprochement took place. I think of the Hebrew School as something that brings us closer together. We understand each other, even though we have separate synagogues. We also have joint meetings now. We didn't have them when I was young. I knew the Sephardim played tennis in Scharloo but I didn't belong there. That barrier is now gone." ◄

6 Living a Jewish Life As Much As Possible

The Ashkenazic Jews could not maintain all of their religious traditions on Curaçao. Their stores had to stay open on the Sabbath and kosher food was difficult to get on the island. They soon held services in their own synagogue, though, since they did not feel welcome in the Sephardic synagogue. They also founded a Jewish social club.

Not Really Welcome in the Sephardic Snoa

Some of the Ashkenazic Jews started living in Punda immediately after their arrival. Here stood a magnificent synagogue from 1732, which was owned by the Sephardic orthodox community of *Mikvé Israel*. Yet, the equally orthodox Ashkenazim seldom if ever attended services there. This was not only because the Ashkenazic and Sephardic rites differ from one another or because an Ashkenazic service is more informal than a Sephardic one. They did not go there primarily because they did not feel welcome. After all, why would those poor wretches from Eastern Europe sit among the 'well-to-do' of Curaçao? As one of the interviewees put it: "When you went to the synagogue in Punda, you had to wear a coat and tie; otherwise they wouldn't let you in. None of us had a decent dress coat, much less a tie."

But the fact that the Ashkenazim felt ill at ease inside the 'aristocratic' synagogue or *snoa* was not their only reason for staying away. According to Isaac Emmanuel, the rabbi for *Mikvé Israel* from 1936 to 1939, the Sephardic congregation would not accept Ashkenazic Jews as members. They were afraid that, over time, the newcomers from Eastern Europe would force their own traditions and rites on them.[85] A rule like this, of course, did not exactly make the Ashkenazim feel welcome in the *snoa*. Besides, there were other differences that explained their hesitance to visit it. *Mikvé Israel*, for instance, had had an organ since 1866. In an orthodox Ashkenazic *shul* or *shiel*, having such musical accompaniment in the services was unthinkable.

Later on, according to Emmanuel, the Ashkenazim were allowed to become members of *Mikvé Israel*, but only on the condition that for the first ten years they would not stand for election to the *parnassim*, the board of the Sephardic orthodox congregation. From here on they refrained from applying for membership. Though they did not have an official congregation yet, the Ashkenazim did have their own prayer room and a social club.

Some of them, however, did occasionally go to the *snoa*, such as when they were invited to a class mate's bar mitzvah (a religious initiation ceremony). Others never did, simply because outside school they seldom if ever had any contact with the Sephardim. Ida Hirschberg did have frequent contacts with Sephardic children when she was a child (see Chapter 16), and she and her family regularly attended the *snoa* to celebrate the Sabbath. But they did not have the same background as most other Ashkenazim. The family came from Dresden, spoke German at home and was better educated than many Eastern European Jews. Ida didn't learn Yiddish until she lived in Japan during the war and came in contact with Russian Jews (see also the portrait in Chapter 8).

"My parents were assimilated. We even had a small Christmas tree when we first arrived from Europe. I also attended the Protestant Easter services and the Roman Catholic midnight mass. My parents had no problem with it. I, in turn, took non-Jewish friends to the *Seder* (the Jewish Passover meal) at our

The Polish shochet Gersz Szmukler. (photo: private collection of Frieda Geller-Faerman)

The building on the Bargestraat where the Ashkenazim established their first synagogue is now a ruin. (photo: Jeannette van Ditzhuijzen)

house. We celebrated all the Jewish holidays. We were Jewish, but not very religious. My children, too, have all been raised as Jews."

Their Own Prayer Room in the Bargestraat

The Seibalds, who were one of the very first Ashkenazic Jewish families on the island, cherished their religious traditions. It is very probable that, after arriving on Curaçao, they gathered with other pioneers to hold services at home. A synagogue is, after all, not absolutely necessary for holding a prayer service. Soon the newcomers came together for prayers under the leadership of a Polish man named Gersz Szmukler, who arrived on the island around 1928 and was a *shochet* (ritual slaughterer). The other Jews helped him to sell merchandise so that he could earn a living.

In 1930 there were sufficient numbers of Ashkenazic Jews on Curaçao to justify having their own place of prayer. So they rented the first floor of the house at Bargestraat 1/13. This street lies on the edge of Scharloo, where most of the Sephardic Jews lived, and could be reached from Punda, home to the majority of the Ashkenazim, via a bridge over Waaigat Bay. Szmukler, who lived behind this building, also assumed the tasks of the chazzan, the cantor that leads the services.

The room was filled with folding chairs and, on the Sabbath and the Jewish holidays, services were held here. Men and women sat in separate sections, as is common practice in an orthodox *shul*. As Dora Suchar-Cheis remembered, the men wore Panama hats when they went to the synagogue. "They were in fashion in the 1930s, as were white suits."

Although the community was tight-knit, things were not always smooth sailing. Bruno Linder, who arrived in 1933 from the Polish city of Sniatyn, remembered that his father Elias had a conflict with the *shiel* at a certain point. This is why he attended the Sephardic *snoa* for about a year; Bruno accompanied him a couple of times.

Sometimes the Ashkenazim said their prayers in other locations. Isaac Kisilevich remembered, for instance, that the men used to come to his father's business for the *Yahrzeit,* literally meaning 'the time of year': on the anniversary of a person's death, at least ten men come together ('forming a minyan') to keep the memory of the deceased alive and to say prayers. This can take place in the synagogue or in someone's home. The store owned by Chaim Kisilevich, *La Buena Ventura* on the Madurostraat, was centrally located and therefore a practical location for the Jewish merchants.

Shared Jewish Cemeteries

The newly arrived Jews did not have to search for a Jewish cemetery. The Sephardic Jews had created two of them long ago, which the Ashkenazim could also use: the older of the two, *Beth Haim* from 1659, now lies under the smoke of the refinery; the newer cemetery is located near Punda, at *Berg Altena*. Both cemeteries are owned by *Mikvé Israel-Emanuel*. The Ashkenazic congregation has purchased burial space in Berg Altena for its members.

As far as can be ascertained, Sarah Szmukler, the shochet's wife, was the first *Polako* to die on the island. She died in 1937 and was buried at Berg Altena. Two years later, Haim Gandelman from Noua Suliță was laid to earth at the old cemetery Beth Haim. In total, approximately fifteen Eastern European Jews are buried there. Since the early 1950s, the Ashkenazim have buried their dead nearly always at Berg Altena. One of the exceptions was Beila Libman-Jufe, who was buried next to her husband Aron at Beth Haim in 1963. He had died in 1951.

In his book, former Rabbi Emmanuel mentioned how he performed the burial rites for the Ashkenazic Jews in the late 1930s. "Without charge", he added.[86] Later, his successor, Isaac Jessurun Cardozo, took over the task. It wasn't until 1954 that the Ashkenazim employed their first rabbi, Nathan Schächter.

The Sabbath is No Longer Sacred

Fairly soon, the religious ban on working on Saturday was abandoned. As peddlers, the Ashkenazim could undoubtedly decide for themselves whether or not to sell their wares on the Sabbath. Leon Seibald remembered, for instance, that his father almost never worked on the Sabbath. But once they acquired stores, things changed. Closing the store on Saturday was equivalent to economic suicide and so they simply kept the store open, Sabbath or no Sabbath. Tila Gerstenbluth-Cheis: "Everyone opened their stores on Saturday and so you had to keep up with the rest. Financially, it was essential."

To make it easy for the storekeepers, the normal Saturday Sabbath service was held so early (at 6 or 7 in the morning) that the men still had enough time after the service to open their stores. It was not until the arrival of Rabbi Yeshurun in 2000 that this custom was brought to an end and the Saturday Sabbath service was not held before 8 in the morning anymore.

Only one Ashkenazic store, *Casa Keis*, has a Sabbath closing history. When one of the daughters of the strictly religious Ana Cheis-Aklipa became seriously ill, Ana promised to become *shomer Shabbat* if her daughter was restored to health. The girl recovered and since then Ana's store was closed on the Sabbath for many years – because someone that is *shomer Shabbat* adheres strictly to all the rules surrounding the Sabbath. Among the Sephardic Jews in the 1930s, the store *El Globo* owned by Benjamin and Sol Delvalle on the Heerenstraat was the only one closed on Saturday.[87]

Eating a Little (Less) Kosher

As the ritual slaughterer, Szmukler provided the kosher chicken. He had to slaughter the chicken so that almost all of the blood flowed out of the body immediately, since Jews are not permitted to consume blood. Many people still remember the sickly smell of the slaughtered chickens at Szmukler's house behind the synagogue. Fanny Sprung-Weisinger recalled that each Thursday she and her mother would go to the *shochet*. The chickens that her mother kept in the garden were taken along to be slaughtered by Szmukler.

Kosher meat was not available, but the Cheis sisters remembered that in the early years their mother would make meat 'close to kosher'. Mrs. Cheis would buy meat from the butcher that had not been slaughtered according to Jewish rules. She would then wash and salt the meat, the way it was done with meat slaughtered in a kosher manner. The salt drew the remaining blood out of the meat. Thus, the meat was 'a little kosher'. According to Dora Suchar-Cheis, her mother did this partly to teach her children about the kosher rules. "When I lived in Trinidad later in life, where kosher meat was also unavailable, I did exactly the same."

Apart from chicken, kosher products were rarely available on the island and importing them was expensive. Only the store owned by Grynsztein (see Chapter 4) had kosher cheeses and sausages. For this reason, single men – and later their families – found it difficult to eat kosher like they had been used to in Europe. Bruno Linder remembered that his family in Sniatyn always strictly ate kosher. "But I don't think you could eat kosher on Curaçao at that time." Most Jews ate kosher only on Jewish holidays, if at all. The problem of eating kosher was, of course, also experienced by the Sephardic Jews.

But the Jews did continue to observe certain other rules on Curaçao, such as preparing meat and dairy products separately. Pork, crab, shrimp, lobster etc. were of course strictly forbidden.[88] Nevertheless, several Jews recalled that they did eat pork at home.

Still a Spick-and-Span House at Passover

Apart from the adapted store times and eating a little less kosher, most Ashkenazim observed the Jewish traditions and celebrated all the holidays. The less religious Jews too honored the Jewish traditions. Virtually every Ashkenazic family celebrated the beginning of the Sabbath on Friday evening by ritually lighting candles. If people attended the synagogue on Friday evening at all, it was mainly men, wheras women primarily went on the most important Jewish holidays.

Nearly everyone interviewed spoke of how, prior to the celebration of *Pesach* (Passover), their mother – religious or not – would clean the entire house so that not a crumb of bread or cake could be found. During *Pesach*, nothing could be in the house that contained a leavening agent or had come in contact with a leavening agent.[89]

So the Jewish tradition was and still is important for the entire group. Despite some limitations the truly religious Jews certainly tried to live in the most Jewish manner possible. In the early congregation they were often the leading figures. The Romanian brothers Wiznitzer, Abraham, Salomon and later Moishe, fulfilled this role, for example. They had ties with the strict orthodox Jewish movement, Hassidism, from Wiznitz. The Polish Linder family also took

A few of the Club Union founders in the early 1930s. From left to right: Max Hirschberg, Chaim Causanschi, Joske Faerman, Samuel Brandes and Jan Groisman. (photo: private collection of Ida Aminoff-Hirschberg)

Club Union members in the synagogue on the Bargestraat. Standing, from left to right: Morris Gandelman, Bruno Linder, Samuel Pimsler, Joske Faerman, Max Peicher, Nata Crivosei, Josef Rabinovich, Chaim Kisilevich, Bernardo Metsch, Haim Causanschi and Jacobo Fruchter. Seated, from left to right: Salomon Seibald, Elias Linder, David Adlerstein, Boris Bryczka, Gersz Szmukler, Hersch Cheis, Saul Crivosei, Moishe Seibald and Selig Seibald. In the foreground: Aba Grynsztein and Jozef Seibald. (photo: private collection of Isaac and Lily Kisilevich-Bonaparte)

the lead in the faith. And Salomon Seibald had been *gabai* (the one that organizes the *shul* services) for the congregation almost his entire life, as is written on his gravestone.

Gathered Together at Club Union

In 1933, several Ashkenazic men founded the Club Union, a social-cultural association with a Jewish religious background. The founders were Joske Faerman, Max Hirschberg, Samuel Brandes, David Adlerstein, Samuel Pimsler, Shlom Milstein and Jan Groisman.

The Club Union bylaws received royal approval from the governor on 26 July 1935. According to the bylaws, the Club's mission was "to promote enjoyable social intercourse between its members and to give support to those who need it". To this end, gatherings, conferences and dance parties, among other things, were organized. The members paid a five-guilder deposit plus a monthly fee of 2,50 guilders. Women were considered as associate members. They were not required to pay a deposit or membership fee and were allowed to visit the Club as often as they wished. Anyone who failed to pay their membership fees for three months lost their membership 'without further appeal'.

According to Emmanuel, the Ashkenazic Jews that had emigrated to Central and South America had similar social clubs there.[90] Club life on Curaçao in the first half of the 20th century flourished. The oldest social club was *Club de Gezelligheid*, which had both white Protestants and Sephardic Jews as members.[91] Via a social club, people stayed abreast of the latest news and sometimes the members passed books around among themselves. The Ashkenazim probably also exchanged Jewish newspapers, such as the *Forwarts,* the Yiddish-language immigrant newspaper that was distributed from New York. Nachman Grynsztein remembered that his mother received seven Yiddish-language newspapers from America each week by surface mail.

Sports and theater usually played a role in the social clubs as well, but at Club Union that was not initially the case because - except for the first year – the Club did not have a roof over its head until around 1940. In that first year, 1934, the Ashkenazim rented a property from Aron Abraham Abady, a Jewish immigrant from Beirut. It was a large house at Penstraat 14, just outside Punda. The rent amounted to 2,400 guilders per year and had to be paid in advance. Where the Club members met after that is not clear. Marie Brandes recalled that her parents always played cards at different people's homes. The Ashkenazic Jews could also frequently be found playing cards at her mother's restaurant. She said the card games were organized under the auspices of Club Union.

Starting in 1940, the Club found a home at Hendrikplein 3 in Punda, where there was also space for theater performances. The plays almost always had a Jewish religious slant.

Things were going well for the Ashkenazim. By the time the Second World War broke out, they were firmly established on Curaçao. They had their own synagogue and Club, and they had risen far above the status of 'poor wretches'. The Wiznitzers, the Taubers, the Sterentals, the Metsches, the Spritzers and the Fuhrmanns – to name but a few families – had finally made it. They were well on their way, in the words of Herman Tauber, to becoming 'the best' on the island. Their success could be attributed to hard work, sometimes by the entire family, frugality and the ambition to climb up the ladder of prosperity.

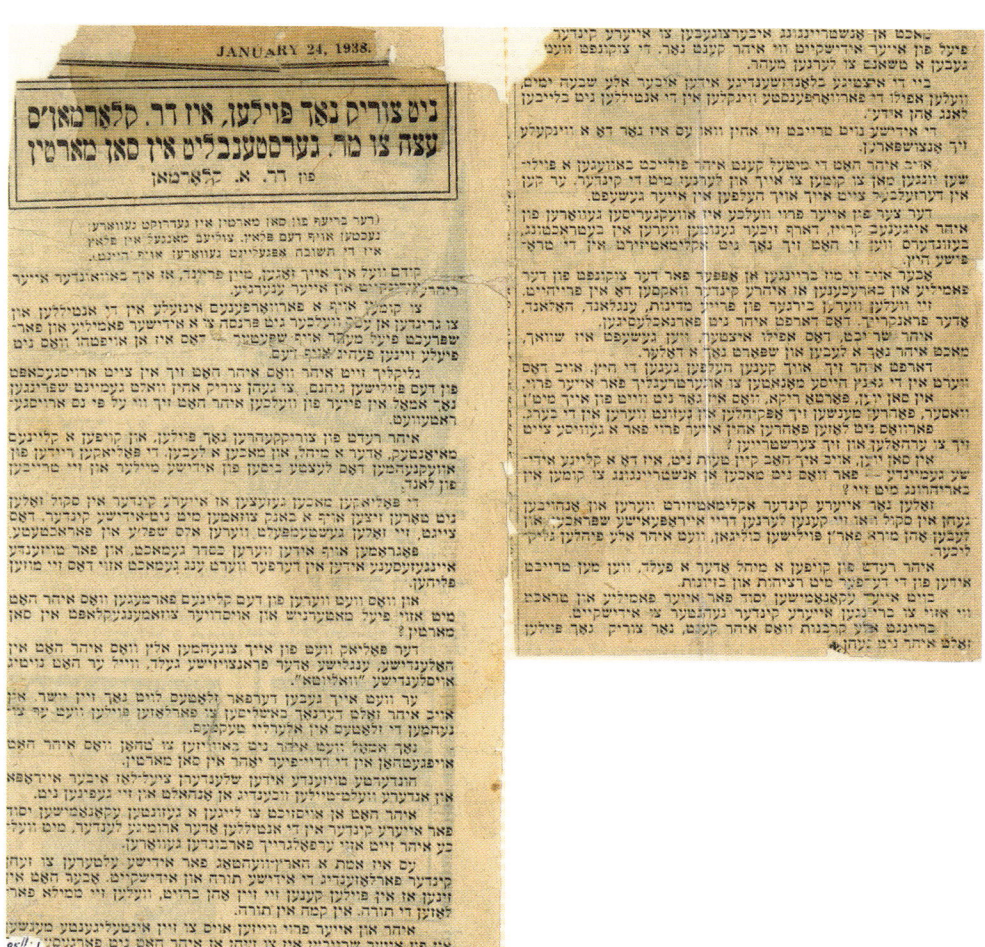

The answer from dr. A. Klarman to the letter Isaac Gerstenbluth sent to the Jewish Journal in 1938. (from the private collection of the late Bill Gerstenbluth)

▶ The Faith of Isaac Gerstenbluth (Poland, 1898-1950)

The importance of faith for some Eastern European Jews can be deduced from a letter written by Isaac Gerstenbluth to the *Jewish Journal* in New York. After living on Curaçao for over a year (see the Prologue), the Polish grain merchant Gerstenbluth returned to Europe around 1931 for health reasons. But the stock market crash of 1929 meant that he could not earn much in the grain trade there. So he decided to head west again. This time he journeyed to Sint Maarten, where he started a fabric store on Front Street around 1935.

In 1937 he was able to have his family join him on the island. At the time, only a handful of Jews were living on Sint Maarten, and the island had not had a synagogue since the hurricane of 1819. His son Bill (Jacob Gabriel) recalled that on the High Holidays of Rosh Hashanah and Yom Kippur, two or three Jews would come from Saba and Sint Eustatius. Together with the Jews of Sint Maarten, they then had a sufficient number of men aged 13 or older to form a minyan and hold a prayer service. "That was held in our house or in a hotel room."

Although, for the rest of the year, the family tried to live a Jewish life as best as they could using their own prayer books, father Gerstenbluth did not like the idea of his children growing up in a non-Jewish environment without a synagogue. He also worried about his daughter, who had reached marriageable age but did not have the chance to meet Jewish men.

So in 1938 he wrote a long letter to the American *Jewish Journal* asking for advice. He explained his situation and seriously proposed that he would have to return to Europe. The letter and the reply to it were published in the newspaper. In view of the approaching war, the rabbi advised him absolutely not to return to Europe. "If you cannot find a rabbi that will come to Sint Maarten to give your children Jewish lessons, then come here, where there is a Jewish environment", was his advice.

And that's what happened. In 1941, the Gerstenbluths were given a visa – due to the war, very few Polish people were in a position to make use of the immigration quota set for the United States – and the family moved to New York, where Gerstenbluth set up an export business in textiles. His son Bill was to work for the company at a later stage. They did business with a range of countries in South America and had several large clients on Curaçao, such as Herman Gärtner of *La Aurora* and *La Economia*, Bernardo Metsch of *Casa Bernardo* and the Cheis family of *Casa Marco* and *Casa Keis*. This is how Bill met Tila Cheis. In 1953 they married and the couple set up house on Curaçao. ◂

Part III

The Second World War

7 Jewish Refugees Interned on the Islands

During the Second World War, Jewish refugees from Europe tried to reach Curaçao by ship. But they were not welcome. Those that did arrive on the island were interned – despite the protests of the Jewish community.

Jewish Germans and Austrians rounded up

On 10 May 1940, Germany invaded the Netherlands. Due to a six hour time difference, people on Curaçao already knew that the Netherlands were at war on 9 May. The very same night, Governor Gielliam Wouters had all Germans and Austrians on the island rounded up. To the dismay of the local Jews, this group held 23 fellow Jews,[92] including the Austrian physician Dr Julius Benesch and photographer Fred Fischer, also an Austrian.[93]

Some of these foreigners who had been detained were initially locked up in the Hendrik School in Pietermaai for a few hours. Isaac Kisilevich, who was not yet eight years old at the time, remembered it well. He lived across from the school and saw that some of the detainees were still wearing pajamas. Fanya Gandelman-Becher rode to school with her father the next day. "Suddenly, we saw an army truck driving in front of us full of people. Some of them were only wearing underclothes. Fred Fischer was among them. A Jew! We did not understand. Only later did we hear that Germany had invaded the Netherlands."

The foreigners were taken to Bonaire to be interned there for the duration of the war.[94] In the first few months, the Jewish men were kept together with the Germans, some of whom explicitly sympathized with the Nazis. After complaints had been made about this situation, the Jews were separated some time later and taken to a camp on the Bonaire plantation of Guatemala, later also referred to as the Jewish Camp.[95]

The Jews interned on Bonaire, it should be noted, were not part of the group of Jews that had emigrated to Curaçao from Eastern Europe during the years 1926-1937. They were German and Austrian Jews who just happened to be on the island when the war broke out and who just happened to hold the wrong nationality. The aforementioned Mr Fischer, for example, worked on board a KNSM ship as a photographer. Because he was making a film about Curaçao, he had been given a temporary residence permit for the island. Another internee,

The Gandelman family in 1933. From left to right: Moses, father Haim, Marco (who died in the war), mother Ana and Basia. (photo: private collection of Basia Bitterman-Gandelman)

the German Hans Sollinger, worked in Almelo for a company that had seconded him to Curaçao as a representative in 1939. These Jews thus escaped the Holocaust in Europe, but on Curaçao, they were considered to be enemies of the state because of their nationality.

For the Roman Catholic and Protestant internees pastoral care was provided in the internment camp. Since Bonaire had no Jewish residents, there was no synagogue or rabbi. This privation was particularly felt at the celebration of Yom Kippur (Day of Atonement), a High Holiday in the Jewish Calendar. That is why the interned Jews asked the Protestant church council for permission in October 1940 to use the Protestant church of Kralendijk for their service. They celebrated the Day of Atonement there that year.

More Jews interned on Bonaire

A group of 17 Jewish refugees, also originally from Germany and Austria, was added to the Jews interned on Bonaire on 6 July 1940. They had been traveling on the KNSM ship *Hermes* from Europe to Chile. Halfway there, another regime took over Chile, and the visas already granted were revoked. On 7 June 1940, the ship moored at Curaçao, where the passengers applied for political asylum, but were refused.

The captain then took them to Panama, and passengers that had enough money to stay there, remained. The Dutch consul tried to gain entry into Chile for the other passengers. The attempt failed, so less than three weeks later they were put on the KNSM ship *Crijnssen*, headed for Europe.

Again the ship moored at Curaçao and once again the refugees asked for asylum. This time the KNSM and the Government reached a compromise: the shipping company would bear the costs of internment (50 cents per person per day) for as long as the war lasted. As soon as the war ended, the KNSM would ensure that the refugees were taken to their respective countries of origin or to another country. Because these Jews were German or Austrian nationals, Governor Wouters considered them to be enemies of the state and they were taken to the internment camp on Bonaire.

Of the 17 refugees on the *Crijnssen*, two families remained on Curaçao after the war: Max, Erni and daughter Elvira Kywi from the German city of Dortmund, and Alfred and Erika Schnog. After the war ended, Schnog began the car dealership *Cordia*. His brother Leo joined him later, and also became a car dealer.

In 1961, the name of Max Kywi was on the membership list of *Shaarei Tsedek*, the Ashkenazic Jewish congregation that was founded in 1958. According to Kywi's granddaughter Yvonne, her grandparents had not been allowed to become members of *Mikvé Israel* after the war because they were German Jews. After hearing this, her grandfather didn't want to join anymore, but his wife absolutely did not feel at home with the Ashkenazim. Like her daughter, Elvira Kywi, she considered herself to be a 'German Jew' and absolutely not an Ashkenazi.[96]

Before the journey to the Western Hemisphere, Elvira had lived in a children's home on the Kalverstraat in Amsterdam, while her father was a prisoner in a camp. According to her daughter Yvonne, she loved her life as an internee on Bonaire. Apparently, she experienced it as the best time of her life. When later on the internees were granted greater freedom of movement, Elvira's father Max started working as a watchmaker for the Curaçao jewelers Spritzer & Fuhrmann. There, he became a colleague of the Curaçao Sephardic Jew Max de Castro, with whom Elvira fell head over heels in love, marrying him at the age of 16. The Kywi family now owns an optician's store on the island.

A Boat Full of Refugees Interned on Curaçao

At the beginning of October 1941, the Spanish ship *Cabo de Hornos* arrived in Curaçao's harbor. This passenger ship sailed to Curaçao regularly, but this time it was crammed full of refugees from Europe. According to the newspaper *Beurs- en Nieuwsberichten* of 7 October, the situation on board was heartbreaking: "A ship that was built to carry perhaps two hundred people at most is now packed full with many hundreds more. Quite a few of them are Jewish refugees who have been forced to flee Europe because of their faith. They are on their way to Argentina. These Jews have a horrific existence on board that ship."

"For their third class passage, these Jews have had to pay more than Canadians paid for their first-class tickets. On board there is a shortage of drinking water and sanitary facilities. Any one that manages to press through the mass of people on the boat has tears in his eyes because of the overwhelming misery encountered on the way. It is inhuman."[97] One of the Jewish passengers died while the ship was moored in the harbor. He was given a burial on the island according to Jewish rites.

A month and a half later, on 19 November 1941, the ship returned, again with Jewish refugees on board; 86 in all. Both Brazil and Argentina had denied them entrance. They had visas for Uruguay which could only be reached via these countries. Governor Wouters did not want to grant them entry either. In a telegram dated 13 November 1941, he had reported to the Dutch government in London that Curaçao was not able to house these refugees and it was "all too clear [that] they would never leave the island".[98]

At the last moment, the Jewish refugees, who had come from different European countries, were allowed to disembark on Curaçao. Not because Wouters had changed his mind, but because the Dutch Minister for the Colonies, Charles Welter, had ordered him by telegraph from London to admit the refugees. The international Jewish aid organization JJDC (the Jewish Joint Distribution Committee) had guaranteed it would bear the costs of the internment and this played no doubt a significant role in the turnaround.

The boat refugees had, by that time, been traveling for several months and the ship was not equipped to carry so many passengers. It is not surprising then that some of them were emaciated when they arrived on Curaçao. A few of them even had to be taken to hospital. Wouters had the other passengers moved to a men's camp and a women's camp on Curaçao – at Suffisant and in the quarantine building of Mundo Nobo, respectively.

Limited Freedom for the Jewish Refugees

From the beginning, the entire Jewish community applied enormous pressure to have the Jewish internees on Bonaire freed. Their spokesman was the Sephardic religious leader Isaac Jessurun Cardozo. Initially, his words fell on deaf ears because Wouters stood his ground. He had heard that Jews in Colombia had been caught spying and he was afraid the same could happen on the islands.

After his visit to camp Guatemala on Bonaire in June 1941, the Dutch Minister Welter also urged him to free the Jewish internees. Wouters continued to resist, but under the ministerial pressure and the pressure exercised by the Jewish community on Curaçao, he granted the Jews limited freedom of movement on Bonaire at the end of August 1941.[99]

For Jessurun Cardozo this was not enough, simply because a return to Aruba or Curaçao had not yet been granted. So in May 1942, he sent the Governor another letter in which he explained why the Jews should be freed completely. Several days later, a written letter of support from the Sephardic Jew Salomon Maduro 'and 55 others' followed.

It seemed as though they would be successful. But the (Sephardic) merchants of Curaçao had not forgotten the competition they had come up against from the Eastern European Jews. They were apparently not happy that another group of them would now be admitted to the island. A couple of weeks later, the politician Moisés da Costa Gomez[100] approached the Governor. He let him know that several Curaçao merchants and a leader of one of the Jewish congregations objected to the inhabitants of the Guatemala plantation on Bonaire being freed. Each of them was an Ashkenazic Jew.

Soon after, Wouters was replaced by Governor Piet Kasteel. Kasteel also had his doubts about the reliability of several of the Jews interned, but he didn't want the good ones to suffer because of those under suspicion. That is why he decided on 1 September 1942 to expand the freedom of movement of these Jews from camp Guatemala to Aruba and Curaçao. But – probably due to the objections of Da Costa Gomez and associates – he set a few conditions: they had to report in daily, they could not be outdoors after sunset (sometime between 6 and 7 pm), they needed to have permission to accept work, they were not allowed to start their own businesses and, in their work, they were not to have any contacts with the population. Lastly, the possession of a radio was forbidden. The measures clearly seemed to be aimed at curtailing commercial competition from the refugees. The boat refugees of the *Cabo de Hornos* were also granted this limited freedom.

On the occasion of Princess Margriet's birth on 19 January 1943, one of the conditions was relaxed: from that day onward, the Jewish boat refugees and former internees had to be inside after ten in the evening, instead of after sunset.[101] Later that year, starting 23 November, another restrictive condition was added: the refugees were not allowed to enter a movie theater or another venue of public entertainment. The restriction did not last long, because barely a half year later, on 15 March 1944, all restrictions were abolished.

Criticism of Wouters

After the war, Wouters refused to share the view that it was rather strange, to put it mildly, to detain and intern Jews. In his opinion, his first duty during the war was to protect the islands of Aruba and Curaçao against enemy attacks. Both islands were, after all, very important to the allied air force because the refineries (Aruba had one as well) provided the vast majority of their requirement for kerosene.

In the early 1950s, Wouters told the Board of Inquiry Concerning the Refugee Problem that his reason for refusing entry was that the island was too small to accommodate so many refugees. There were no houses for them and insufficient supplies of food.[102] Besides, he did not know for certain whether these Jews and the others he interned were politically trustworthy.[103] Lou de Jong suggests in his book *Het Koninkrijk der Nederlanden in de Tweede Wereldoorlog* (The Kingdom of the Netherlands in the Second World War) that Wouters' refusal to accept refugees was based on his 'aversion to Jews'.[104]

Incidentally, on 10 May 1940, Wouters did allow twenty Dutch Jewish passengers of the KNSM passenger ship *Stuyvesant* to enter the island. They were also refugees from Europe.[105]

Jewish Aid to Refugees in Transit

Before the war, a small committee had been set up on Curaçao that concerned itself with Jewish refugees who stopped over on the island. After all, many ships called on Curaçao to refuel. The committee, consisting of members of all three Jewish congregations,[106] visited the passengers (Jewish or otherwise) on board the ships and, if necessary, provided them with clothing and medicines. The committee had also provided the refugees on board the *Cabo de Hornos* with daily necessities when their ship called on Curaçao for the first time.

The committee was formalized after 19 November 1941, when the refugees on board the *Cabo de Hornos* were admitted to the island. It was given the name *Joods Hulp Comité* (Jewish Aid Committee) and maintained an office at the *snoa* in Punda. The committee worked closely with the JJDC and also advocated the acquisition of visas for the refugees.

The explicit plan was for the passengers of the *Cabo de Hornos* to leave the island within three months. One month later, 16 of the displaced persons had indeed left for another destination. Yet after four months, the majority of the passengers were still on Curaçao. It wasn't until sometime in 1945 that all the Jewish passengers had finally left the island. Three had died during or shortly after the war. They are buried at the Jewish cemetery *Beth Haim*. The last of them to die, the German woman Anna Jakobowitz, passed away on 5 August 1945.[107]

Up to and including December 1944, the JJDC sent nearly 40,000 American dollars to the island to pay for the living costs of the *Cabo de Hornos* passengers. The Jewish Aid Committee paid the extra costs for medicine, school fees, hospital admission and baby food.[108] The committee also ensured that the children of those interned on Curaçao could attend public schools during the day and eat with Jewish families at lunchtime.

Dutch Refugees Working on Aruba and Curaçao

Although Governor Wouters was of the opinion that Curaçao did not have sufficient housing and food to take in the Jewish boat refugees during the war, his successor Kasteel in 1943 looked for qualified personnel among the Dutch, partly Jewish refugees that had ended up on Jamaica. These refugees were housed in Camp Gibraltar, which the English initially had built to house refugees from Gibraltar. So it was not an internment camp and the camp residents were able to move freely in and out of the camp.

Among the 125 Dutch citizens that came to Aruba and Curaçao from Jamaica in 1943 for work[109] were the Taytelbaum family from the town of Veere in Zeeland, the Zadoks family, and the Silbiger family, all Ashkenazic Jews. Mr

Taytelbaum became a government doctor on Curaçao. Almost immediately after the start of the war, the Taytelbaums had escaped from the Netherlands. Initially they went to France, still unoccupied at the time, where they lived for two and a half years. With a range of other refugees, both Jewish and non-Jewish, they then sailed to Jamaica via the Spanish port of Vigo. The well-known Curaçao architect Ben Smit also came to Curaçao via Jamaica. In the early 1950s, he designed the store premises for several *Polakos*.

▶ ## Marco Gandelman (Noua Suliță, 1919 – 1945)

Marco Gandelman. (from: History of the Jews of the Netherlands Antilles *by Isaac and Suzanne Emmanuel)*

Curaçao has a road named George Maduroweg and one named Boy Ecuryweg. Both the Curaçao native George Maduro and the Aruban Boy Ecury were actively involved in the resistance in the Netherlands – and both paid for their involvement with their lives. The Ashkenazic Jew Marco Gandelman (still) has no street named after him on the island. But like George Maduro and Boy Ecury, he helped defend his – new – homeland, the Netherlands. He died at the age of 26 in a German camp.

Gandelman had lived on Curaçao for only some 7 years when he left for Amsterdam to attend the Joodsche HBS (a college-prep school) there.[110] According to relatives, in 1939 he went on to a *Yeshiva*, a school that trains people to become a rabbi, cantor or religious teacher. Remarkably, this program was made possible by members of the Sephardic community, probably because his father had just died that year.

Gandelman apparently served in the Dutch army during the war since, in November 1945, the Red Cross reported that Gandelman had been imprisoned in a prisoner-of-war camp. The camp was located in Cieszyn, some 70 kilometers southwest of Auschwitz, on the border between present-day Poland and the Czech Republic. Gandelman reportedly died here. According to a fellow Curaçao prisoner, Isaac Yohai, he had contracted typhus. ◀

8 Daily Life during the War Years

The Jewish community – both Ashkenazic and Sephardic – was thoroughly aware of the suffering encountered by fellow Jews in Europe. They prayed together for their salvation and made donations. Otherwise, life continued as usual. There were parties with Jewish soldiers from the United States, and the Ashkenazic youth founded their own club.

No More Contact with Families in Europe

Although, during the war, Curaçao was not occupied by enemy troops and the Dutch flag continued to wave valiantly, some things did change. First of all, the contacts the Eastern European Jews had maintained with their families back in Poland and Romania were terminated abruptly. There was news about the fate of the Jews in Europe, but no one knew anything about how their own family was doing. In 1944, 26 letters were received from Poland and 13 from Romania. In the other direction, no letters or packages were brought in that year to be sent to Europe.[111]

Some Ashkenazic Jews had been in Europe just before the war broke out and this often proved to have been the last time they saw their families. Dora Suchar-Cheis: "Many members of our family had stayed behind in Romania at that time. In the early days we still had contact with them, but during and after the war contact ceased. We did not even know whether they were still alive or not."

Because imports from the Netherlands and the rest of Europe almost entirely dried up with the outbreak of the war, there was a shortage of food in the beginning. Rationing was unnecessary, however, because soon initiatives were taken to import food from the United States. After the Americans entered the war following the attack on Pearl Harbor (7 December 1941), the supply of goods from America also became limited. For this reason, the traders sought other suppliers in South America.[112] A large part of the clothing and fabrics that the Ashkenazim imported and sold no longer came from Japan, as it had prior to the war, but from Brazil.

Warm Welcome for the Jewish-American Soldiers

The islands of Curaçao and Aruba were vitally important to the Allied Forces because of their refineries. German submarines in the seas around the islands, therefore, tried with all their might to attack the refineries. For this reason, blackout measures were put in place on Curaçao during the evening and nighttime hours. Furthermore, the entrance to Anna Bay was sealed with a steel net so that no submarines could enter the bay.

To defend the island, British troops were initially stationed on Curaçao, to be relieved on 11 February 1942 by the Americans, who stationed a total of 4,600 troops on the island[113]. They were different from the British largely because there were a large number of Jewish men among the American soldiers, often of Ashkenazic descent.

The Ashkenazic community on Curaçao took these soldiers under its wing. The soldiers regularly attended the Jewish prayer services and they were welcomed into Ashkenazic homes. Chaim Jacob Geiger remembered that they came to his parents' house to eat, and that they also brought food with them that his mother then prepared.

The Ashkenazic (and the Sephardic) Jews invited the Jewish soldiers to join them at home for Jewish holidays. During the last year of the war (and perhaps more often), a community *Seder* was organized on Passover for the American soldiers in the Club Union building.[114] This was probably a *Seder* shared by all three congregations. The soldiers put up a good show and didn't come empty-handed. Nearly all the Ashkenazic Jews interviewed still had fond memories of the matzos that the American soldiers brought with them at Passover to share around.

The Jewish soldiers also came to Club Union, recalled Dora Suchar-Cheis. "It was a lot of fun. We sometimes sang Hebrew songs and we went out on the town together." For their part, the Curaçao youth attended the chic parties thrown by the American recreation center of the USO (United States Organiza-

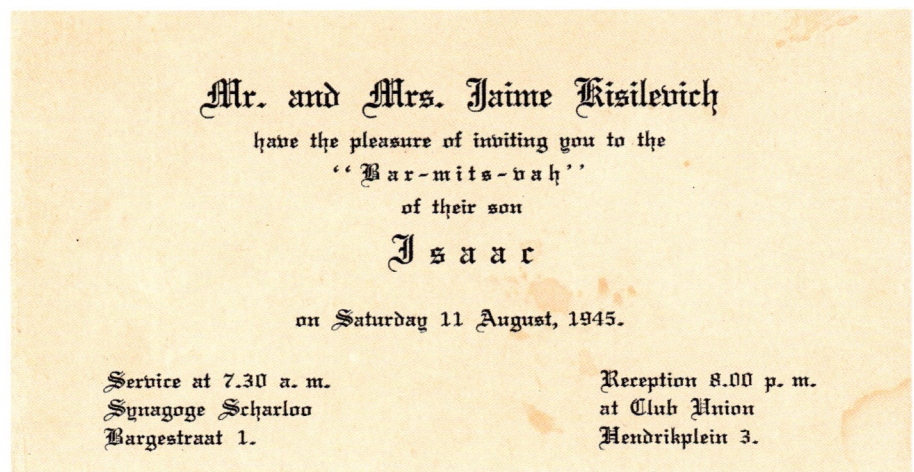

Bar mitzvah invitation. *(from the private collection of Isaac Kisilevich)*

The Becher family in 1942 at the wedding of Bernardo Metsch and Tonia Altnaj. (photo: private collection of Liza Seibald-Becher)

tion), on condition that their fathers had no objections. Fanya Gandelman-Becher was never allowed to go there, even though she was 19 by the end of the war. She and her girlfriends did hang out with the Jewish soldiers though and, in the end, three Ashkenazic Jewish girls married American soldiers: Rachilde and Saartje Haber, and Pesa Silberstein.

The Jewish soldiers from America were also welcome on Aruba. On the occasion of Purim in 1943, for example, nearly all the Jewish soldiers were invited to a big party at the Aruba Country Club (see also Chapter 15).

Wartime... but Business is Booming

Despite the blackouts and the lack of imported goods from the Netherlands, the island suffered little during the war. The refinery continued to operate fully, there was a surplus of work available and therefore also money in circulation. The *Curaçaosch Verslag* even referred to a 'high standard of living' on Curaçao in 1942.[115]

The Americans purchased items in the Punda and Otrobanda stores, and the sailors brought their uniforms to the laundry established by the Ashkenazic

Jew from Poland, Gershon Becher, on the Columbusstraat in Punda. The merchants certainly had no reason to complain about their turnover. Again, people had plenty of money and, because of the good connections with South America, the supply of goods did not stagnate. In 1943 the merchants did better business than they had in 1942 and business in 1944 was also fairly good. According to Van Soest[116], audits conducted by the tax inspector on eight merchants (two dealing in foodstuffs, three in dry goods and three in drinks) showed that their net profits in 1943 were no less than 350 per cent higher than they had been in 1939.

The war years did not, therefore, present an obstacle to the Ashkenazic tradesmen. Herman Tauber, who had come from the Polish city of Sniatyn in 1933, went to the United States for the first time in 1940. He had just turned 21 and was working with his brother Leon in the clothing store that Leon had begun in Otrobanda. In New York, on 14th Street, he saw a sign with the words *Business in millions, profit in pennies* displayed in big letters. It made a deep impression on the young Tauber, who immediately made the words the motto of Tauber Hermanos (The Tauber Brothers). "I really wanted to do a large volume of business, but be satisfied with little profit." During the war, the Tauber brothers already had their own agency in New York and, yes, their business flourished.

Praying Together for the Netherlands and the Jews

In the years leading up to the war, the Ashkenazic Jews and the Sephardic Jews still did not, or rarely, come together socially. But once they heard about the atrocities suffered by their fellow Jews in Europe, they closed ranks. Immediately after war was declared in 1940, the members of the three Jewish congregations held a common prayer service in the *snoa* in Punda. They prayed for the Netherlands and their allies and for a quick victory over the enemy.

A year and a half later, their persecuted and murdered fellow Jews in Europe were at the forefront of their minds. Governor Piet Kasteel had declared 2 December 1942 a national day of mourning and prayer; a day on which the victims of the Nazi regime were remembered. Again, the members of the three congregations came together in the *snoa* of *Mikvé Israel*. During a restrained ceremony, the *shochet* Gersz Szmukler spoke on behalf of the Ashkenazim. He also recited the *El Malei Rachamim*, a prayer for the repose of the souls of those killed in the massacres.

Several weeks later, on 29 December, the Curaçao Jews organized a mourning and prayer day to 'implore God's mercy for the terrible fate' that awaited the Jews at the hands of Hitler. In this case, the Jews held a remembrance prayer service in their own synagogues. Later on that day, the three congregations gathered in the Roxy Theater in order to express their grief together and to protest against the persecution of Jews. According to the monthly newsletter of *Mikvé Israel*, Punda looked deserted on that day because all the Jewish stores were closed.

In the Roxy Theater, where every last seat was taken, Governor Piet Kasteel was one of many that spoke to those gathered. Others were Msgr Verriet of the

Club Union on the Hendrikplein. Top row, from left to right: Ita Meit, Ms. Ehrlich, Ovsia Groisman, Berta Becher, Chaim Kisilevich, Herman Tauber, Marco Cheis, Samuel Silberstein, Berta Wuhl, David Leib Wuhl, unknown, Isaia Dorer and Jose Faerman. 2nd row: Ernö Spritzer, Leo Sterental, Max Peicher, Moises Meit, Jan Groisman, Israel Baumgarten, Samuel Brandes, Elias Linder and Haim Causanchi. The row beginning in front of Samuel Brandes: Lea Meit, Esther Causanschi, Leon Tauber, Sara Groisman, Isaac Groisman, Manea and Zalman Aron Josub. Seated, from left to right: Rosa Spritzer, Manya Groisman, Max Hirschberg, Nettie Brandes, Frieda Hirschberg, unknown, Sonia Kisilevich, unknown. (photo: private collection of Isaac and Lily Kisilevich-Bonaparte)

Roman Catholic Church and Rev Eldermans on behalf of the Protestants. The gathering concluded with everyone singing the *Wilhelmus*, the Dutch national anthem.

The Ashkenazic and Sephardic Jews of Aruba showed solidarity with their fellow Jews on Curaçao and closed all of their stores at 12 noon on 2 December. Several non-Jewish stores closed their stores too. In the afternoon, a special service was held in San Nicolas.

On 29 December, the Aruba Jews held a protest meeting in their own Country Club building (see Chapter 15). This was led by the musician Max Tak, who had fled the Netherlands and had come from Curaçao specially for the meeting.[117]

Enjoying the Time Off

The social venue of the Ashkenazic community was Club Union in Punda (see also Chapter 6). Each Sunday, when the stores were closed, the Jewish families would congregate there. It was the best place to meet and catch up on each other's lives. According to Dora Suchar-Cheis, it was always a wonderful occasion, for the young people as well. They would go on to a film from there, take a stroll through Punda or walk along the Rifwater across the Floating Bridge.

Chaim Jacob Geiger recalled that, in addition to the Club, the Jewish men would meet during the war at other places too. "They also met at my father's house. We had a very old gramophone and records with Jewish singers. Everyone would sing, drink and eat."

On the weekend people would also go swimming. Many Ashkenazic families already had a car and, like many other Curaçao families, they would pile into it on Sunday and head for Jan Thiel beach. After that they would go to the Club.

The Jewish Youth Had Their Own Club, too

Initially, nothing special was organized for the children of the Jewish pioneers. But in 1942 many of them had reached an age at which they wanted to play soccer, chess or a game of ping-pong. There was of course the Curaçao Sports Club (CSC), whose members were Protestants and Sephardic Jews, but for the Ashkenazim, joining this club at the time was apparently a step too far. They preferred to keep company with their own kind. Only one or two were members of the CSC, such as Ernö Spritzer, who, compared with the other newcomers, had a considerable degree of contact with the Sephardic Jews.

So the time had come for a special youth association: the Maccabi Jewish Sports and Culture Club. This club was founded on 12 January 1942 (and gained royal approval in January 1945) and was meant for Jewish young people aged 12 and upwards. The initiators were Pinhos Meit and Nioma Causanschi, among others. Of course, all over the world there were (and are) Jewish sports and culture clubs named Maccabi. In Czernowitz and Noua Suliță, for example, from where a great many of Curaçao's Jews had come. According to Esther Gal-Jessurun Cardozo, the daughter of the Sephardic leader from the Netherlands, the name *Maccabi* alludes to a Zionist orientation. The name is derived from Judah the Maccabee, an important leader in Jewish history.

Esther became a Maccabi member in 1944, one of the few Sephardic Jews to do so. She said her father thought it was a good idea "because I would be in the company of only Jews there". Artie Goudsmit, from the Netherlands, was also given a warm reception within Maccabi. He had lost his parents in the war and had come to the island via Cuba. After his arrival, he quickly became active in this youth club and later on in Club Union as well.

Each of the persons interviewed had warm memories of Maccabi. This association gave the Ashkenazic children more opportunities for entertainment. But, according to Sonia Causanschi-Zonenschain, not all the parents supported such a club. She recalled how much effort it took before the youth got their own sports field in the Van Engelen district. According to the *Maandblad voor Israelitische Huisgezinnen op de Nederlandse Antillen* (Monthly magazine for the Israeli Households on the Netherlands Antilles) that wasn't realized until mid 1945, and it was, at least partly, Jacobo Fruchter's doing.

From that moment on, they played sports outside to their heart's content,

As the chazzan's daughter, Esther Jessurun Cardozo became a Maccabi member. (from the private collection of Esther Gal-Jessurun Cardozo)

also against other Curaçao clubs, particularly soccer and volleyball. They had already played table tennis before. Leon Seibald: "We didn't know the first thing about tennis. We saw the youth playing tennis in Scharloo at the csc. So what did we do? We took up ping-pong." There were also several excellent chess players among the younger Ashkenazim. So chess lessons and (starting in 1944) chess competitions were organized as well.

The quarters used by Maccabi, Club Union on Hendrikplein, started to become the place to be during the war years. Here, the young people could meet. Fanya Gandelman-Becher recalled that she always went to the Club directly from school – she attended the *Algemene Middelbare School* (Public High School) located on the same square. Non-Jewish friends also went along. "We would talk to each other there or do our homework. At the end of the afternoon, we would walk to the Columbusstraat around the corner where my father's laundry was, and then he would drive us home. This was because we had been living in Van Engelen, far outside Punda, since 1936."

The Sephardi Isaac Jessurun Cardozo was closely involved with Maccabi. As the religious teacher he knew the young people from the Jewish classes at school. From the first issue of Maccabi's newsletter, *Shomer Hanóar* (Watchman of the Youth), dated 1 February 1944, it appears that Jessurun Cardozo taught the Maccabi members the Hebrew language and culture. Maccabi also organized musical and cultural evenings, with a lecture at least once a month, as reported in the first issue of *Shomer Hanóar*. Around 1945 a Maccabi choir was set up under the baton of the conductor of the *snoa*, David Capriles.

On the initiative of José Abady, Maccabi also regularly held *Oneg Shabbats* (Joy of the Sabbath). These are informal meetings for young people which are usually held on Saturday afternoons.[118]

The Maccabi members maintained international contacts as well. In 1945, for instance, they received a visit from seven Jewish students from Argentina who were on their way to Palestine, and from three Palestine students that were passengers on a Norwegian ship. The latter group told the Maccabi members what it was like to live and work in Palestine.[119]

▶ Ida Hirschberg (Dresden, 1923)

Wedding of Ida & Salomon. (photo: private collection of Ida Aminoff-Hirschberg)

"We left Germany when I was three years old. We went to Paris, where my brother was born. From Paris, the family moved to Cartagena, in Colombia. My parents were very adventurous and were looking for a new life. Both of them were well-educated, my father had studied at the Cracow University, my mother had graduated from the gymnasium in Dresden, where she had grown up. I believe they were fairly well-off. I think my mother's parents had a furniture store in Dresden. In Cartagena my father operated a movie theater with a distant cousin of his. Then my mother became pregnant again. She didn't want the baby to be born in mosquito-infested Cartagena. So we returned to Europe, to Brussels, where my father's brother was studying. While my mother waited to give birth to the baby, she enrolled in a course to become a beautician. This would give her a future, as she discovered later on Curaçao."

"After the baby was born, my parents wanted to return to Cartagena, but because they had given up everything there, it meant they would have to start all over. So they left the three children (my brother Lucien, baby Victoire and myself) behind in the care of Roman Catholic nuns at a boarding school just outside Brussels."

"It was early 1930 and the ship to Cartagena stopped at Curaçao. My parents went on a short sightseeing tour while the ship refueled. The Jews they met on the way asked them what in heaven's name they thought they

Ida Hirschberg. (photo: Jeannette van Ditzhuijzen)

were going to do in Cartagena. 'Stay here', they were told. 'You don't need a visa, there are plenty of jobs around, the Dutch government is good and there are excellent schools.' So they returned to the ship, picked up their luggage and stayed on the island. They found a room and my father returned to Europe to pick us up. We, the children, lived in Belgium for approximately six months in all. We arrived on Curaçao later in 1930."

"In 1939, a fire broke out in the well-known Curaçao movie theater Cinelandia. My father went there to help take furniture out of the neighboring house. The balcony collapsed, he fell with it, with a cabinet ending up on top of him. He lay in a coma for a long time after that and we had to close his business."

"Before the accident, during the engagement party for Tonia Metsch, I had already met Salomon Wiznitzer from Romania. He had just returned from Japan, where he had been on business. He danced with me and apparently fell head over heels in love with me. He even asked me to marry him, but I said 'No, I have just turned 16 and I don't want to marry yet'. For my father's recovery, we went to Santo Domingo in 1940. First we spent a week in the city with friends and then went to the mountains. One day a taxi pulled up and Salomon stepped out with a large box of chocolates. He was 'on his way to Japan' and again asked me to marry him. I was absolutely not in love with him, but I was a good daughter. His suggestion was clear: he would take care of my family now that my father could no longer work. We organized a Jewish wedding in Santo Domingo and my father married us. It was a small affair, but I did wear a wedding dress. They had searched the entire city for it. After that we traveled for some eight hours to Haiti so that we could conclude a civil marriage at the Colombian consulate and arrange a passport for me, because my father had become a Colombian citizen in Cartagena. We then traveled by ship to Panama, where Salomon's brother Schaye lived, and then on to New York. That's where my husband purchased goods for the business. We traveled first class, because the Wiznitzers were already financially well off."

"Next we traveled with friends to Harbin in Manchuria for Schaye's wedding, and from there on to Kobe, in Japan. In Kobe we planned to stay a couple of months to buy goods for the business. We lived there in a guesthouse run by a Russian lady, who fed us breakfast, lunch and dinner – so I had no housework to do. But when the war broke out, it became increasingly difficult to find a ship to take us back home. It wasn't until December 1941 – by that time I was heavily pregnant – that we boarded a Japanese ship that would take us to Curaçao via Panama. We had been underway barely a week when the ship suddenly turned around and headed back to Japan. It was 7 December and the Japanese had just attacked Pearl Harbor, we were later told. Consequently we were forced to spend the duration of the war in Japan. We could not travel, so we played cards the entire day. Later we met Syrian, Iraqi, Egyptian and Russian Jews there. I do not remember there being a synagogue, but we did have a very friendly social group. Fortunately, we were treated well as foreigners. The Japanese authorities considered us as friends of the government because my husband had been born in Romania. They also broadcast on the radio that all foreigners that were still in Japan were guests in the country and therefore should be left in peace. During our stay I gave birth to a second child. A year after the liberation, in 1946, we were able to return to Curaçao." ◀

Part IV

The Second Half of the 20th Century

9 The Ashkenazic Community Expands

After the war, the Ashkenazic community started growing. One reason for this was the fact that Jewish refugees from Europe joined family members already living on Curaçao. Furthermore, marriage partners were sought and found outside the island's population.

Aid to Jewish Emigrants in Transit

After the war, many survivors of the Holocaust did not want to remain in Europe. A large number of them tried to build a new life in Palestine, but some of them preferred to emigrate to North or South America because often they had family there. Ships bound for the Americas continued to refuel on Curaçao, so the emigrants often stayed on the island for short or longer periods. In such cases, the Jewish Aid Committee, which was founded during the war, served as an information center. It continued to operate at least until 1951 and it ensured, for example, that fellow Jews in transit were given shelter and food with Jewish families within the local community. Marie Brandes: "We would receive a telephone call from the HIAS (Hebrew Immigrant Aid Society). The people would stay with a host family for a couple of weeks and then continue their journey."

Sonia Kisilevich and Ida Hirschberg from the women's association OSE, *Œuvre de Secours aux Enfants* (see Chapter 16), assisted them in their search for housing and ensured the immigrants were given a warm welcome. The Monthly Magazine for Israeli Households on the Netherlands Antilles dated September/October 1947, for instance, reads: "In the hotel, many members of the Club "Union" came in the evening to show their concern. Extra fruit and delicacies were provided to entertain the guests and the children were made to feel especially welcome."

The Committee also provided financial support and, if necessary, searched for information in Europe about the family members of the Jews (temporarily) staying on the island. To fund their activities, the committee published an *Israëlitische Almanak* (Israeli Almanac) a couple of times after the war with facts and particulars about the three Jewish congregations on the island.

Family Reunions on Curaçao

Not everyone was passing through. There were also Jews that had chosen Curaçao as their final destination, usually because they had family on the island with whom they had sought contact from Europe in advance. Yet admission to the island had become more difficult. You had to demonstrate that you had employment waiting for you; otherwise you would not be welcome.

That's why Janina Katz (see also the portrait in this chapter) and her father Jehuda, with his second wife, could not remain permanently on Curaçao. They had come to the island – where Janina's cousin Tonia Metsch-Altnaj lived – after the war from Poland via New York. After a short stay, Jehuda Katz and his wife continued on to the Dominican Republic; Janina, who was 15 at the time, first stayed with her cousin for a couple of months, where she was looked after like a sister. She then journeyed to an aunt living in Bloomington (in the United States), where she attended school for approximately a year.

While on Curaçao she had met Marco Cheis, the owner of *Casa Marco* on the De Ruyterkade. He followed her to America, asked her to marry him and so, at 16, she left and traveled to Curaçao for the second time. She later divorced Marco and married the Sephardic Jew Armando de Marchena. In the mid 1950s, her father joined her on Curaçao.

Rachel Koch ('Lucca') was not yet 18 when she arrived in 1948. Her uncle, Wilu Weisinger, made it possible for her, her parents and four other family mem-

In 1936, the Kisilevich family returned briefly to Romania so that the family living there could see the children born on Curaçao. This photo was taken in Romania (from left to right): Manea Faerman, Sonia Kisilevich and Fanny Faerman. Manea came to Curaçao in 1937; Fania in 1948. (photo: private collection of Isaac Kisilevich)

bers to leave Romania after the war, as it was becoming increasingly more communist. She still remembers clearly what her first impression of Curaçao was: as if she had landed on another planet. "It was an enormous culture shock in every way. And we had to learn to speak three new languages: Dutch, Papiamento and Spanish. In Czernowitz and Bucharest, where we had lived previously, we had our own houses of prayer. Admittedly, we did not attend services often, but the idea that they were there for us was comforting. When I asked where we would pray on the Jewish holidays, I was told that the Ashkenazim did not have a synagogue. The services were held in the Club, where we normally went for our social gatherings. And the services would be led by a chazzan or cantor, who would come from Venezuela especially for the occasion."

On arriving at the airport on Curaçao, Lucca and her family were met not only by uncle Wilu and his family. According to her, it was the custom for nearly the entire Ashkenazic community to welcome newcomers at the airport. It made Lucca giddy, when she saw the extravagance and the chic clothes in the shops. After the war in Czernowitz, after her life in a ghetto, the flight to Suceava and then to Bucharest, this island indeed came across as a completely different world.

The Faerman Family

A special reunion on Curaçao took place for the Faerman family. Theirs was a large family consisting of a mother, Rachel Faerman, and her six children: her son Joske and daughters Esther, Tauba, Fanny, Manea and Liza. The mother, Rachel, came to Curaçao in 1939 via Trinidad (see Chapter 15), where Joske and Manea were already living. Liza lived on Trinidad; the three other daughters had remained in Romania.

One of these three, Fanny, was married to Samuel Fruchter. Like thousands of other Romanian Jews, she and her daughter Gitta were transported from Czernowitz to a camp in Transnistria. Starting in November 1941, Romanian Jews were herded together there on the order of the Romanian General Ion Antonescu. With little food or water and under dismal sanitary conditions, the Jews spent the duration of the war in the camp, that is if they were not murdered or did not succumb to one of many contagious diseases. The grandfather of the aforementioned Lucca Koch died of starvation in this camp.

But Fanny and her family survived. They were repatriated to Czernowitz after the war, where Fanny gave birth to daughter Frieda. In the meantime, her husband had been sent to Siberia by the Russians, but he managed to jump off the moving train just in the nick of time.

As soon as it became remotely possible, Fanny and her family escaped Romania with her sister Esther and her husband Adolf Katz, who had been with them in the camp in Transnistria. They had wanted to go to Curaçao, but traveled initially to the Dominican Republic via Trinidad. The men did not (yet) have jobs waiting for them on the island and so they would not be admitted to Curaçao. In the meantime the family on Curaçao found work for them so that the two families were finally allowed to settle permanently on the island around the beginning of 1948. Samuel Fruchter, who was a dentist by profession, started to work part-time as a caretaker at *Mikvé Israel*. He also worked in the store of his brother-in-law, Joske Faerman. Adolf Katz was able to find a job at *La Esquina* in Otrobanda, the store owned by his brother-in-law, Zalman Aron Josub.

Tauba had gone into hiding in Czernowitz during the war. Since her husband, Zelik Sztam, was from the city of Lodz (Poland), he was apparently not registered for deportation to Transnistria. The couple left in 1947 for Venezuela and finally made it to Curaçao in 1949. The last sister came to the island from Trinidad: Liza, who was married to Isaac Vorona.

Frieda Fruchter, Fanny's daughter, only later realized how unusual it was that she had grown up in the midst of so many family members. "I had the distinct privilege as a Jewish child on Curaçao of having a very large family. All of them were my uncles and aunts and my cousins. That was uncommon for most Jews on the island. It took me a long time to realize that I did not know my father's family. They were never spoken of. I believe I was around the age of nine before I discovered photographs of his family, who had not survived the war.'

All told, it took a lot of effort to bring all the Faermans to Curaçao. According to Joske's daughter Frieda Geller-Faerman, Michael Gorsira, Curaçao's lieutenant-governor since 1951, was partly responsible for the family being reunited on the island. Finally all together again, the Faerman family emerged as a very close-knit clan. Within the Jewish community, they were called *the royal family*. They lived within walking distance from one another and evening after evening they would all sit together and talk on one family's balcony. Manea's son Willy:

After his arrival on Curaçao, Adolf Katz was able to work for his brother-in-law in La Esquina. (photo: private collection of Frieda Pais-Fruchter)

Liza Vorona-Faerman and her son Shura traveled to Curaçao at the end of 1938 with grandmother Rachel Faerman. They were refused admission to the island. It wasn't until 1950 that the Vorona-Faerman family was reunited with the other members of the Faerman family. (from the private collection of Willy Aron Josub)

"We didn't need anyone else in the community. The children were there, my grandmother was there and we all spoke Yiddish to each other. We felt independent, like a community within a community."

At parties, the Faermans always sat together, recalled Fanny's other daughter Emily. "The families in the clan were friends and the family as a whole formed a single front to the outside world." The fact that the four sisters always remained very grateful to their brother Joske and sister Manea undoubtedly played a very important role in these close relations. After all, they had spared no trouble or expense to rescue them from the turmoil of Eastern Europe.

The Jessurun Cardozo Brothers

In addition to these Eastern European Jews, after the war Jews came to the island from the Netherlands as well. They also tried to create a new life for themselves. This was the case for David Jessurun Cardozo, the Sephardic chazzan's brother. During the war, David and his family had gone into hiding in the Netherlands. In 1946 they started a new life on Curaçao.

Although David's brother Isaac was usually called rabbi, he was actually a chazzan or cantor. He had never attended the rabbinical seminary, but had been trained by his father-in-law. David, on the other hand, did attend the Amsterdam seminary *Ets Haïm* to be trained as a rabbi. This is why he could substitute for his brother when Isaac went on vacation. After Isaac left for Israel in 1956, David served as a rabbi at *Mikvé Israel* until his death in 1960. Both brothers always dedicated themselves to the Ashkenazic congregation, which had no rabbi or chazzan until 1954. Many Ashkenazic couples were therefore married by one of the Jessurun Cardozo brothers.

David was also a lawyer and on Curaçao he worked as such just across from the door to the *snoa*. In the postwar years, he arranged Dutch citizenship for a large number of Ashkenazic Jews by personally taking their papers to The Hague. Some of them did not become Dutch citizens until long after the war. Herman Gärtner, Bernardo Metsch and Charles Fuhrmann, for example, were naturalized in July 1949; the brothers Leon and Jozef Seibald received their papers in November 1954.

Looking for a Bride Outside the Island

Around 1950, the Ashkenazic community numbered 70 families, some 180 people, according to the Israeli Almanac. A total of 200 Jewish families lived on the island, which came down to approximately 600 people. But by marrying partners from outside the island, the Ashkenazim quickly increased their numbers. Some of them, such as Abraham Wiznitzer and Moishe Seibald, went to Israel to find a wife. Moishe was 44 when he departed, promising not to return without a wife. He did marry there, in 1954, with Rachel Landskroner from the Romanian city of Noua Suliță. Wiznitzer also sought and found a wife in Israel.

Others met their future wives during a business trip abroad. This is how Herman Tauber met his Polish wife Miriam Indich in New York. During the war, she initially lived in a Polish ghetto. "After that I went to Germany under an assumed name using an Aryan passport. I worked for the Germans there. Then after the war I worked for UNRRA (United Nations Relief and Rehabilitation Administration) and from them I received a letter of recommendation for the United Nations in New York. My mother and I subsequently traveled to New York, where I was indeed able to start working for the United Nations. Shortly thereafter, I met Herman and a year later we married."

What surprised her most about the Ashkenazic community on Curaçao was the fact that everyone got along very well and respected one another, even though they were all competitors in business. "It was a wonderful thing. They did everything for one another. We were one big family."

▶ ### Fania Kirzner-Schusterman (Mikaszewice, 1922)[120]

"Mikaszewice was not a large city. It was more like a *shtetl* (small Jewish town) located in Poland at the time. Its residents were not very religious people, but the Jewish stores were closed on the Sabbath. My mother Fania attended a Polish school. As a child, she spoke Yiddish at home and Polish at school. In the afternoon she attended Hebrew lessons."

"My mother had just turned 16 when the war broke out. She virtually became an orphan because after that she never saw her parents again. Her father sent her behind the lines to Russia so that she could stay ahead of the advancing Germans. There she found work in a laboratory where food was inspected for senior military officers and other dignitaries. They were afraid that they would be poisoned. It meant that my mother had access to food, because there were always leftovers – such as a range of meats and chocolate – while the population at large went hungry. Officially the food was supposed to be destroyed, but of course that didn't happen. My mother took it with her to trade it for other things. She traded it, for instance, for a warm overcoat or shoes, or used it to buy her way out of problems."

"My mother lived relatively well in Russia. She thought the system there was awful, but the Russians were friendly. Often people who were com-

Fania Kirzner-Schusterman in her store, David's on Heerenstraat. (photo: Sherman de Jesus)

plete strangers would help her find food, shelter and warm clothes. It didn't take her long to decide to leave Russia as soon as the war was over. But when the war ended, she first wanted to return to her parents, because she did not yet know they had been killed. My father, whom she had met by that time, tried to change her mind. But she was stubborn and set off on the journey without the necessary papers. The journey home became very difficult. But she had food with her, so she could buy her place on a train from the conductors. She later told me: 'Now that I know what the dangers were, I also know that I should never have set off in the first place.'"

"She jumped off a moving train and thus came very near the Jewish cemetery in her home city, where landmines were still buried. Walking through the minefield, she reached her parents' house, where she found a stranger wearing her mother's shoes. Her parents' clock was still hanging on the wall. The Germans had set up their headquarters in the house during the war."

"When she was told that no one had survived, she was unable to speak for an entire week due to the shock. She then returned to Russia, where she heard that her brother Leib, affectionately called Lobke, was still alive. So in the middle of the winter, she went to retrieve him in frozen Siberia. It was an extremely dangerous trip because, in Stalin's Russia, you needed special travel papers in order to move around. Traveling without these documents might lead to immediate execution. More or less against his will, she took her brother with her and together they boarded a train, without papers. On the way they were picked up. But due to a bluff by her brother with a fake pistol and the acting performance of my mother, they were able to get away. Later, they were detained a second time. This time my mother pointed out the fact that her brother was a war veteran, had fought heroically and was seriously wounded in one arm; in this way she convinced the authorities that they had to let them pass. So they once again escaped detention and on different trains – picking up my father on the way – they headed for Germany. By pretending to be Greeks, they successfully crossed the German border without papers. After that, soldiers in the American sector sent my father back a couple of times, but at a certain point they did succeed. In 1946 they settled in Germany."

"Because they could not prove who they were, they spent another two years as displaced persons in the DP camp Feldafing located in southern Germany. The Americans had placed the Jews there and the camp residents were happy to have a roof over their head. My parents were married in Germany and from that camp they sought contact with my mother's aunt Hanah Wuhl on Curaçao. They arrived on the island in 1948 – two weeks before my birth – after a difficult journey via the Netherlands. Though the war had taken its toll on them, they were willing to roll their sleeves up and start working hard. My uncle Leib Schusterman initially went to the United States. He finally came to Curaçao in the 1960s. He had changed his name to Leo Shuman by that time." ◄

Janina de Marchena-Katz (Chorostków, 1932)

"When the war broke out, the Russians came. They arrested all the bourgeoisie, all the people that were rich or owned land. Thus, they deported my father to Siberia because he was bourgeois. And they confiscated everything. In the meantime we stayed at my grandmother's house. It didn't take long before the Russians left and the Germans arrived. They sent my brother Bumek to a labor camp in Kamionka and I remained behind with my mother, sister and grandmother. At a certain moment – I was nine years old – they said that all the Jews were to be rounded up and deported. The city had to be made *Judenfrei*. A lot of people hid in bunkers, including my mother, my sister and I. But my grandmother said that she was not leaving because her house was *gebensjt*, i.e. blessed. Therefore she erected a double wall behind which she and a couple of neighbors could hide."

"Unfortunately, the Germans opened the bunker we were hiding in. 'Juden 'raus', we heard them say and they took us all to the city center. Once there, my mother told me that I should simply walk away. 'We are older and will be fine, but you are still young'. So I began to walk and remembered the rabbi's house, where I hid under the floor. Everywhere I heard the Germans screaming: 'Juden 'raus, verfluchte Juden 'raus'. I must have fallen asleep, I don't know, but when I awoke it was sometime in the early morning. There was not a living soul on the street. Nothing moved and I thought to myself 'What should I do?' I went to my grandmother's house, broke through the double wall and there she was, still alive and healthy."

"The city had now been declared *Judenfrei*, which meant we had to leave and go to Ternopil. My grandmother was 80 years old, she had asthma, she coughed continually, was actually dying and I had to take her with me to Ternopil on foot; it was very difficult. In Ternopil we stayed with a family, I no longer remember who they were. My brother sent someone from the labor camp to pick me up. I had to leave my grandmother behind with that family; she was too old to travel further, and I never saw her again. My mother and sister and all the others had already been taken to an extermination camp, where they were killed."

"My brother Bumek then took me to Kamionka, where I was placed with the women. Though it was outside the labor camp, we were under the authority of the Ukrainian police. We stayed there until it became too dangerous. Friends of my brother feared a raid would take place. So Bumek and his friend Sam Halpern took me to two sisters a couple of kilometers further on. I cried and said: 'I'll stay there only if you stay as well, and ran after my brother. But he told me 'Go back. You have to.' Soon after that, on 10 July 1943, there was indeed a raid on the camp and my brother and hundreds of other Jews died. Sam Halpern escaped in time. Bumek had asked him to take care of his little sister if he did not survive."

"After a couple of months, the sisters said that they could no longer keep me. Where was I to go? Then I remembered that my brother had some

Janina de Marchena-Katz. (photo: Frans de Graaff)

friends. I went to them, but of course they were also afraid of the Germans. I spent the night with them and the next day they sent me to another village, two hours away on foot. There was a family living there with a sick mother and a small child. They needed someone to look after the child. It was snowing and I started walking. I wondered what I would do if they did not want me. Fortunately, I was allowed to stay with them to help out and I could sleep on a mattress on the floor. One day the neighbors came by – real Jew-haters. 'Death to all Jews', they said. I sat there and thought, 'The first thing they will do is murder me'. But I had nowhere to go. The lady with whom I lived later asked me whether or not I could pray, that is whether I was Catholic. She also thought that I made *piroshkis* (pastries with filling) just like the Jews. But I assured her that that was how the Polish made them. She suspected I was a Jew, I am certain of that."

"When I had been there for about a month, the Russians returned because the Germans had retreated. I was putting the cows out to pasture and suddenly I saw Sam Halpern. I asked him immediately where my brother was. He was in the army, he said, safe and alive. He didn't want to take my hope away. I then returned to my brother's friends. They were no longer afraid and let me stay with them. I helped them with everything. They were very kind and made a dress for me from a *tallit* (prayer shawl). One day I saw an old man walking toward me. He hugged me, but I had no idea who he was. 'I am your father', he said. 'Don't you remember me?' But I remembered him as a young man before the war. He took me to Ternopil where he contacted family living in the States and on Curaçao. They arranged papers for us so that we could go there." ◄

► Joseph Frankel (Komárom, Slovakia, 1925)

"We were not traditional Jews. Though we observed the Sabbath rituals on Friday evening, we seldom went to the synagogue, except for the High Holidays. We had a kosher kitchen and at home kept milk and meats separated. But I think that my mother did this mostly to please her mother. At the neighbor's house, for example, I regularly ate sausage or pork. We didn't eat those things at home, but did eat them at other

Joseph Frankel (photo: Jeannette van Ditzhuijzen)

people's houses. We were also given Christmas presents by the neighbor across the street and we would then sing Christmas carols."

"As a boy of ten, I was a member of the extreme right Jewish movement *Betar*, the predecessor of *Irgun* in Israel. In this Zionist movement, religion was a secondary matter. We learned more about how to use firearms and how to defend ourselves. When I was eleven years old, my parents sent me to a school in Győr, just across the border in Hungary. I lived with a cousin of my mother's. During vacation periods, I traveled home on a bike, some 40 kilometers. I actually lived two lives: a Zionist life within *Betar* and a non-Jewish, Hungarian life in Győr."

"While I was at school, my parents were deported. I only heard about it when I wanted to go home. I managed to acquire fake papers that I used to go to Ostrava, in Czechoslovakia. There I joined the partisans. I was 16 years old, one of the youngest members. Toward the end of the war, most of the members of my brigade were dead. I escaped and traveled on foot to Prague, some 250 to 300 kilometers away. It took me a week to get there, perhaps ten days. Fortunately, I did not look like a Jew. From Prague, via a wide range of adventures with the Germans and the Russians, I went to the place of my birth, Komárom. All of my family and friends had been deported. I did not know whether my mother was still alive, so I went to Győr. There, too, all the Jews were gone."

"What was I to do? I spoke to a man from Budapest who was looking for people from *Betar*, people who spoke their language and had guts. He wanted me to help him smuggle Jews to Palestine. I didn't have anything else to do, so I went with him. After that, I took people from various camps – Mauthausen, Buchenwald, Auschwitz – to the American side of Austria. There they were placed in a refugee camp of the UNRRA (United Nations Relief and Rehabilitation Administration)."

"We were unable to get to Palestine, so after that, funded by the UNRRA, I traveled to Belgium with many other Jews. There was a camp there as well, but it drove me crazy. I had nothing to do. With a mechanic and a carpenter from Komárom I took the train to Brussels, where we found work and a place to sleep. It was there that I met a Hungarian musician who played in the Philharmonic Orchestra of Brussels. One day he gave me a ticket to a concert. Dressed in clothes he had lent me, I went to the concert. There, I got into conversation with baroness Van Harinxma thoe Slooten, the Dutch ambassador's wife. Two weeks later, I received an invitation for a cocktail party at the embassy. I borrowed suitable clothes again and went to the party. The ambassador asked about my language skills and proposed that I come to work at the embassy to set up the library. That was in 1947. I still had contact with the illegal Zionist organization *Betar*. It didn't become legal until 1948."

"The ambassador and his family were like a family to me. One day he introduced me to the new ambassador of Cuba. He was looking for someone who could speak a few languages. At the time I was stateless, but the Dutch Embassy gave me a document stating that I worked for them and in The Hague I was given a laissez-passer as a courier in the diplomatic service. So in February of 1949 I left for Cuba to work at the embassy."

"There was a large Jewish community there, but initially the Jews did not accept me because I did not speak Yiddish. They simply did not believe that I was Jewish. Finally, I met my wife Helen there and in 1950 we married. I then resigned from my job at the embassy and started a business selling liquor to all the embassies. I knew everyone and met a large number of people, including Fidel Castro and Rómulo Betancourt, who later became President of Venezuela again."

"In 1959 I got myself into trouble. At the request of the ambassador of Guatemala, I delivered a letter to Guantánamo Bay and on my return to Havana I was accused of being a courier for Castro. Soon after that I was being threatened and, as a result, I fled the island First I went to America. Later I traveled to Curaçao, where my wife had been born. Thanks to my connections at the embassies, I acquired a Haitian passport. We lived on Aruba for a time, but in the end returned to Curaçao." ◀

10   The Rise and Fall of Social Life

The primary meeting place of the Ashkenazic Jews was Club Union, which moved to a newer and better location in Scharloo after the war. The social life of the youth revolved around Maccabi. In preparation for possible emigration to Israel, even a farming course was launched.

Club Union and Maccabi

Club Union and Maccabi flourished in the postwar years. The entire social life of the Ashkenazic community was concentrated in these organizations. The Club opened in the evening around half past seven, when the members would play cards, chess or billiards. Lectures were also given and you could take Hebrew lessons. On Sundays there were films for young and old.

From the late 1940s, Yiddish theater groups from South America regularly came to the island with music, plays, comedy performances and magic acts. Nachman Grynsztein: "They gave performances in the Club. I attended them with my mother and heard those people sing." Ida Hirschberg thought she remembered that the actors were actually on the way to other destinations. Because the ships had to refuel on Curaçao, they would perform for the Ashkenazic Jewish community, where they were warmly welcomed. The Sephardim did not attend the performances because they did not understand Yiddish.

The popularity of the Club Union is obvious from the number of members in 1962: out of a total of 117 Ashkenazic families, 105 were members of the Club, while only 92 families were members of the religious congregation that was established in 1958 (see Chapter 11). The close relationship that the Ashkenazic community had with Club Union as the main social venue lasted until the 1970s. Claire Fixman-Seibald, a teenager in those years: "The Club was fantastic. We were very Jewish-minded. Not that we went to synagogue each Saturday, but we did jump into the car with the family every Sunday, rain or shine, to go to the Club. Once there, we would play dominos and eat. And we had the best parties there. All the Jews came together. It was a lot of fun – always."

There were only a couple of Ashkenazim that seldom or never came to the Club or the synagogue. Benjamin Riks and Carlos Roitman, for example, both of whom had a non-Jewish partner and thought that that would not go down well in the community. And then there was Samuel Frimmerman, a friendly but shy man that also stayed away from the Club and the synagogue. Only when one of the congregation members personally handed him an invitation to her son's *bar mitzvah*, he did show up. It was the only time that he visited *shiel*.

Breakfast at Club Union (photo: private collection of Bill and Tila Gerstenbluth-Cheis)

Breakfast at Club Union. From left to right: Abraham Wiznitzer, Tila Gerstenbluth, Samuel Fruchter and Herman Gärtner. (photo: private collection of Bill and Tila Gerstenbluth-Cheis)

The wedding of Gitta Fruchter and Pinhos Meit in 1955 in the Sephardic snoa. (photos: private collection of Frieda Pais-Fruchter)

A New Accommodation in Scharloo

In 1949, Club Union moved from the Hendrikplein to its own beautiful property at Scharlooweg 41, which was built in 1879. The official opening took place on 9 December 1950. In what used to be the living room (the *sala* in Curaçao), there were comfortable chairs with attractive seats and a floor lamp. On the wall hung portraits of Theodor Herzl, the father of Zionism, David Ben-Gurion, the first prime minister of Israel, and the reigning Dutch Queen Juliana. From this room you could go through a small space and end up on a patio, a common feature in Scharloo's older houses. On both sides of this patio were several rooms, and the board of the Club met in one of them. In the middle of that room was a large conference table surrounded by leather chairs. Here was also a library with various newspapers, such as the Yiddish-language *Forwarts* and *Der Tog-Morgen Journal* from New York. Also available were *The Jerusalem Post* from Israel, the *Nieuw Israëlitisch Weekblad* from Amsterdam, the local newspapers *Beurs- en Nieuwsberichten* and *Amigoe*, plus several magazines.

Another room was used as a card room, where the various card clubs met on their fixed evenings. Tsale Kirzner remembered that Marco Cheis, Saul Ghitman and Herman Gärtner were always playing cards. "There was a lot of smoking and it smelled like an old gentlemen's room."

To the left at the back was the Club's canteen: a bar with stools and a kitchen behind the bar area. On the other side of the patio, one of the rooms was set up as a classroom for the Jewish Moria School (see Chapter 12). This classroom was later moved to the synagogue next door, after which the room was set up as a billiard room. Nearly all the men and boys played billiards and there were even competitions. Butchie Wiznitzer: "I still remember how I and the boys from the Hebrew School learned to play billiards before and after class."

For dance parties and other parties – such as *bar mitzvahs* and weddings – the *sala* was used. General membership meetings and board elections were also held there. New Year's Eve (not the Jewish new year) was of course celebrated there with plenty of fireworks – as is the tradition on Curaçao – followed by dancing in the *sala* and behind the patio.

Also behind the patio was a stage for theatrical performances. The children from the Jewish school were not the only ones to perform there. Several local and foreign theater companies, such as the aforementioned Yiddish theater groups, also used this 'theater', which, according to the Monthly Magazine for Israeli Households on the Netherlands Antilles, could seat 500 people.

The land behind served as a sports field. In the evening it could be illuminated and, thanks to the lines drawn on the ground, the boys could play basketball and volleyball there. Later, tennis matches were also played under the supervision of Isuhar Meit.

Kosher Cooking for the Club

Socher and Fania Kirzner, who arrived in 1948 from Europe, ran the Club's canteen. Their son Tsale: "They wanted to improve their finances and were not afraid of hard work. In the daytime, my father worked in various stores. And because we lived near Club Union, the congregation asked my father if he would run the Club. My mother made pastry and snacks, such as croquettes and kosher hotdogs. They earned the most money by selling food, because the congregation did not pay them much. It was a difficult time. My father worked two jobs for approximately ten years." Later Socher Kirzner would play an important role on the board of the congregation.

After the Kirzners, Fanny Sprung-Weisinger was active in the Club. "I sold kosher food there, organized bingo for the women and card game evenings for the men. On Sunday, a film for the children and a Jewish film for the adults were shown. I gave the profits that I earned to a good cause."

Isaac Kisilevich also worked for the Club for a couple of years. That was in the 1960s and, just like the Kirzners, he worked someplace else during the day – i.e. in a business in Otrobanda. "At the Club I worked behind the bar and sold drinks and cigarettes to the members. I earned some extra money doing this. I also had to make sure that the building was kept clean. Every Monday evening was poker night and on the weekend people came to the Club to eat. My mother prepared the food."

New Start for Club Union

The Club continued to be the social center for the Ashkenazic community until around 1982, when the building in Scharloo was sold. The adjoining synagogue, consecrated in 1959, was vacated in 1986. The synagogue then moved to the Lelieweg (see Chapter 14), but there was no longer a separate building for the Club. This brought an end to the regular meetings of Club Union. There still seemed to be a need for Club activities, though, and so in 1990, under the presidency of Paul Morón, the Club rose from its ashes. On Sundays the congregation members would come together again, only now on the Lelieweg.

From old editions of KOL, *the Voice of Shaarei Tsedek*, the congregation's bulletin that has been published since 1992, it seems that occasionally films were shown and that the congregation organized children's activities. On Mother's Day, there were bake contests, and on Father's Day rallies were held. On Purim and other religious holidays, there were also activities , such as quiz games. But the older generation thought the Club on the Lelieweg did not compare with the wonderful times they had spent in Scharloo.

The children that were born 'after Scharloo' hold a different view, evidenced by Annette Morón's memories of the 1990s. She could still picture the covered patio with the plastic tables and chairs and the two old ping-pong tables. "On Sundays you would come back from the beach, shower and dress very quickly to go to the Club. The older women would play cards or Rummikub, or just talk. Or all three at the same time. The men played dominos and at the end, say at about seven-thirty, the buffet opened. Everyone brought something along and the theme changed each week, Italian or Chinese for example. It was always a lot of fun."

Women at Club Union. From left to right: Rachel Poplicher, Cily Weisinger, Tila Gerstenbluth, Janina Cheis, Mary Sterental, Sylvia Ghitman, Sonia Causanchi, Marietta Lachs, Rosita Zonenschain and, seated at the front, Becci and Tonia Metsch. (photo: private collection of Bill and Tila Gerstenbluth-Cheis)

The End of Club Union

The final blow for Club Union came in 1996 when Rabbi Poupko was contracted by *Shaarei Tsedek*. Because the Club no longer had a canteen like it had in Scharloo, the custom was for congregation members to take turns bringing food to the Club. Rabbi Poupko demanded that this food had to be kosher. At the school, too, only kosher food was allowed to be served.

He therefore stood by the door at a Purim celebration where hotdogs were being served and sent the bread back because it was not kosher. None of the parents had considered this, simply because on Curaçao at the time kosher bread[121] was unavailable. But he stuck to his guns, so that was the end of the hotdogs.

On the other hand, Poupko did try to acquire kosher bread after that. He approached a baker called Ashley, who was willing to make space available in his bakery so that kosher *challes* could be baked for the congregation. Over these braided bread loaves the *bracha* (blessing) is said at the start of the Sabbath, on Friday evening. For Poupko no amount of effort was too much and he was always personally present when Ashley baked *challes* to make sure everything was done according to the rules. Ashley was not a Jew, but because he was a Seventh Day Adventist, his shop was closed on the Sabbath.

Annette Morón remembered that – at her request – baker Ashley also baked *challah* with chocolate chips. *Hamantaschen* were also made at his bakery – triangles of dough, which were usually filled with plums and nuts and were eaten on Purim. Annette: "On an island, you have to make do with what you have and baker Ashley baked as kosher as was possible on Curaçao."

Until 2011, the former Club Union building housed an accountants' office. After that the Directorate of Foreign Relations was temporarily housed in this building. (photo: Jeannette van Ditzhuijzen)

Officially, the Club was never closed down, but due to Poupko's strict policy on food, the Club Union died a quiet death. After all, not all the Ashkenazim cooked kosher, and as a result of Poupko's requirements some of them stopped coming to the Club on Sundays. Something else that undoubtedly played a role in its demise is the fact that now there was much more entertainment to be had on the island – both Jewish and non-Jewish – so there was no longer any need for a Jewish club.

Annette's older brother Adam had such fond memories of the Club that in 2002 he and several contemporaries tried to bring the good old times back to life. As members of the youth organization BBYO (see Chapter 12) they organized a domino tournament at which both Ashkenazic and Sephardic Jews were welcome, young and old. "We created a lot of publicity for it, but in the end only twelve people came. Despite the poor turnout we had a fun evening, but we had really expected to attract more people. That was a disappointment."

A year later, the BBYO also tried to breathe new life into the Purim party. Adam Morón: "We divided the hall in two parts, one for the young people and one for the older crowd. It was a success. But when we tried to organize it again in the following years, each time it had to be called off at the last moment due to different circumstances."

Maccabi: Combining the Practical with the Pleasurable

The youth association Maccabi did not keep going as long as the Club. It stopped probably sometime in the mid 1950s. Until then the Maccabi members met in the rooms of the Club, first on the Hendrikplein and later in Scharloo. Each Friday after school, they went to the Club to play records and dance. And on the weekend, they often set out together on some adventure.

Almost all Ashkenazic young people who were Maccabi members after the war remembered camping at Boca Tabla or the picnics on Knip beach and Westpunt. With around 20 people, they rode toward Westpunt in a large truck. Hammocks and tents were taken along, as were chaperones, often the parents of Isaac Kisilevich. Liza Seibald-Becher: "We went swimming and in the evening we would sing Hebrew songs around the campfire." Nioma Causanschi was older than most of the Maccabi members and he invariably drove the truck, which he rented or even borrowed from Teofilio Cuales.

Maccabi also organized parties for the Jewish holidays such as *Sukkot* (Feast of Tabernacles), *Hanukkah* (Festival of Lights) and *Purim* (Feast of Lots). Until her departure to Israel in 1953, Lucca Koch played the accordion on these occasions while the young people sang Israeli songs at the top of their voices. During such festivals, money was often collected for good causes.

In this way, after the war the Maccabi members collectively saved money for the purchase of a 'synagogue ambulance' for Israel. The ambulance served as a mobile synagogue with prayer books, *tefillin* (prayer straps, also called phylacteries) and other necessities for a Jewish service. At the same time, it also contained a stock of medicine and food for the refugees and displaced persons in the postwar camps. The ambulances were meant not only for the camps in the liberated areas, cities where the synagogue had been destroyed or ransacked during the war would also receive 'synagogue ambulances'. Later, of course, ambulances were sent to the new land of Israel. On Curaçao, some Maccabi members donated their pocket money for the ambulance. Others, who already had a job, donated a part of their salary. The proceeds of one social evening at the Club raised the remainder of the 2,600 dollars needed for the ambulance.

On 26 January 1952, Maccabi celebrated its tenth anniversary with a reception and a party. The Monthly Magazine for Israeli Households on the Netherlands Antilles was somewhat critical of the youth club. It pointed out the fact that both married people and 12-year-old children were members. The magazine also wrote about the 'once so flourishing club of our Jewish youth' and implied the club lived on its fame from days gone by. "And on a full cash box that could be spent on a wide range of useful causes if only the management were more inclined to do so."[122]

The 15th anniversary may have been the last to be celebrated. What is at least certain is that the members marched in the procession celebrating Queen Juliana's visit in 1955. Maccabi also took part once or twice in the carnival parades that had been organized on Curaçao since 1949. Fela Seibald-Meit and Clara

An impression of a camping weekend of the Maccabi members. (photos: private collection of Liza Seibald-Becher)

Goudsmit-Meit still clearly remembered that the youth association had portrayed a kibbutz during one of the parades, complete with a truck and rifles. The participants were dressed as soldiers.

According to the newspaper *Amigoe* dated 5 April 1957, Maccabi took part in the volleyball competition that year. Not long thereafter the club must have stopped operating. Lily Kisilevich, born in 1940, could still remember the closing down meeting, but does not remember exactly when that was.

She did remember that in those years another youth group was operating. It was shortly after 1955 when her cousin Sunye Meit came back from Brasilia where his family had lived for a time. He was a member of *Ha-Shomer Ha-Tsair*, a progressive, Zionist youth movement and he formed a youth group on

Synagogue ambulance paid for by Maccabi members. (photo: private collection of Esther Gal-Jessurun Cardozo)

A SHTETL UNDER THE SUN

Traytel Oberman from Poland was active within Maccabi; later he became the gabai for the congregation. (photo: Frieda Geller-Faerman)

Curaçao for Ashkenazic youngsters. He taught them Zionist ideals, Israeli dances and partisan songs. According to Lily, the membership included Henri and Robert Gärtner, who had lived in Israel, Esther Grynsztein, Lina Aron Josub, Fela Meit and Rita Wiznitzer. "It was a small group, but we were very active, even though it only lasted two or three years. Sunye actually wanted to go to Israel himself, but he had to help his father in the store."

Agricultural Classes in the Hachsharah

Several enthusiastic Maccabi members came together in April 1947 in an agricultural program, *hachsharah* in Hebrew. The training program, which was given all over the world, was meant for the pioneers (*chalutzim*) who wanted to emigrate to Israel to work in a kibbutz. The Curaçao pioneers were between 16 and 20 years old and they met every Sunday on a field at Kas Kòrá, near Van Engelen. Under the supervision of Adolf Haber from Sniatyn they learned how to farm and to breed cattle. The Sephardic leader, Isaac Jessurun Cardozo, taught modern Hebrew, the language of the new state of Israel founded in 1948. The lessons were held in the open air; if the weather turned bad, the pioneers could meet in the wooden house that they had built and painted themselves.

According to the Monthly Magazine for Israeli Households on the Netherlands Antilles dated May/June 1947, the *hachsharah* had actually existed since 1945. But because they had not yet found a suitable piece of farmland, it took until 1947 before they could get started. After that they encountered a new problem:

Hachsharah, from left to right: Jochanan Taytelbaum, Lea Groisman, Manfred Klug, Otilia Kisilevich, Rabbi Jessurun Cardozo, Molka Weisinger, Aba Grynsztein, Esther Jessurun Cardozo, Isaac Kisilevich, Martha Kisilevich and Adolph Haber. (photo: private collection of Esther Gal-Jessurun Cardozo)

there were no water pipes, which meant they could not yet sow seeds. Finally the pipes were provided and the students could enthusiastically sow and plant. Each day, a group went to the field to water it. Their first harvest was a bunch of radishes. During the Hanukkah celebrations of Maccabi (end of 1947), they were sold and the money went to care for Jewish children in Palestine. The radishes brought in no less than 100 guilders.

One of the initiators of the *hachsharah* was José Abady, a Sephardic Jew whose family came from Beirut (see Chapter 14). He left in 1947 for America to train further in agriculture. He planned to go to Israel after that. From Maccabi he received a watch as a farewell gift.

Aba Grynsztein also emigrated to Israel. According to his brother Nachman, he was inspired to do so at Kas Kòrá. Another *hachsharah* member, Isaac Kisilevich, left for Israel in 1950, where he volunteered for the Israeli air force. After three and a half years, he returned to Curaçao. The agricultural project only lasted a few years at most.

Hachsharah: Hebrew lesson in the open air. From left to right: Isaac Kisilevich (with back turned), Rabbi Isaac Jessurun Cardozo, Martha Kisilevich, Otilia Kisilevich (Isaac's niece and sister), Molka Weisinger, Manfred Klug, Adolph Haber, Aba Grynsztein, Esther Jessurun Cardozo and Lea Groisman (with back turned).
Hachsharah: Aba Grynsztein and Molka Weisinger weeding at Kas Kòrá.
Hachsharah: preparing the seed-beds with, from left to right, Manfred Klug, Adolph Haber, Isaac Kisilevich, Jochanan Taytelbaum and Aba Grynsztein.
(photos: private collection of Esther Gal-Jessurun Cardozo)

Curaçao: a Small Shtetl

Altogether, the decades after the war were the best of times for the Ashkenazic community on Curaçao. It was a time full of social activities and a time when everyone in the community visited everyone else at home. Most of the stores were Jewish and on the High Holidays Punda was deserted because all Jewish stores – those of the Sephardim included – were closed. Tsale Kirzner called the close-knit Jewish community of that era 'a kind of microcosm'. "We sometimes argued, but two days later the disagreement was forgotten. Curaçao was actually just like a small *shtetl*."

▶ Mark 'Butchie' Wiznitzer (New York, 1949)

"The children of the Ashkenazic community on Curaçao who grew up together in the 1950s generally had a fantastic youth and developed a strong Jewish identity. And regardless of the places our lives led us to, the ties with Curaçao remained strong. We could attribute this wonderful youth we all had to the fact that we grew up without personal memories of the discrimination against Jews in Eastern Europe or of the Holocaust. During those years, we had not yet been confronted with the colonial heritage of Curaçao and the social tensions that became painfully clear on 30 May 1969. And as offspring of a new elite class we enjoyed the privileges of our parents' economic success."

"As a child I attended the Hendrik School across from Cinelandia. I was the only Jewish boy in the class. In the afternoons I met my best friends in the Hebrew classes at the Moria School. They were Isaak Sitzer, Larry Becher, Fannie Weinstein, Willy Josub, Mark 'Mono' Bonaparte, Meyer Grynsztein, Tsale Kirzner, Reny Metsch, Paulette Tauber and Esty Fruchter. There were also two boys from Holland, Jopie Moffie and Salko de Wolf, and the American boy Andy Lindauer. I was the youngest person in the group and my nickname was 'Butchie', actually a typical Curaçao name for a boy. That is why everyone thought that I was a real *yu'i Korsou*, someone who had been born on the island. The children in my class played together at each other's houses and we celebrated our birthdays together. On Sunday, we all went to the social activities of Club Union."

"I think the Jewish identity of our group was primarily formed by Nathan Schächter, our rabbi, chazzan, *moreh* (teacher) and *shochet*. At the Jewish School he taught us to speak Hebrew with a modern accent, which sounds much sharper than the liturgical language that our fathers had learned at *cheder* in Europe. He and his wife Rozika also organized cultural activities at Club Union. So on Saturday afternoons we would learn Israeli songs and dances. On the religious holidays we would perform plays for the entire community. From our parents we had learned the *Yiddishkeit* of the Old World. But the rabbi imbued us with a love for the newborn state of Israel, where our ancestor's prayers and dreams had been realized."

"The Jewish community was one big family. For example, Isaak Sitzer, the oldest boy in the group, accompanied our family around 1955 on our first vacation to Bonaire. Only one of my friends, Tsale Kirzner, lived in Scharloo like us, and together we would play 'cowboy' or 'adventurer' in the *mondi* – land covered with cactuses and thorn bushes – behind Club

Mark 'Butchie' Wiznitzer. (photo: Jeannette van Ditzhuijzen)

Union. I always felt at home with my friends' families. Sometimes I would stay with them for lunch or dinner, for instance the family of Fajwel and Ida Becher, who had six children, or the Metsch, Josub, Tauber and Cheis families."

"In 1960 my parents divorced and my mother, my two sisters and I moved to New York. After that I would return to Curaçao on each vacation. In the morning I would work for my father Salomon Wiznitzer, in *La Confianza*. The rest of the time I spent playing with my friends. But starting in the 1960s, more and more friends moved to Israel, America or the Netherlands. One of the first was Isaak Sitzer, who fought in the Six Day War of 1967 in Jerusalem. In the end, out of the entire group, only Willy Josub remained on the island, where he worked in *Casa Moderna*, his parents' business."

"After I graduated from university in 1975, I was invited to work for the American State Department. My father and my uncle Abraham had always hoped that one of their sons would take over the business. Unfortunately that didn't happen and they finally had to close *La Confianza*. But my father, who left Romania as a teenager without graduating from high school, was naturally very proud of the fact that his son had earned a university degree and had entered the prestigious world of diplomacy. It was all made possible because of his hard work." ◀

11 Their Own Shiel and the Old Traditions

As the Jewish congregation grew, the Ashkenazim could afford their own synagogue. Eating strictly kosher continued to be a difficult challenge, though. Also, driving a car on the Sabbath was no longer a taboo for everyone, the distances were simply too great to do otherwise. Thus, the Ashkenazim observed their religious traditions as best they could on Curaçao.

Marrying in the Sephardic Snoa

Until 1954 the Ashkenazim did not have their own rabbi. To a certain degree, some Ashkenazim considered Isaac Jessurun Cardozo, appointed chazzan at Mikve Israel in 1939, to be 'their' rabbi. The younger Ashkenazim knew him from the religion classes at school and the Hebrew lessons he taught the Maccabi members. The parents greatly appreciated the fact that, during the war, he had devoted himself to improving the lot of interned fellow Jews, many of them Ashkenazim.

Because the *shiel* on the Bargestraat was not particularly presentable and was too small to accommodate large groups of people, some Ashkenazim set aside their reluctance to attend the *snoa* during festive occasions such as *bar mitzvahs* and weddings. Chaim Jacob Geiger, for example, had his *bar mitzvah* in 1945 in the Sephardic *snoa*. He was certainly not the only one to do so during those years.

A year earlier, Clara Libman and Joske Faerman had wanted to marry in the *snoa*. But Joske's friends advised him that in that case probably no one would attend. The Ashkenazic Jews of that generation – despite their appreciation for Jessurun Cardozo – were convinced that the Sephardic Jews did not know how to properly observe those kinds of occasions. That is why the couple got married in Club Union on the Hendrikplein after all.

It wasn't until three years later, in 1947, that the very first Ashkenazic wedding was held in the synagogue of *Mikvé Israel*. It was the wedding of Dora Cheis and Philip Suchar. Dora's father had sent her to her sister Rosa in Caracas. Dora: "He hoped that I would meet someone there I could marry." The plan worked, because at a party she met Philip Suchar, a Jew from Trinidad. Just like her, he originally came from the Romanian city of Herţa.

The Sephardic Rabbi Jessurun Cardozo married Liza Becher and Jozef Seibald in 1950 in Club Union in Scharloo. (photo: private collection of Liza Seibald-Becher)

Dora: "At the synagogue on the Bargestraat we did not have a rabbi and I was a good friend of Jessurun Cardozo. Our wedding was also the first one to be catered. It took place in the Piscadera Club, where the Hilton Hotel is now." Although the marriage was blessed in the Sephardic *snoa*, the guests were all Ashkenazim, except for Atilio de Marchena, the man who had stood by Dora's father at the very beginning. The Jessurun Cardozo family, of course, also attended.

In 1953, Dora's sister Tila was also married in the *snoa* by the Sephardic chazzan's brother, David Jessurun Cardozo. Tila explained that a rabbi or chazzan is not absolutely necessary for a Jewish wedding, but she and others were simply fond of the Jessurun Cardozo brothers. "I always thought the *snoa* was beautiful and now I was standing in it myself. Normally, we never went there, only when we were invited for a *bar mitzvah*." Her eldest sister Rosa was married by the Ashkenazic *shochet*, though not in the *snoa* or *shiel*, but in Club Union.

Shaarei Tsedek: a new congregation with a new shiel

In 1949, the Ashkenazim left the *shiel* they had rented on the Bargestraat since 1930.[123] After that, for a long time services were held in the building of the Club in Scharloo. It wasn't until 1955 that the Ashkenazic Jews were to purchase the

Nathan Schächter was rabbi from 1954 to 1960. (photo: private collection of Leo Wiznitzer)

The synagogue building in Scharloo. (From: History of the Jews of the Netherlands Antilles *by Isaac and Suzanne Emmanuel)*

The official consecration of the synagogue in Scharloo on 18 February 1959. (From: History of the Jews of the Netherlands Antilles *by Isaac and Suzanne Emmanuel*)

building next to the Club, at number 39. Just like the Club, this had originally been a residence (from 1881) and the board decided to submit both buildings to a rigorous restoration and renovation. During the restoration, the colorful Portuguese tiles on the walls of number 41 were retained. The architect wanted to remove them, but the president of Club Union, Jan Groisman, insisted that they be spared.

In the *shiel*, a double door separated the worldly from the religious section. Across from this door, against the wall that was more or less in the direction of Jerusalem, stood the cabinet containing the Torah scrolls, the *aron kodesh*, with a *menorah*, the seven-branch candelabrum, in front of it. Just inside the entrance, to the left and right, stood low mahogany tables with prayer books. The women sat in the back row. As is common in orthodox Jewish synagogues, they were separated from the men, in this case by a low wooden partition (the *mechitzah*). Initially, the doors and windows stood open during a service. Later, the synagogue had air conditioning.

The new *shiel* could accommodate 186 people[124], in 1959 114 families (approximately 350 people) were members of the congregation. This congregation, the Curaçao Ashkenazic Jewish Congregation of *Shaarei Tsedek* ('Gates of Righteousness'), had been founded one year earlier. It is noteworthy that at the start of the 21st century, the word 'orthodox' was added to it. Since then, the congregation has called itself 'Shaarei Tsedek' Ashkenazic Orthodox Jewish Community.

On 18 February 1959, the birthday of (at the time) Princess Marijke, Rabbi Nathan Schächter officially consecrated the new synagogue. Schächter had arrived from Israel in February 1954, after the *shochet* Szmukler had died in 1953. Schächter stayed until 1960. Different dignitaries attended the consecration ceremony: Governor Anton Speekenbrink, lieutenant-governor Michael Gorsira, Prime Minister Efrain Jonckheer, Maurits Goudeket of *Emanu-El* and Chazzan David Jessurun Cardozo of *Mikvé Israel*. Johannes Holterman, who was to be a bishop a couple of months later, also put in an appearance.

In 1959, Fela Meit and Leon Seibald were the first couple in the new synagogue to stand under the *chuppah*[125]. Rabbi Schächter performed the marriage ceremony. A quarter of a century later, Leon Seibald, as the president of *Shaarei Tsedek*, was to place his signature on the contract selling this same building.

Shiel Services: a Friendly Anarchy

According to Tsale Kirzner, the services in the *shiel* in Scharloo often trod a middle way between a real service and a friendly gathering. "During the services, people would cheerfully discuss the latest (business) news. Often the rabbi or the one leading the service would become irritated, demonstrably stop the service, look around sternly with admonishment in his eyes and sometimes bang on the table with his fist. When the congregation had quieted down, it usually wasn't long before things got out of hand again. In the meantime, children walked in and out; they even played tag. It was a friendly sort of anarchy. Much more relaxed than it is now."

On 15 January 1956, a new Torah was consecrated. The Torah was a gift from Herman Tauber in memory of his family members who had died during the war. From left to right: Lupe Bonaparte (with glasses), Selig Seibald (with glasses), Muñe Crivosei, Szmul Silberstein (with Torah), Abraham Schmidt (with Torah), Adolf Katz, Moishe Meit and Wilu Weisinger. (photo: private collection of Frieda Pais-Fruchter)

In Kirzner's eyes, the Saturday morning service was special. As mentioned earlier, it began as early as 6 or 7 o'clock so that the storekeepers could go to Punda or Otrobanda afterwards and open their stores on time. "This Saturday morning service was a tour de force in efficiency. It had to be done quickly, at supersonic speed, because afterwards the congregation was in a hurry to get to the city. Often they had not yet eaten breakfast, so after the service a glass of wine, tea or coffee was served. I still remember clearly the elongated yellow tins of Portuguese sardines that were eaten with white bread. Usually the Seibald brothers supplied them generously."

The sardine tins also appeared at the Friday evening services. They were taken from the cupboard by *gabai* Moishe Wiznitzer, together with salted crackers and whisky, *bromfen* in Yiddish. Anyone who showed up early for the service could drink a glass of spirits and eat a snack.

Celebrating the High Holidays

In those days it was primarily men and boys that came to the synagogue on the Sabbath. Not so on the High Holidays of *Rosh Hashanah* (Jewish New Year) and *Yom Kippur* (Day of Atonement). On those days absolutely everyone came to the synagogue, even women and children. Sometimes a choir was formed especially for these holidays. In the bulletin of *Shaarei Tsedek* for July 1975, for example, Rabbi Martin Levin called on adults and teenagers to come to practice and sing in the choir for *Rosh Hashanah* and *Yom Kippur*. He already conducted a *Shaarei Tsedek* children's choir at that time.

Furthermore, the congregation almost always had (and still has) a chazzan come over from abroad especially for these holidays. Lies Linder-Jessurun Cardozo remembered that the congregation went by the stores of the Ashkenazic Jews in advance, "To collect money for a chazzan". Later, the money for this was taken from the member's contributions.

An unusual spectacle during the High Holidays was the bidding by the male congregation members for the *aliot*. An *aliah* (plural *aliot*) is the honor, given to congregation members of reading from the Torah during these holidays. They paid for this honor and the money thus collected went towards the benefit of the congregation; just as money is collected in Protestant and Catholic churches during the offertory. The *aliot* involve larger amounts in a lump sum, though.

The bidding was done just like at an auction. The 'auctioneer' – for years the *gabai* Josef Rabinovich and later Traytel Oberman – tapped on the *bimah* (from which the Torah is read) and when the Yiddish phrase *zum ersten mul, zum zweiten mul und zum dritten mul* was spoken, the honor went to the highest bidder. In those years, the Tauber, Metsch and Seibald families regularly bid against one another. Charles Fuhrmann also got involved. Dressed in his white suit, he would usually bid so much money that no one could or wanted to bid higher, out of respect for this businessman, who always came to the congregation's aid when needed.

Most of the visitors to the synagogue considered this somewhat chaotic auction as the non-official part of the service. Everyone walked in and out of the building at will, to the irritation of the rabbi or chazzan. They disapproved because reading from the Torah, which began after the auction, was the highlight of the service. But after the 'spectacle' of the bidding, the children usually walked away. They often strolled over to the *snoa*, where a service was also being held. During the bidding, many of the women would already have left for the Club next door. "We didn't count, anyway", some commented about the services in those days. "We had things to do at home, such as lighting the candles. It didn't really bother us. We had grown up that way."

But men also took the opportunity to slip away unnoticed. The auction was increasingly seen as a prelude to the intermission that was traditionally inserted after the reading of the Torah. Because of the disorder created by the auction, the congregation stopped auctioning off the *aliot* to the highest bidder sometime in the 1970s or early 1980s. Instead, the custom was adopted of having the person who was given the honor of reading from the Torah – which could actually be anyone – determine for himself how much money he could afford to give.

Delicious Snacks on Yom Kippur

Yom Kippur is the most important day of the Jewish calendar. It is the day on which people repent for what they have done wrong, both against their fellow men and against God. Just like the Sabbath, Jewish holidays begin traditionally at sundown on the previous day. On the eve of *Yom Kippur* all men over 12 and women over 13 begin a period of fasting that lasts until sundown the next day. They may not eat or drink anything during this time. Wearing leather shoes is another taboo.

The evening service is called *Kol Nidre*, after the prayer with which the service begins. The next day, on *Yom Kippur* proper, Jews come to the synagogue early, where they remain for prayer the entire day, with a break of roughly one hour. At the end of the day, at sundown, the fast ends with shared snacks and drinks in *shiel*. These delicacies are usually sponsored by congregation members. In the past, they were made at home and for a long time the Tauber and Seibald families competed in making the most delicious food and drinks. Even today, many remember how, in the 1960s and '70s, at around 6 in the evening, the outside doors of the synagogue would swing open. "First the station wagon of the Tauber family would pull up and one of the two waiting tables would be filled with home-baked pies and cakes, such as *Honig Leikach* or honey cake, and *Fluden,* a hearty pie with walnuts and raisins", said one of the interviewees. "Then the car of the Seibald family would appear, from which delicacies just as tasty were taken." Between the two tables stood a table with (alcoholic) drinks. After the rabbi or chazzan had blown the *shofar* for the last time, the members of the congregation would elbow their way around the tables to sample the fare on display: which pie was the most delicious this year?

Sharon Seibald remembered that in the 1970s a Sephardic girlfriend of hers came with her to *shiel* especially to taste these delicacies on *Yom Kippur*.

No Cars on Yom Kippur?

For traditional Jews, driving a car on *Yom Kippur* is forbidden. "But you are allowed to take the boat", remembered Bruno Linder. Those who lived in Otrobanda therefore could ride across Anna Bay to Scharloo in a ferry. "The boat moored just in front of our house. Usually we walked back home, but occasionally we took the boat and that was kosher." His contemporary Dora Suchar-Cheis remembered that in the 1940s people who had moved to the outlying districts stayed the night of Yom Kippur in the city so that they didn't have to take the car. "Some of them stayed with us above the store in Punda. The next day we would all walk to the synagogue."

Older Ashkenazim still remembered that in those days it was usual for the young people first to go to their own synagogue for *Kol Nidre*. Thereafter they would walk as quickly as they could to the *snoa*, because the *Kol Nidre* prayer there began a little later. The solemn atmosphere in the *snoa*, which was lit by candles only, and the elegantly dressed ladies appealed enormously to the Ashkenazic youth. After *Kol Nidre*, the youngsters would always stroll down the Rif, the girls usually singing.

The Wiznitzer families in Scharloo often had overnight guests during the High Holidays as well. Up until sometime in the 1960s, they had lived near the

Moses and Abraham Wiznitzer in the synagogue in Scharloo. (photo: private collection of Leo Wiznitzer)

synagogue. At that time, almost all the other Ashkenazic Jews had moved to the outlying districts. Karen Cheis remembered that, in those years, her family and the Tauber and Metsch families always stayed in the Plaza Hotel in Punda during *Yom Kippur*. "In the morning, a suitcase with clothes would be taken to the hotel and in the evening we would take the car to the synagogue. After *Kol Nidre*, we could then return to the hotel on foot. The parents went to their rooms and the children – we were teenagers at the time – stayed for a while longer at the swimming pool talking to one another. We couldn't really do anything else, because watching television or doing other things was not allowed on *Yom Kippur*."

Despite the tradition of not driving a car on Jewish religious holidays, as Tsale Kirzner remembered it, Scharloo was always full of gleaming American cars around that time. All of them were owned by Ashkenazic Jews. For example, the Seibalds came by car, because according to Claire Fixman-Seibald her family lived some distance outside of Scharloo (near Caracas Bay) and, in view of the distance, they had no other choice. "During the intermission of the services, we walked with the Gerstenbluth children over the bridge to Punda, where their grandmother lived. This meant that we did not need to drive back and forth to the Caracasbaaiweg and we would spend a lovely time at her house."

Today, there are still Ashkenazic Jews that come to the synagogue on *Rosh Hashanah* and *Yom Kippur* on foot. Mainly to keep up the tradition.

Adapting Traditions to Curaçao Conditions

Although the Sabbath was seen as a workday and the stores were open, some Ashkenazim preferred not to drive a car. Elias Linder was one. He didn't even light a cigarette on that day. His daughter-in-law remembered how he continually consulted his watch at the end of the afternoon on Saturday to see if evening had arrived so that he could light up again.

The Zonenschains too were traditional and refused to take the car to the synagogue. After they moved outside the city center, they hardly ever went to *shiel* anymore, which was located in Scharloo until 1986. When old Leib Zonenschain did go, he would stay the night in a hotel. Until one night he became sick. After that he said "God forgive me, but from now on I'm going to the synagogue by car." Thus, the Ashkenazim continually adapted their religious traditions to the local circumstances.

The same was true with regard to keeping kosher. On postwar Curaçao, it was still not easy to keep an entirely kosher kitchen. Almost everything had to be imported. At Lucca Koch's house they mainly ate kosher chicken slaughtered by her grandfather. Just like Szmukler, he was a *shochet*. By then imported kosher beef was available, but she said it tasted like nothing by the time it made it to the table.

She remembered that a range of kosher products was available in Grynsztein's store. Among other things, he imported kosher pastrami, salami and herring. And of course matzos for Passover. But eating one hundred per cent kosher was simply impossible. For Lucca's grandfather, who came with the family from Romania in 1948, the lack of kosher food was one of the reasons to move to Israel for good in 1953. Lucca and her parents also moved to Israel at the time.

Things became easier in the 1950s. The Ashkenazic Jews traveled more often to America for business and family visits. So it became possible for them to return with deep-frozen kosher meat and other kosher products. Thus Bill Gerstenbluth on returning from New York brought back kosher meat for his family and the rest of his relatives. The family did not yet have their own freezer, so the meat was stored in the freezer units of the slaughterhouse in Parera.

Shlogn Kapores

While eating kosher was problematic, other religious traditions from Eastern Europe were easier to maintain. Many Jews who were born in the 1940s and 1950s remembered with some horror the ritual of *shlogn kapores*. This Jewish tradition is officially called *kapparot* (atonement). The day before *Yom Kippur*, the Jews symbolically transfer their sins to a live chicken. To that effect, the chicken is swung in a circle above the head three times while a special prayer is recited. Then the chicken is ritually killed and eaten, or given to the poor.

It is an old tradition which these days is still practiced primarily by ultra orthodox Jews. From the stories told, one can conclude that it was also practiced on Curaçao. Parents used to hold the chicken above the heads of their children. Since then, Karen Cheis, for example, almost never eats chicken. "I once witnessed the chicken being slaughtered. I will never forget that moment. After that I always hid under the table during *shlogn kapores*." Benny Seibald was terrified of this ritual. "For a small child, it was a bizarre custom which our parents apparently brought with them from Poland."

Frieda Geller-Faerman remembered that it was still done as late as 1967. "I was pregnant with my first child at the time and in that situation, instead of a chicken, they hold an egg above your head. I think my father performed the ritual. That was the last time."

Rituals Surrounding Birth and Death

An important religious tradition, the circumcision, was also held onto. According to Jewish law, boys must be circumcised when they are eight days old. That was not easy on Curaçao, where no *mohel* lived, i.e. someone that is authorized to perform the circumcision (*brith milah*). So regularly, a *mohel* had to come over to carry out this important ritual which may even take place on the Sabbath.

Paul Ackerman remembered that in the 1930 he and other Ashkenazic boys were circumcised by the Sephardic Jew Luis Ricardo. In the postwar years, a *mohel* often came from Caracas or Aruba, and sometimes even from as far afield as Miami. Lies Linder-Jessurun Cardozo: "If you were lucky, there was a *mohel* already on the island to circumcise another baby and you could split the costs of his travel and accommodation.

If a *mohel* was not available, the circumcision was performed by a doctor or surgeon – such as the Austrian doctor Julius Benesch, who died in 1962, or later the surgeon Paul Ackerman, both of them Jewish. But when Lies and Salo Linder had their first son circumcised by the Curaçao GP Dr Bonnema the in-laws frowned upon it. Three months later, Lies and Salo traveled to Aruba with their son and Lies' father to have the boy circumcised for a second time, more or less symbolically, by a Jewish doctor. Jessurun Cardozo said the prayers at the ceremony. The papers testifying to the fact have been carefully kept.

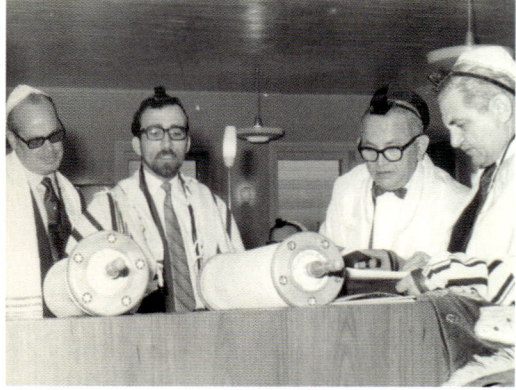

Leo Wiznitzer reading from the Torah during his bar mitzvah in 1967. To his right, behind him, is his father Abraham Wiznitzer. (photo: private collection of Sonia Racin-Kirzner)
The bar mitzvah of Izzy Gerstenbluth in 1970. To the left: Abraham Wiznitzer and Saul Ghitman. Right: Reading from the Torah with, from left to right, Armando de Marchena, moreh Truzman, Abraham Wiznitzer and Bill Gerstenbluth. (photos: private collection of Bill and Tila Gerstenbluth)

For this ritual, the Ashkenazim initially rented the 'chair of Elijah', a special chair used for circumcisions, from the Sephardic congregation. Since the 1980s, they have owned their own chair of Elijah, a replica of the chair the Sephardim use.

The end of life is also surrounded by traditions. The body is ritually washed and then the deceased is wrapped in a simple white burial shroud. Members of the *chevra kadisha* (holy society) ensure that these rituals are performed. This group of volunteers, consisting of five to six people, then lay the deceased in the casket. Women prepare women, men prepare men.

If someone has died abroad, it is tradition for a large part of the Ashkenazic community to go to the airport to welcome the casket carrying the body of the deceased. After Salomon Wiznitzer had died in a hospital in Miami in 1994, his widow and three children had his body brought back to Curaçao for burial. His son Butchie: "The feeling of a close-knit community came back completely when I saw all of my old friends standing at the airport to greet us. I had lived in America for more than 30 years by then and had not seen some of these friends for many years. But they took over the casket from us and performed all the rituals that accompany death. The week following the burial, they also looked after my family."

Tsale Kirzner said that the community also used to show concern during serious illnesses and that it still does to this day. "Everyone was touched personally by it and they would visit the sick many times with heartfelt intentions. The entire community, almost without exception, attended burials. Also, when people had financial and personal problems, the community would advise and assist them."

Bar Mitzvah, Confirmation and Bat Mitzvah

According to Jewish law, boys reach adulthood at the age of thirteen years and one day, when they become a *bar mitzvah* (son of the commandment). From then on, they may read from the Torah. In Eastern Europe a *bar mitzvah* was nothing more than a religious ritual that was performed without preparation during a 'normal' service and without festivities afterwards. On Curaçao, too, a *bar mitzvah* initially went by without much notice. But during and after the war this changed and *bar mitzvahs* became big celebrations just like in America. When Isaac Kisilevich, for example, became a *bar mitzvah* in 1945, printed cards were sent out in which everyone was invited to a reception at Club Union.

Bat mitzvah (daughter of the commandment) marks the religious adulthood of Jewish girls at the age of twelve years and one day. Nowadays, in liberal congregations, girls officially become *bat mitzvah* in the synagogue, but in the liberal Temple even the boys did not become *bar mitzvah* until the early 1960s. They only did what was called confirmation, often in small groups. After the founding of the common Hebrew School in 1962 (see Chapter 12), both the Ashkenazic and Sephardic students were confirmed in the *snoa*; including the

Bar mitzvah invitation. (from the private collection of Bill and Tila Gerstenbluth)

girls. According to Esty da Costa-Frankel, it was nothing more than an official conclusion of the school term. "A type of alternative *bat mitzvah*. Because neither *Mikvé Israel* nor *Shaarei Tsedek* had the practice of celebrating *bat mizvahs* at that time."

In 2002, the first Ashkenazic girl officially became *bat mitzvah* at *Shaarei Tsedek* (see the portrait in Chapter 12).

Who Pays the Rabbi?

Both congregations often had to make do without a rabbi and/or chazzan. For a small congregation on a remote island, it is simply not always easy to find a rabbi in another country. The Ashkenazic congregation had the added problem of finances. In 1855, the government had declared the religious leaders of *Mikvé Israel* officially equal to Protestant ministers.[126] This meant that, since that time, rabbis and chazzans have received a stipend from the government coffers, like Christian ministers. By the time the Ashkenazim founded their own congregation in 1958, this had changed. The change was related to the self-government that the Antilles were granted in 1950.[127] This autonomy meant that the islands were given their own national laws, which no longer left any room for subsidies for (new) religious communities.

In the early 1950s, the Jewish congregation in formation on Aruba (see Chapter 15) had already appealed several times to the 1855 provision. But they received no funds from the national budget either. At *Shaarei Tsedek*, too, the members of the congregation had (and still have) to cover the costs of a rabbi.

Bar mitzvah of Ruben Seibald in the synagogue in Scharloo and the party afterwards in Club Union next door. (photos: private collection of Liza Seibald-Becher)

Mikvé Israel-Emanuel, though, still receives an allowance from the government for a rabbi simply because this congregation is traditionally entitled to one. But the allowance falls far short of paying the salary of a rabbi or chazzan.

To hold services in *shiel*, a rabbi or chazzan is not absolutely necessary. In their absence often one of the elder men assumes responsibility for reading from the Torah and leading the prayers. The same is true in the Ashkenazic congregation on Curaçao. Men who often took on the leadership at a *shul* service were, for example, Abraham Wiznitzer, Bill Gerstenbluth, Socher Kirzner, Herman Gärtner and Jacob Gelber.

▶ **Benny Seibald (Curaçao, 1955)**

The Seibald family. Standing, from left to right: Susan, Jozef, Fanea, Leon and Rachel Seibald. Seated, from left to right: Morris, Liza, Salomon, Benny, and Moishe Seibald. (photo: private collection of Liza Seibald-Becher)

"My father Moishe and his brothers were very much oriented toward the synagogue. There was not a single holiday that was not celebrated, even the least important ones that we now sometimes let pass unnoticed. The celebrations included all the traditions attached to these holidays. Everything was set aside for these celebrations. If you had to cut palm branches for the *sukkah*,[128] you simply did it. It took priority. They regularly went to the synagogue and always attended services on the important religious holidays."

"But were they religious? I remember that the store opened later on the day so that they could first go to synagogue. But they still worked on the Sabbath. And we were not kosher at home. As I understood it at the time, that had to do with the fact that we had domestic help. They were allowed to keep *treife* (non-kosher) food in the fridge. I do not know when we also started to eat *treife*, but we did and were therefore not kosher at home. Except when it was Passover, then the entire house was cleaned and the normal tableware was replaced by special tableware that we only used during Passover. Then we ate only kosher meat. If I was caught chewing gum, I was told that it was not kosher. During the religious holidays this suddenly became very important."

"I also went to synagogue. I had to. Although I don't remember it being unpleasant. And I don't remember us going every week. But my father and uncles went every week. I felt very comfortable there and we had a lot of activities at the Club. The social part of religion played a large role in my life. We went to Club Union for the religious holidays and for activities. On Sunday we went to the movies and there was always food. You would meet your friends there. Almost all of my friends were Jews – Ashkenazic Jews. You saw them at the Club; our parents socialized with one another. Contacts with people from the Sephardic congregation did not come about until later." ◀

12 A Jewish School and Other Jewish Education

In the first decades there was hardly any Jewish instruction on Curaçao. It wasn't until 1950 that the young Ashkenazim began to receive a serious Jewish after-school education. First in their own school, nearly exclusively Ashkenazic, and later in collaboration with the Sephardim. There were also religious gatherings and clubs for the young.

Religious tuition yes, but no cheder

Some of the children had been used to attending a *cheder* in Eastern Europe, where they attended Jewish classes (often after school). Bruno Linder went to the *cheder* in Sniatyn from the age of five. It wasn't until he was six or seven that he went to a Polish elementary school. On Curaçao in the 1930s and 1940s, there were no special classes for children in for example Hebrew and Jewish history. Linder: "When I left Poland in 1933 as an eight-year-old boy, my Jewish education actually came to an end. I vaguely remember that my brother Felix and I attended Jewish lessons by the *shochet* a couple of times."

As of 1936, Rabbi Isaac Emmanuel of the Sephardic congregation *Mikvé Israel* took the first step towards providing Jewish education. He began religious instruction at the Hendrik School for the Jewish students, both Sephardic and Ashkenazic.[129] The classes were only an hour a week, but it was a beginning. Later on, the girls from the Wilhelmina School also received such instruction. After Emmanuel's departure in 1939, Isaac Jessurun Cardozo, originally from the Netherlands, took over these teaching duties. In 1941, a total of 85 Jewish students were attending the religion classes.[130]

'Preserving the children for Judaism' at the Moria School

Things really became serious when the Moria School was founded at the end of 1950. Its full name was the School for Religious Education and General Knowledge of Judaism "Moria". The school was named after Mount Moria, better

Children at the Moria School in 1953. Left side, 1st row: Mark Bonaparte, Samuel Jessurun Cardozo and Louis Metsch. 2nd row: Mayerlin Becher and Trixie Groisman. 3rd row: Rolaf and Nachama Jessurun Cardozo. 4th row: Esther Grynsztein and Debbie de Vries. Right side, 1st row: Larry Becher and Tsale Kirzner. 2nd row: Fanny (Fanchika) Weisinger, Elka Ehrlich and Judith Becher. 3rd row: Frieda Faerman and Frieda Fruchter. 4th row: Lina Aron Josub and Fela Meit. 5th row: X de Vries. (photo: private collection of Frieda Geller-Faerman)

known as the Temple Mount. At the Moria School, the Ashkenazic children received after-school instruction in Jewish religion, history and the Hebrew language once or twice a week in the afternoon. Considerable attention was also given to the development of a Jewish identity.

The first lessons began on 2 January 1951 with 63 students. Appeals made in the Monthly Magazine for Israeli Households on the Netherlands Antilles show that the school was intended for children from all three congregations. Thus, the annual report for 1951-1952 stated that it "is our obligation to convince, on a large scale, *all* Jewish families on Curaçao that they can only preserve their children for Judaism if they send them to the Jewish school "Moria"." Nonetheless, photographs from those years show almost exclusively Ashkenazic children. Only a couple of Sephardic children attended the Moria School; among them those of David and Isaac Jessurun Cardozo.

Initially, the Moria School was housed in the Club Union building in Scharloo. When the building next door was converted into a *shiel*, the classroom

Children of the Moria School in the early 1950s. Upper right: Jacques Behar, diagonally behind him: unknown. Standing, from left to right: Shirley Gärtner, Clara Meit, Fanny Weisinger, Bella Aron Josub, unknown, unknown, Molca Weinstein, Gitta Fruchter, Nachman Grynsztein, Robert Gärtner (?) and Henry Gärtner. Next row, from left to right: Fela Meit, Lily Bonaparte, Fanny Ehrlich, Johnny Wachter, unknown, Sigmund Kurtsberg, Lina Aron Josub, Rita Wiznitzer, Victor Abady (?) and unknown. Next row, from left to right: unknown, Mark Bonaparte, Max Djament, Tsale Kirzner, Willy Aron Josub, Louis Metsch, Frieda Fruchter, Isaac Sitzer; in front of him Meyer Grynsztein, Judith Becher, Nora Wiznitzer; behind her Mayerlin Becher and Elka Ehrlich. (photo: private collection of Isaac and Lily Kisilevich-Bonaparte)

Children from the Moria School around 1953. 1st row seated, from left to right: Judith Becher, Louis Metsch, Elka Ehrlich, Tsale Kirzner, Mark Bonaparte, Fanny Weinstein and ? Cohen. 2nd row, from left to right: Nachama Jessurun Cardozo, Rolaf Jessurun Cardozo (?), Mayerlin Becher, Frieda Fruchter, Trixie Groisman, Broertje Jessurun Cardozo and Larry Becher. Standing, from left to right: Debby de Vries, Esther Grynsztein, Lina Aron Josub, Fanny Ehrlich, Deborah Jessurun Cardozo, Rabbi Jessurun Cardozo, unknown, Fela Meit and Nachman Grynsztein. (photo: private collection of Isaac and Lily Kisilevich-Bonaparte)

Children from the Moria School in 1956 in the sukkah. (photo: private collection of Frieda Pais-Fruchter)

moved to a space behind the prayer area. Tsale Kirzner remembered precisely what the classroom looked like: "At the front, in the middle, stood an impressive desk with a blackboard on the wall behind it. The classroom was divided into two rows of school desks of the old fashioned kind with an inkwell with a sliding lid in the middle. At the back stood a large book cabinet containing the Talmud and other books with gold bindings. Hanging on the wall was a map of Israel and the Hebrew alphabet."

Isaac Jessurun Cardozo was the school's principal and he also taught classes. At the end of 1954, the Ashkenazic rabbi, Nathan Schächter, took over as principal. He often got help from Fania Kirzner, who had mastered Hebrew and substituted for Schächter when he was not on the island. Her son Tsale remembered the magnificent Bible stories by Schächter and the Verkade box containing Israeli postage stamps. "If you had done your very best at school, the box appeared and you were allowed to select a beautiful stamp from it."

Looking Like Fools During the Purim Celebration

Ivan Becher remembered Schächter as a strict, but good teacher. "He was very much involved in theater and had a beautiful voice." The rabbi and the children performed plays on the occasion of Jewish festivals, such as *Hanukkah* and *Purim*. In 1954, the children gave a performance of *Megilat Esther*, the story of Queen Esther.[131] For the costume balls or plays performed on the occasion of *Purim*, usually a biblical theme was chosen. Children dressed up, for example, as Queen Esther or they portrayed a candle.

Morris Seibald remembered that sometimes things went differently. It was at the time of Chaim Abramovic, who was *moreh* or teacher from 1961 to 1963. When he taught classes at the Moria School, he decided that the students should be allowed to determine the *Purim* festival theme themselves. Morris Seibald: "We came up with the theme of 'monkeys'. Our mothers sewed the costumes, we obtained chimpanzee masks and we even invented a story: one of the students, Berny Cheis, supposedly came from Venezuela with a sack full of cod. During the performance, he had real fish from the fishing boats with him and it stank to high heaven."

On the day of the performance, the proud grandmothers and grandfathers naturally sat in the first row. They were very shocked when a troop of 'monkeys' appeared on stage. The elderly ladies Wiznitzer and Schmidt gasped, particularly when the 'monkeys' also started making strange sounds. Morris Seibald: "Fairly soon thereafter, Abramovic left the island. With this performance, he had made a very bad impression on the older generation."

The departure of the rabbi was a real shame, Morris Seibald thought. In his eyes Abramovic did a 'fantastic' job in preparing the boys for their *bar mitzvah*. This rabbi had also established a boys' choir with both Ashkenazic and Sephardic boys. "Before the Jewish High Holidays, we practiced in the evenings in the Moria School classroom and it sounded incredibly good."

Morris' cousin Ivan Becher also thought it was awful that Abramovic had to leave. According to him, Abramovic had come up with the monkey theme himself. It was his way of punishing the Moria School children for the fact that they had behaved so badly during classes. "Because monkeys obviously had nothing to do with *Purim* and we looked very foolish in our tights. We did, indeed, always

Purim party at Club Union. From left to right: Nora Wiznitzer, Esty Fruchter and Clara Tauber. (photo: private collection of Frieda Pais-Fruchter)

behave very badly in his class, but we were the same outside of class. Actually, we were constantly testing how far we could go with him. But we never intended for him to be dismissed. Because, despite everything else, we learned a lot from Abramovic, more than we learned from his successor, Rabbi Hirsh Zelkovicz. Zelkovicz could simply not keep order. Abramovic also organized a lot of things for us outside the classroom. We went swimming and picnicking with him, as well as playing sports. After he returned to Israel, he became a taxi driver there."

With the Sephardic Children to the Hebrew School

The Moria School was closed in 1964 because in that year the Ashkenazic Jews entered the Hebrew School.[132] Rabbi Simeon Maslin from *Emanu-El* had founded this Jewish school in 1962 for the children of the Sephardic congregations. The school had some 50 students and was housed in several classrooms that were rented from the Römer School[133]. Students attended Hebrew School twice a week in the afternoon for an hour and a half until the age of 13.

To accommodate the 105 students that now attended the school, more

Class at the Curaçao Hebrew School in 2009. (photo: Jeannette van Ditzhuijzen)

space was needed. So the now merged Sephardic congregation rented a residence on the corner of the Gladiolenweg and the Mahaaiweg. Classes began on Monday, 5 October. Norman Swerling, chazzan from 1964 to 1967 at the liberal Temple *Emanu-El* and later at *Mikvé Israel-Emanuel,* served as principal.

On behalf of the Ashkenazic congregation, the Polish Rabbi Hirsh Zelkovicz served as teacher. He was only a short time on the island, from February until the end of November 1964, and had absolutely no experience with children. Some of them therefore had a field day in his classes. Most of the students remembered him as someone that always walked through the city dressed neatly in a suit, someone that considered visiting the governor and attending official receptions as extremely important. But according to Tsale Kirzner, he was also a very erudite man. He himself preferred to go to the Friday evening services because Zelkovicz' sermons were so good. After his departure the Ashkenazic congregation had no rabbi for a couple of years. During this time, several members of the congregation served as teachers.

In October 1967, *Shaarei Tsedek* welcomed a new rabbi, Menachim Fitterman. He did not approve of the Ashkenazic children being taught in the same building as the liberal Sephardic youth. So until the arrival of *moreh* Truzman in 1969, the congregation members of *Shaarei Tsedek* once again took on the task of teaching. Lily Kisilevich-Bonaparte was one of them. "I taught the small children the alphabet and also taught Bible lessons. But when I realized that they were asking me more than I actually knew, I stopped. Otherwise, I would have done more harm than good." In the absence of a religious leader at *Shaarei Tsedek*, Fanny van der Elzen was regularly asked to teach. Particularly in the 1980s and 1990s, when *Shaarei Tsedek* had to make do without a rabbi for a number of years (with short intervals).

So the collaboration between the two congregations did not always run smoothly. The Sephardic Jews for instance were not happy about *moreh* Truzman's qualities. Because *Mikvé Israel-Emanuel* did want to maintain the common school, the solution was sought in having separate classes: Truzman taught the 32 Ashkenazic children while the 19 Sephardic children were taught by Chazzan Pavel Slavensky from *Mikvé Israel-Emanuel.*

In 1972 the school moved to the Gladiolenweg, where it still is up to the present day. When the young rabbi, Martin Levin, arrived at *Shaarei Tsedek* two years later, it seemed that he did not approve of the teaching methods of the much older Slavensky from *Mikvé Israel-Emanuel*. But, according to Lily Kisilevich-Bonaparte, Levin did a lot of good for the youth. "He was a good speaker and he made everyone very enthusiastic. Yet he also courted controversy."

Learning outside the classroom

Levin got along much better with Slavensky's successor, Rabbi Philip Bentley. Together they reorganized the Jewish school. Over the years, extra-curricular activities were also organized (partly under parental supervision), such as climbing Mt Christoffel or making *Seder* plates in a pottery.

The students also celebrated *Hanukkah* and *Purim* together. Traditionally *Hanukkah* was celebrated at Club Curaçao in Scharloo, the club that nearly all Sephardic Jews were members of. The activities on the occasion of *Purim* took place at Club Union. For the young, there were a range of games to play and at the end of the evening it was announced which child had the best costume.

Starting in 1977, every year (lasting up until 2009) a pseudo *Seder* was organized at Passover for all the Hebrew School students. In the 1950s, the Moria School had also held a youth *Seder* a couple of times. The *Seder* is the first evening of Passover that is linked with certain traditions and rituals, of which the *Seder* meal is an important part. The purpose of the youth *Seder*, according to Rabbi Yeshurun from *Shaarei Tsedek,* is to prepare the children for the *Seder* at home. "They learn the best known Pesach songs, are given a foretaste of the traditional *Seder* food and become familiar with the *Haggadah*, the story that accompanies Passover, about the slavery and subsequent liberation of the ancient Hebrews. Thus, they can participate much better in the *Seder* at home."

In 1955 Rabbi Yossi Feintuch from *Mikvé Israel-Emanuel* introduced the *High Holiday Food Drive*. This involved students from the school taking food packets to poor island families during the High Holidays. Some still remembered how they asked family and acquaintances for cans and food packages. They then took them to school and everything was distributed among people in need. Sometimes *Ayudo Sosial* (a social organization on the island) came to pick up the food in a van. "One year we collected so much food that they had to drive back and forth seven times", a former student remembered.

Adam Morón said that during the tenure of Rabbi Tayvah from *Mikvé Israel-Emanuel* a large number of fruit trees were planted in the garden of the Hebrew School. That was in the 1990s. Under his supervision, the students planted these trees during Tu B'Shevat.[134]

Becoming Friends Because of the Hebrew School

In the mid 1990s, the Hebrew School hit a bad patch. The orthodox Rabbi Poupko from *Shaarei Tsedek* did not go down well with the liberal Sephardic congregation and the collaboration between the two congregations almost came to an end. Poupko, who began serving as rabbi in 1996, was too inflexible in the eyes of the Sephardim and, in reaction to his Hassidic views, several students left the Hebrew School.[135] In a letter addressed to *Shaarei Tsedek*'s president, Aron Abady, the president of *Mikvé Israel-Emanuel* wrote that this had never happened before and that Poupko was unsuitable for teaching at the Hebrew School.[136] The rabbi left in 1997.

Yet, one positive consequence of having a common school was the fact that, beginning in the early 1960s, the Sephardic and Ashkenazic children saw and spoke to one another more often. They knew each other from Hebrew School and there was no longer any reason to look down on each other. Nachman Grynsztein: "I always saw the school as a link between us. We knew each other, even though we went to different synagogues."

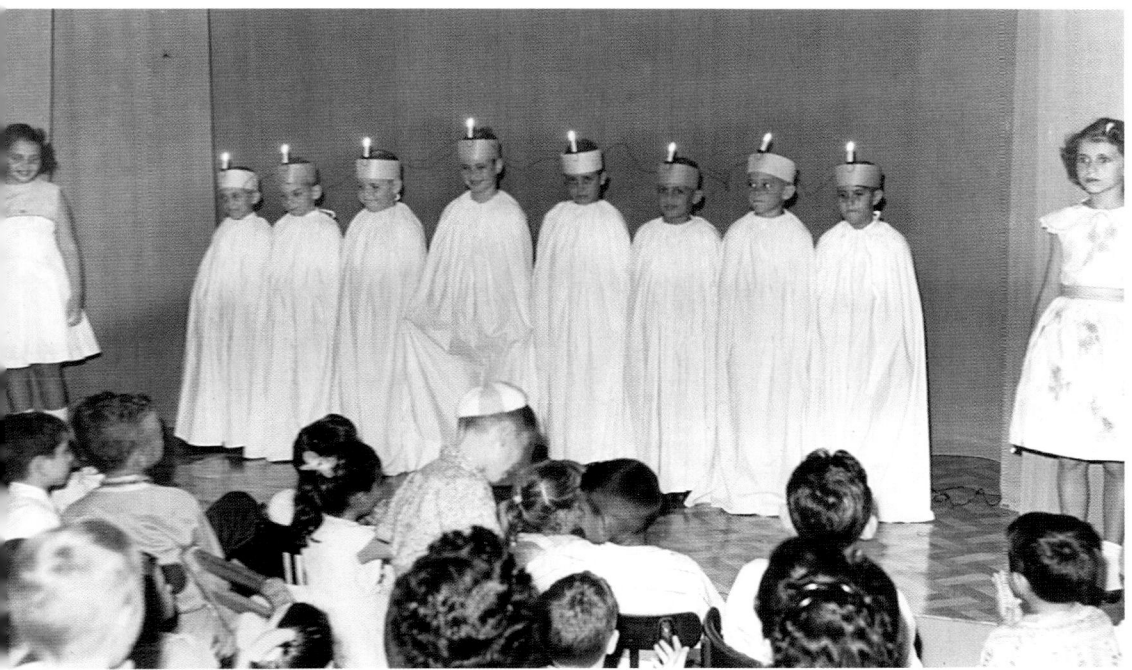

Hanukkah in Club Curaçao. (photo: private collection of Liza Seibald-Becher)

Up to the present day, the Hebrew School is seen as an important link between the Ashkenazic and the Sephardic congregations. When Paul Morón took over as president at *Shaarei Tsedek* in 1990, his predecessor, Leon Seibald, urged him to keep the common Hebrew School going above all else. "He said I should not change it in any way because the children of the two congregations got to know one another at school. They met not only as fellow students, but also socially. There they could become friends, in Leon's view." As soon as a problem arose that threatened the Hebrew School, Leon came to Paul to tell him again: 'Don't touch the Hebrew School.'

Because both Sephardic and Ashkenazic Jews have declined in numbers in recent decades (see table 1), by 2011 the school had no more than some 7 children ranging in age from three to thirteen. Classes were held from Monday to Thursday, each child seven years and older attending the Jewish school twice a week, those younger attending once a week.

The curriculum was and still is set up in joint consultation between the religious leaders of the two congregations. Until 2010 they both taught classes in reading, writing and understanding Hebrew, the ABC of the Jewish faith, Jewish history, Zionism and prayer. Shaarei Tsedek's rabbi left for Miami in that year and became a part-time rabbi.

The classes in Jewish customs and Jewish faith were kept very general in nature and the teachers did not delve too deeply into the subjects. This was because of the ideological differences between the more orthodox Ashkenazim and the liberal Sephardim. The traditional approach to Judaism was more general in nature, but according to Rabbi Yeshurun it brought the students in contact with the rich history of Judaism and its ceremonial aspects. "This approach works well in a common Hebrew School."

Torah Island

The Johan van Walbeeck School on Mahaai is a public elementary school, but in the 1950s and 1960s, so many Jewish children (Ashkenazic and Sephardic) attended the school that the three congregations made joint attempts to ensure this school was closed on Saturday. This would allow the Jewish children to honor the Sabbath much better. According to the monthly bulletin of *Emanu-El*, a petition was submitted to the Island administration in August 1963, but in later bulletins this subject was never discussed again. Apparently the attempt was not successful.

In the 1990s, Curaçao had a second Jewish school for a time, called Torah Island. It was founded by Laurie Abady, a *Shaarei Tsedek* member. She thought that her children should have Jewish classes more often than the usual four hours a week at the Hebrew School. Torah Island was attended by both Sephardic and Ashkenazic children, supplementing the Hebrew School classes. After the Abady family moved to America at the start of the 21st century, Torah Island was closed.

Oneg Shabbat Celebrations at School and at the Rabbi's Home

Apart from the Jewish education they received at school, the youth were involved in the faith in other ways as well. They regularly came together for *Oneg Shabbat*, informal Shabbat celebrations (see also Chapter 8). In the 1950s they were held at the Moria School, for which the parents took turns providing snacks. Bread with sardines was a regular delicacy. Mirjam Schipper-Moffie, who has since returned to the Netherlands, still thinks back to the *Oneg Shabbats* in Scharloo every time she sees or smells sardines.

At the end of May 1954, no fewer than a hundred young people attended the *Oneg Shabbat*. Some of them even had to stand.[137] The Moria Choir sang Shabbat songs and the Israeli Consul in New York, Reuven Dafni, gave a lecture on 'living and working in the state of Israel'.

In the 1960s, the extremely popular Chazzan Norman Swerling and Rabbi Maslin organized *Oneg Shabbat* gatherings in their homes. According to Izzy Gerstenbluth, Maslin was a charming, erudite and highly educated man. "Every Saturday afternoon, the young people from all three congregations met at his house. We all loved going there, because Swerling was popular with the young." Sometimes there were as many as 25 children present.

Esty da Costa-Frankel also has good memories of the meetings. "Stories were told and just before sundown a prayer was said to celebrate the end of the Sabbath. We were then allowed to hold the braided candle in turns. I still remember the sweet-smelling spices."

In 2008/2009, *Oneg Shabbat* was held again in the synagogue for children aged three to eight each Saturday. It was organized by two Israeli girls who came to Curaçao in 2008 via a special program offering religious girls an alternative to conscription in the Israeli army. The two girls also taught classes at the Hebrew School and assisted the youth organization BBYO (B'nai Brith Youth Organization).

Contacts via the AGY and the BBYO

In the 1960s, the children of the various Jewish congregations also came in contact with one another through the Jewish Youth Group AGY (*Achim Gam Yachad,* All Brothers Together). Announcements in the monthly bulletin of the Temple *Emanu-El* show that Rabbi Maslin founded the AGY in 1961 for the children of the Sephardic congregations who were fourteen and older. The Ashkenazic children joined them in 1963 and from that time there were two chairpersons, one from each congregation.

According to Tsale Kirzner, the arrival of a group of Jewish young people from America was the highlight of the AGY. It was in December 1964 and, together with Rita Chumaceiro from *Mikvé Israel,* he was the welcoming chairman of the AGY. "It was a wonderful and informative experience to get in touch with teenagers from another country and to hear about their interests."

Altogether, the youth club existed for only a couple of years. In 1969 the B'nai B'rith Youth Organization (BBYO) was established, which is still active. Ivan Becher was the first chairman. Over the years the BBYO has also organized various exchanges. These days, the members (ranging in age from 13 to 18) meet each week in a renovated garage at the Hebrew School on the Gladiolenweg.

▶ ### Annette Morón (Curaçao, 1990)

"I was the first Ashkenazic girl that became *bat mitzvah*, a religious adult, in *shiel*. Among the Sephardim, that was common practice at that time. The women had equal rights. After the *bat mitzvah*, they were allowed to wear a *tallit* and to read from the Torah. Among the Ashkenazim, things were different and, initially, there was some doubt as to whether a *bat mitzvah* was possible in *shiel*. My grandparents, too, thought it was a very strange innovation, but then my grandfather did some research and he could not find a ban on it anywhere. Fortunately, I had my heart set on doing a *bat mitzvah*, though preferably in *shiel*. I felt somewhat ill at ease with the idea that I would have to wear a *tallit,* and at a *bat mitzvah* in the *snoa,* that was required."

"Once my grandfather had assured himself that it was permitted, he helped me enormously. He and my father sought out prayers for me and from those I selected two prayers I liked. Then I had to practice, practice and then practice some more, because you want to recite the prayer well.

Annette Morón (photo: Adam Morón)

I practiced with Paola Tayvah, the wife of the rabbi at *Mikvé Israel-Emanuel*. She was a bit of a feminist, but she did not pressure me about anything. She wanted me to study the Torah chapter for that day and understand it. We spent hours together poring over that chapter."

"So I did not read from the Torah. I did, however, hold a *d'var Torah*. That is a type of discourse in which you explain the *parashah*, the Torah chapter for that day. I wanted to find a link between the chapter and my own ideas about it. The *parashah* was about kosher food and my grandmother's mother was one of the first people on Curaçao that kept a kosher kitchen."

"I also wanted to contribute something to the community as a sort of giving back tradition. That is why I chose to work with autistic children for a long time. It was my contribution as an adult woman to the Curaçao community. Being Jewish is simply a part of my life." ◄

13 Doing Business in Good and Bad Times

Some twenty years after they had arrived on Curaçao, the Ashkenazim had become successful and prosperous. Their businesses thrived and they threw large feasts and parties. But they also had to cope with their share of bad times: the riots of May 1969 and the devaluation of the Venezuelan bolivar in 1983. Following these setbacks, the East Indians took over many stores.

Minding the Store

Business was good after the war. More than that: Curaçao experienced a boom period with full employment, high wages and thriving trade. By that time the Ashkenazim owned a large number of the stores in Punda and Otrobanda and they were doing very well. Around 1945, for example, nearly three-quarters of the dry goods stores was in the hands of 'Poles, Syrians and Bombayers'. The word 'Pole' is undoubtedly a too literal translation of the word *Polako* and must be understood as Ashkenazic Jews. Of the six jewelry stores on the island at the time, three were owned by 'foreigners'.[138] Two of these, *Weisinger* and *Spritzer + Fuhrmann*, were Ashkenazi-owned.

Opening new businesses was not an option for the Ashkenazim because, according to the 1946 rule for setting up establishments, this was reserved only for Dutch subjects or people who were born on Curaçao. In 1945 the Dutch Attorney General had warned the Governor of possible undesirable consequences of this latest rule: "… then the *Polako* (Eastern European Jewish) children will gain an opportunity that one perhaps does not want them to have."[139] The children of *Polakos* born on Curaçao, after all, often did have the Dutch nationality and could therefore open a store.

The 'old' business elite, though, were happy about the new rules. In a letter written in 1944 the Chamber of Commerce had informed the governor that they had wanted the 1937 ban on foreigners opening stores to be maintained. The 'invasion of immigrants who were fiercely competitive due to their cheaper life styles' was too fresh in their memories. In the eyes of the Chamber of Commerce it was these foreigners who were to blame for the bankruptcy of several businesses in the early 1930s.[140]

Foreigners therefore were still required to apply for a license to operate a new store. As mentioned earlier, until a few years after the war, most of the Ashkenazim were stateless – i.e. they were officially foreigners. That is why people thought twice before parting with a store, because it would mean instantly losing the business license.

Luckily for the Eastern European Jews, they had established most of the stores before the war. So this rule was only a problem for the immigrants that arrived on the island after the war. On the other hand, these newcomers often had family living on Curaçao who could employ them. Because, just as not all Sephardic Jews were rich, not all Ashkenazim owned their own businesses. Some of them were employed, often in stores owned by *Polakos*.

Trading in 'Porcelain, Perfume, Cigars and Tobacco'

A trade register was introduced in 1944 and every shopkeeper was required to register his business with the Chamber of Commerce. Like everyone else, the Ashkenazim dutifully filled in the registration forms – stating when they had arrived, when they had started their business and especially, what they sold. Usually it was 'dry goods' (clothing and fabrics), yet a letter from the Department of Social and Economic Affairs written in 1950 to the Chamber of Commerce

The opening of Bechers on 18 August 1959. The man wearing the bow tie is the owner: Fajwel Becher. (photo: private collection of Ivan Becher)

Linder's store in Otrobanda. (photo: private collection of Diane Liebeskind-Linder)

reveals that *La Estrella* at Heerenstraat 24, for example, had sold a whole catalogue of products since 1940. In addition to clothing, it sold 'penknives, silver cups, cabin trunks, clippers, ink, woolen blankets, alarm clocks, lighters, briefcases, smoking pipes, watches, pencil boxes, hat boxes, baby boxes', and much, much more. It was a complete department store. The owner of *La Estrella* was the Romanian Samuel Pimsler, one of the founders of Club Union.

Likewise, the *Oranjewinkel* of Rachmiel Geiger from Sniatyn located on the Heerenstraat 19 since 1941, sold 'cosmetics and fancy articles' in addition to women's and men's clothing. In an advertisement put in the *Israeli Almanac* in 1948, Geiger also announced that he was the 'sole representative' for the Helena Rubinstein's cosmetic products. The El Continental store on the Heerenstraat, started during the depression years by the Polish brothers Max and Jacobo Fruchter, had also been expanded considerably. Initially, they mostly sold dry goods. In 1954 'trade in porcelain, perfume, cigars and tobacco' was added, according to the Chamber of Commerce documents.

The Wiznitzer brothers ran *La Confianza* on the Columbusstraat, a wholesale company plus store. Business boomed and in 1952 they built a commercial building that was modern for those days, on the corner of the Columbusstraat and the De Ruyterkade (today this building is used by the Girobank). The Wiznitzers could afford such a new building: just after the war, they reported to the Chamber of Commerce that they had invested 582,999 Curaçao guilders of their own capital in the company. That is considerably more than the 24,000 guilders that Adolf Haber invested in 1945 in his *New York Store*.

For an impression of the amount of money involved: in 1944 only 12 of the nearly 23,000 Curaçao taxpayers had a taxable income of more than 100,000 guilders. A total of 48 persons earned more than 50,000 guilders, while the majority reported an income between 1,700 and 4,000 guilders.[141]

In 1952, the Wiznitzer brothers had this modern building constructed in Punda. The photo was taken in 1985. (photo: private collection of Leo Wiznitzer)

Abraham Wiznitzer in his store La Confianza in 1955. (photo: private collection of Leo Wiznitzer)

Like some other Ashkenazim, the Wiznitzers later also had businesses in the Free Zone next to the harbor. The Free Zone was established in 1957. Products sold there were exempt from import duties as long as they left the island and were therefore not sold on Curaçao.

On the other side of Anna Bay, in Otrobanda, *Tauber Hermanos* were gradually expanding their empire. During the war years, the brothers were already active in New York and later, in the 1960s, they established agencies in Hong Kong and Taiwan. Starting from their first store on the Breedestraat in Otrobanda, the brothers Leon and Herman Tauber bought up several buildings in the neighborhood in the 1950s and 1960s. One of them was the building in which the '*Ellis en Dania*' store was located. They also bought Elias Linder's *soda fountain*.

Jackpot! The American Cruise Tourists Arrive

The storekeepers' business was not limited to high-earning Curaçao customers. Regularly, American cruise ships sailed into the harbor of Curaçao. On board were invariably hundreds of Americans eager to spend money. Since the establishment of the Shell refinery on the island, increasing numbers of cruise ships called on Curaçao because of the inexpensive fuel. In 1953 more than 16,000 cruise passengers visited the island, rising in 1960 to more than 45,000, nearly three times as many.[142] This was in part due to the revolution in Cuba. After Fidel Castro and his followers had seized power there in 1959, American cruise ships were no longer allowed to call on that popular destination.

Yet, things were going well even before the Cuban revolution. Between 1946 and 1952, the number of dollars spent by Americans on the island tripled. And of every dollar spent, more than half disappeared into the cash registers of storekeepers.[143]

So 20 to 25 years after their arrival on the island, things were going very well indeed for the Eastern European Jews. In *A Reason Why,* Lucca Koch writes that around 1950 a great many of the Ashkenazic Jews had two or more live-in maids and lived in big houses.[144] Her uncle came to pick her and her family up at the airport in 1948 in his car. To her great surprise, her aunt – a woman! – was behind the wheel.

Weddings and *bar mitzvahs* were big celebrations in those years. Initially, they were held at the Club, later at the hotels. For a *bar mitzvah* at the time, the entire community, friend and foe alike, was invited, as well as any non-Jewish acquaintances, business relations and family from abroad. They were lavish events that often had a live band playing and enormous amounts of delicious hot food and drinks.

A honeymoon lasting a couple of months was also fairly common. After his wedding with Gitta Fruchter in 1955, Pinhos Meit traveled through Europe for three and a half months, visiting Paris, Milan, Venice, Amsterdam, etc. In 1955, Lies and Salo Linder spent two months on a honeymoon traveling to Cuba, Mexico and the United States. They ended the trip in New York, where Salo immediately took the opportunity to make purchases for his newly opened store, *Linder* in Otrobanda.

The wedding of Bill and Tila Gerstenbluth-Cheis in 1953. Right: under the chuppah; below: the wedding party and far right: in the wedding car. (photos: private collection of Bill and Tila Gerstenbluth-Cheis)

Credit from the MCB bank

Although the Ashkenazic Jews' relations with the Sephardim in the 1950s and '60s were perhaps somewhat distant – though among young people it was markedly different from what it was among adults – their relationship with the Maduro & Curiel's Bank (MCB) was excellent, as it always had been. The Ashkenazic merchants did good business and received large loans. According to former bank director Lio Capriles, thanks to the success of the Ashkenazic businessmen other sections of the population also came to the MCB. "Generally speaking, the Ashkenazim have had a large and positive influence on the economic activity and future of Curaçao."

Tsale Kirzner thought that the prosperity of the Ashkenazic community would have been impossible without the forward-looking attitude and support of Sha and Lio Capriles. "My father said time and again that he would not have gotten anywhere without the trust that this bank placed in him personally."

The MCB's influence even stretched all the way to the Netherlands. Much later, when Kirzner's father, Socher, was in an Amsterdam hospital, his mother stayed in a kind of family hotel. "By coincidence, she was given a room with a sign hanging next to the door saying the room had been sponsored by the Maduro & Curiel's Bank. To which my father said: 'You see, even here my bank is looking after me.' From his sickbed he repeatedly urged me never to switch banks."

The First Blow: 30 May 1969

The golden years of the 1950s and '60s came to an abrupt end on 30 May 1969. This date marks a turning point in many aspects of social life on Curaçao. It was the day on which Punda and Otrobanda caught fire and many a storekeeper had to watch his life's work go up in flames.

The events leading up to this disaster are complex. Firstly, it was the era of the turbulent 1960s in which students rebelled against everything that smelled of 'the establishment'. The same was true on Curaçao. During their studies in the Netherlands, Curaçao students had become familiar with left-wing politics, with revolution and with demonstrations. Back on Curaçao, they discovered that graduates with a colored or black skin were given fewer opportunities of finding a job than their white fellow graduates. The magazine *Vitó* exposed every abuse it came across in detail. Dutch Shell was the object of an especially fierce tirade. But *Tauber Hermanos*, *Spritzer + Fuhrmann* and the banks in general were laid into as well; the DP (Democratic Party), the white Protestants' party, was also viewed as a culprit in the eyes of *Vitó* and the revolutionary young. They agitated against everything white: the Protestant Curaçaoans, Europeans, Lebanese, and Sephardic and Ashkenazic Jews.

Of course it was true that whites generally prospered during this time. The storekeepers profited fully from the squandermania of American and Venezuelan tourists, while the common islander in the 1960s fared less well. The largest employer on the island, Shell, had increasingly transitioned to automated processes, which led to the laying off of employees. At the same time, wages fell and prices rose. Many, especially colored Curaçaoans, were downright poor. "The tension had been in the air for a year and a half", recalled Tsale Kirzner. "There was a clear and visible inequality."

Stores Looted and Set on Fire

The immediate cause of the plundering that took place on 30 May was a labor conflict. At Shell, laid-off employees could sometimes find a job with a subcontractor to whom Shell outsourced the work. The work was the same they had done in their previous jobs, but for a fraction of the pay they had taken home from Shell. The trade unions decided not to put up with this situation and they demanded higher wages.

Wescar N.V. was one of the subcontractors. Following long negotiations between the trade union CFW (*Curaçaose Federatie van Werknemers* / Curaçao Federation of Employees) and this company, and following several strikes by the employees, all strikers were threatened with dismissal. Frenetic meetings ensued, but despite mediators, a solution was not found. On the contrary, the Shell employees showed solidarity and on 30 May 1969 they, the subcontractors' employees and other sympathizers started to march from the refinery to the city. On the way, stores were broken into and plundered and cars set on fire. White people were the primary targets of their wrath. The hot passions were further inflamed by alcohol looted from the stores. By the time the mob reached Otrobanda and Punda, their ire was given full sway and one store after another was plundered and/or set alight.

Lies Linder-Jessurun Cardozo: "My husband Salo closed the business in Otrobanda on the instruction of the police. When he heard that stones had been thrown through the windows, he wanted to board up the store. We went there together and from a distance saw people walking with bags taken from *Linder*.

Sunye Meit in front of his destroyed store, La Rivièra, following the riots on 30 May 1969. (photo: private collection of Frieda Pais-Fruchter)

Everything was ripped open and on the ground lay the bag containing my father-in-law's *tallit*. Fortunately there were now soldiers around that had chased everyone away and were keeping an eye on things. Salo was afraid that the fire would reach the store. But we were lucky. The fire stopped at the building next to ours. And the looters did not go upstairs where our stocks were."

Casa Seibald in Punda had just closed that 30th of May because Jozef and Leon Seibald were planning to renovate the property. Liza Seibald-Becher: "Our stocks were being kept temporarily in my brother-in-law's store, *Casa Leon* in Otrobanda. That store was plundered. The looters had thrown a lot of stuff off of the balcony down into the street." *Casa Leon* was one of the few stores with riot insurance. According to Leon Seibald, in the months prior to the revolt it was announced that you could take out insurance for that risk and some storekeepers like him did just that.

Isaac Kisilevich had a stroke of luck. The windows of his store *Zigzag* in Otrobanda were broken during the riot. Everything the looters could get their hands on they took. "But I also had money stashed away in the store because on 30 May I was due to pay my staff. Fortunately the looters did not find the tin can containing the money. They also did not touch the stocks on the second floor, so a day or two later I was back in business. I also had light, which most other storekeepers did not."

Casa Salomon owned by Moishe and Salomon Seibald in Punda escaped completely. Benny Seibald: "My father was a small trader. He was very popular, both among the local population and among the Jews. Because he was not super rich, he was not seen as a threat. And he treated everyone well. It seems that local people told the looters: 'Don't touch this store'. Regardless of why, we suffered no damage on the 30th of May." Others were less fortunate. For example, at *La Aurora,* owned by Herman Gärtner, stones were thrown through the windows.

Apart from those mentioned above, the stores owned by Ashkenazic Jews that were hit included *Spritzer + Fuhrmann, Casa José, Casa Los Dos Amigos, David's, Vorona's, La Rivièra* and *Tauber Hermanos.*[145] The Sephardic Jewish stores that were affected were *El Globo, El Louvre, La Modernista, Vreugdenhil* (the wife of the owner was Jewish) and *Hector Henriquez B.* on the Penstraat.

The total damage caused by the riots was estimated at 40 million Antillean guilders.[146] Sixty buildings were destroyed by fire and another one hundred businesses suffered considerable damage due to looting and broken windows. Part of the archives of the Sephardic congregation was also lost. These were various documents kept by Charles Gomes Casseres at his Punda office, which unfortunately burned to the ground.

After the 30th of May many Ashkenazic Jews were facing a serious financial setback. For a number of them, such as Sunye Meit who owned *La Rivièra*, the blow was so fierce that they left the island. According to Eva Abraham-Van der Mark, prior to May 1969 Curaçao was home to 450 Ashkenazic Jews. Five years later, there were only 325 left.[147] Those who remained took out a loan with the MCB which they used to rebuild their businesses. For the most serious cases, several men from the Ashkenazic community went round collecting money. The Ashkenazim still formed one big family, and each of them was ready to help out a fellow Jew at any time.

Not Against the Jews, but Against the Rich

Because a large number of Jewish stores were targeted by the looting mob, people quickly wondered whether this was due to anti-Semitism. This question was almost immediately answered with a wholehearted no.[148] The Jewish stores were targeted simply because in 1969 a large number of the stores in the city center happened to be Jewish-owned.

The aggression was directed against rich white people and the establishment in general, of which the Ashkenazic Jews had become a part. In the eyes of the strikers, the Taubers were an exponent of rich exploiters and that is why they were targeted. So it was not because the Taubers were Jewish, but because they belonged to the establishment and had a lot of money, while the lower class of blacks and coloreds lived in poverty.

According to the 'Commission set up to study the backgrounds and causes of the riots that took place on Curaçao on the 30th of May 1969', the looters and arsonists clearly did not set out to destroy property. Many of the stores were burned simply because the fire spread and not because the strikers had purposely targeted those stores.[149]

Only *Tauber Hermanos* was intentionally targeted. In an interview with Gert Oostindie in 1999, Herman Tauber said that their store was attacked on the 30th of May because *Vitó* had incited its readers against the Taubers. "He [Stanley Brown, *jvd*] only did it to sell copy. He told me as much." Tauber denied that he and his brother had exploited the black employees, as was suggested after the 30th of May. "We employed nearly 150 people, 95 per cent of whom were Curaçao boys. My relationship with my employees was always good. No one ever left us of their own accord. In 1965 I was even given a Royal honor – Officer in the Order of Orange-Nassau – in recognition of my services to the island."[150]

On that 30th of May, Herman Tauber also personally saved old Miss Ellis from the burning building, recalled her nephew Jan Willem Ellis. When the store property was sold to the Taubers, the Ellis family had stipulated that this aunt should be allowed to remain living on the top floor for the rest of her life. When Tauber went to see what was happening at the store, he saw old Miss Ellis standing at the top of the stairs. Tauber: "She was trying to come down. At which point I ran up the stairs, picked her up and carried her back down the stairs."

The Venezuelans: Big Spenders

When the smoke of the 30th of May cleared, the negative effects of the riots became apparent: tourism took a dive because the Americans, who as everyone knows are very afraid of riots, chose to stay away. Initially, the cruise ships avoided Curaçao altogether and preferred to call on Aruba or Sint Maarten. Not for long, though. In 1970, the number of tourists visiting Curaçao was back to the high levels of 1968.

But because of rising oil prices, the number of cruise ships declined in the second half of the 1970s. Curaçao was farther away from Miami than other tropical islands and therefore the shipping companies sought destinations closer to home in order to save on fuel. The top year of 1976 saw some 178,000 passengers come to Curaçao. At the start of the 1980s, the numbers had dropped to between 110,000 and 120,000.[151]

The passengers that came in the 1980s also had less to spend than the rich Americans that had gone on cruises in the previous decades. This was due not only to the fact that taking a cruise had lost some of its aura of exclusivity, but also because at the time the United States were going through a deep economic recession. Stores that were to a large extent dependent on cruise ship passengers, such as *Spritzer + Fuhrmann*, clearly noticed that fewer ships were coming to the island and those that did come brought passengers with less money to spend.

Nevertheless, the merchant class was still doing well. By now, most of the stores profited fully from the boom in the 1970s, when many merchants from Venezuela, came to the island. In the past, Venezuelans had also come to Curaçao for shopping sprees. Transit tourists on their way to Europe often spent several days or weeks on Curaçao. Ships moving between the Venezuelan ports such as La Guaira and Maracaibo also often traveled via Curaçao.[152]

But the consumer tourism of the 1970s was of an entirely different type. The Venezuelans came to Curaçao by air – after 1973 they also came by ferry from Coro – to shop. Nachman Grynsztein: "They came without luggage, bought suitcases here and filled them with things to resell in Venezuela. A lot of money was earned here and our businesses boomed." In the mid 1970s, the average Venezuelan consumer tourist stayed on the island for three days. In that time, he would buy goods worth an average of 360 dollars a day.[153]

Lies Linder-Jessurun Cardozo recalled how, in the evenings after the store was closed, her husband Salomon and a driver took goods to the hotels where the Venezuelans were staying. It was referred to as making *bultos*, said Tsale Kirzner. The goods were packed in linen to make bales (*bultos*) and then they were delivered to the hotels in the evening.

The Venezuelans did not take everything back to their country legally. Sometimes the store owners of Curacao would deliver specially wrapped purchases to the Venezuelan fishing boats moored at the De Ruyterkade. After selling their supply of fruits and vegetables, these vessels then returned home stocked with smuggled goods.

The interior of Spritzer + Fuhrmann above the Ritz cafeteria on the Breedestraat. (photo: private collection of Ralph Spritzer)

A Shtetl under the Sun   **168**

Venezuelans also came to Curaçao to buy specialist articles. Bill and Tila Gerstenbluth had a store in Otrobanda (*Casa Bill*) which primarily sold doctors' and nurses' uniforms, nurses' shoes and other hospital textiles. Bill Gerstenbluth: "The business was good because we sold *White Swan* and other brands that were much more expensive in Venezuela. That is why they came here to make purchases. Ninety per cent of our clientele was Venezuelan."

To a lesser degree, consumer tourists also came from Haiti, Jamaica and Trinidad. These travelers left the island loaded with suitcases, bags and other packages. Ladies unashamedly boarded airplanes with ten hats piled on top of one another; hats that were bound to be resold in their own country.

The Second Blow: the Devaluation of the Bolivar

This booming trade suddenly came to an end. On 25 February 1983 the Venezuelan bolivar was devalued by 60 per cent. This meant that shopping on Curaçao (and Aruba) was suddenly no longer profitable for Venezuelans and they therefore stopped coming to the island. In 1982 some 168,000 Venezuelan consumer tourists had come to Aruba and Curaçao. In 1983, their numbers decreased to only 53,000.[154]

Lily Kisilevich-Bonaparte had opened her store *Chérie* close to the fishing boats in Punda for the specific purpose of selling to the Venezuelans. "When the bolivar fell in value, I sold that store and I went back to my husband's store *Zigzag*, in Otrobanda. *Zigzag* was not affected very much by the devaluation because we primarily sold to the local population. Yet, there were noticeable side effects. When other merchants had fewer customers and therefore earned less, they also stopped buying merchandise from our store. At one point, we employed 13 people at *Zigzag* and they all had to be paid."

Several families took a beating after the devaluation. Sales suddenly plummeted and they had to make cutbacks. Gitta Meit-Fruchter recalled that after 1983 the storekeepers were forced to drastically change their stock purchasing. "For Venezuelan customers, for example, you bought smaller sizes than you did for the Curaçao population. Suddenly you needed to have more white clothes in stock because that's what people on the island wear during periods of bereavement."

In those years the storekeepers could not make a living from the local population alone. Things were going so badly for the island's most important employer, Shell, that unemployment rose to 19 per cent. Three years later, Shell pulled up stakes and left. After that the Venezuelan oil producer PdVSA started leasing the refinery, but things would never be the same.

In these tough economic times, many store owners were also confronted with the lack of a successor to take over their business. In the past it was taken for granted that children would take over their parents' store. But in the 1980s things had changed. Some children had no desire to start working for their parents in the family business. They had headed off to America to study and often did not see the store as a part of their future career. They had seen and experienced close at hand how their parents always had to work very hard, often until late in the evening.

The combination of the rapidly declining consumer tourism since 1983 and the lack of any successor for the business prompted some owners to sell their businesses or to lease them out. Bill and Tila Gerstenbluth-Cheis did just that. Shortly after 1983, they shut down their store and leased out the premises. Tila: "Most of our customers were Venezuelan and it was difficult to recruit local business at the drop of a hat. Because we did not want to incur any debts and preferred to leave with our heads held high, we leased out the store. Our son is a doctor and was never interested in taking over the business."

The East Indians Grab their Chance

The Gerstenbluths continued to live on Curaçao, but a number of other Ashkenazic Jews left the island and moved abroad after the decline of the bolivar. Many went to America to start a new life. Some followed their children, who after their studies had continued to live in the United States. According to the stories told, the exodus was larger than it had been after the riots of 1969.

The East Indians who had come to Curaçao in small numbers starting in 1925, grabbed their opportunity. Up to the 1970s, there were not that many East Indians on the island because, like the Eastern Europeans, they were foreigners and therefore needed a license in order to open a new store. But when the Free Zone opened, they were given the opportunity to establish businesses there and later in Punda as well. To staff these businesses, the East Indians brought in personnel from India. Later, after years of hard work, the latter had saved so much money that they were able, cautiously, to start their own businesses. So they leased the store premises left by the Ashkenazic Jews, some of which, by the way, had been bought up by Marco Cheis and Socher Kirzner, both Ashkenazic.

Socher's son Tsale: "My father often helped these East Indians by acting as their guarantor at the bank. He had enormous respect for these hard-working people and trusted them simply because he recognized himself in them. That is why he was happy to give them a chance that they otherwise would not have had."

So history repeated itself. In the 1930s, the Sephardic merchants from Punda had helped the Ashkenazim in business. Gradually, the *Polakos* climbed up the ladder of success and took over the Sephardic stores. Now the Ashkenazic Jews were helping the East Indians to start their own businesses, after which the East Indians 'took over' Punda. Today, most Punda shops are East Indian, just as in the 1950s and '60s they were Ashkenazic and before that Sephardic.

An interesting detail is the fact that, in the 1930s, the Sephardic Jews had often commented on the simple life style of their Ashkenazic fellow Jews. This was reputed to be the cause of their 'unfair' competition. They also sold items of a cheaper quality, which prompted the local Curaçao population to buy from the Ashkenazic stores sooner than from the existing traders. With the arrival of the East Indians, the story played out again more or less the same. But now it was the

Ashkenazim that complained about the 'cheaper' and uniform product range of the East Indian stores, which gradually began to change the shopping scene in Punda and Otrobanda.

According to the census of 2001, 64 per cent of the Jewish population (both Ashkenazic and Sephardic) in that year still worked in the retail and wholesale trade. More than 83 per cent of the Curaçao population born in India worked in trade as compared with less than 17 per cent of the Curaçao population born on the island.

▶ Spritzer + Fuhrmann

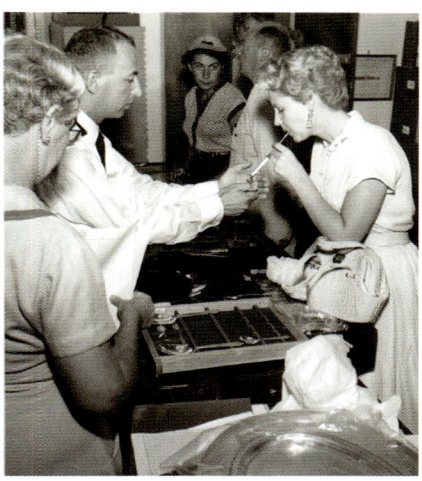

Ernö Spritzer in one of the Spritzer + Fuhrmann stores. (photo: collection of National Archives of Curaçao)

Wolf Spritzer, a watchmaker born in Poland, arrived on Curaçao in 1927. His wife, Rachel Weisz, also from Poland, and their two children followed in 1929 (see also the portrait in Chapter 2). Spritzer began to repair watches in a space a couple of square meters large he rented from Amador Maduro on the Handelskade, on the corner of the Windstraat. He had no more than an open door with a plank fixed between the door jambs that served both as a display counter and a work bench. The store was called *Relojeria Alemana*, which was later changed to *W. Spritzer* because at that time the word 'German' (Alemana) already had an unpleasant ring to it.

Charles Fuhrmann, born in Czernowitz, arrived from the Polish city of Sniatyn two years after Spritzer. He was on his way to Maracaibo in Venezuela with a box of gemstones when he met Spritzer on Curaçao while his ship refueled. Fuhrmann decided to stay on the island and the two men started working together. In 1936, Fuhrmann married Spritzer's daughter Frida.

According to Spritzer's son Ernö, a year later the two businessmen had two stores on Curaçao and one on Aruba. In addition to watches, *Spritzer + Fuhrmann* sold jewelry, crystal, silver, porcelain and luxury gift articles. Due to the large number of foreign soldiers on the island, the stores did very well during the Second World War.

Ernö Spritzer, who was born in 1919, was now also active in the business. He had received a practical education in the branch store on Aruba and the stores on Curaçao. In 1940 he earned an optician's diploma in New York, after which he became the first optician on Curaçao. From the Americans he received the order to make glasses for the troops stationed in the Caribbean region.

After the war, the company experienced a rapid rise in success. The existing buildings were modernized and new stores were acquired. As mentioned early in the chapter, Curaçao was a free port that, particularly from the 1950s onwards, was frequently visited by American cruise ships. The passengers were often rich Jews from New York, eager to spend money, who enjoyed meeting fellow Jews on the island and sometimes even fellow Americans. Ernö, who had become general manager after his father's death (in 1953), made sure that he got to know his customers personally. He engaged them in conversation by offering them a pocket knife bearing the *Spritzer + Fuhrmann* logo. It didn't take him long to work out whether or not they were creditworthy and it was safe to accept their bank checks. In view of the precious objects that were sold, cash payments were rare. *Spritzer + Fuhrmann* prospered. In 1954 a new, four-story main building was built on the Gomezplein. Two of the floors were used for sales. With air conditioning and an elevator, this building was unique for Curaçao. The carillon on the building's front played songs on the days that many (cruise ship) tourists were in Punda.

Once a year, Fuhrmann traveled to Europe on business. In Denmark he purchased porcelain and silver, clocks and watches in Switzerland, and jewelry in Italy and Germany. Ernö took responsibility for the store's logistics.

The winter was *Spritzer + Fuhrmann*'s most important season. Then, most cruise ships called on Curaçao and 90 per cent of their annual turnover was earned in this period. Many crates full of merchandise from *Spritzer + Fuhrmann* were delivered to the ships. Everything was very carefully prepared for delivery. Complete Wedgwood services were already packaged and sometimes a crate contained more than had been ordered so that, if something broke, a replacement would not have to be sent on later.

Spritzer + Fuhrmann's clientele included famous celebrities such as Diana Ross and Elizabeth Taylor. In New York, people talked about the store, its exclusive products and the excellent service. *Spritzer + Fuhrmann* also

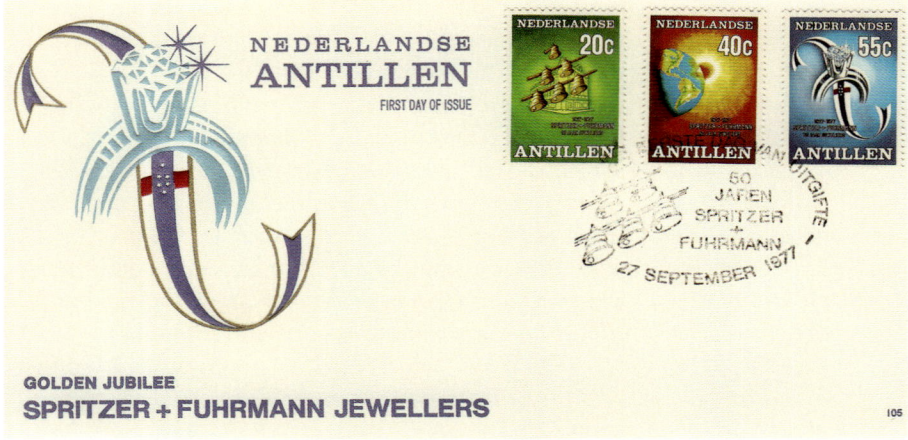

placed full-page advertisements in the *New York Times*. Thus, in America, the island of Curaçao became known as the 'island of Spritzer + Fuhrmann'.

In the meantime, stores were opened on Aruba, Bonaire and Sint Maarten – *Spritzer + Fuhrmann* even had a branch in New York. Initially, customers could go there only for service and repairs. Later it became a sales outlet as well. To attract more tourists to Curaçao and for longer stays, Ernö became one of the driving forces behind establishing Hotel Intercontinental, which opened its doors in 1957. Boutiques of *Spritzer + Fuhrmann* were to be found inside this and other hotels.

The atmosphere in the very first stores on the Heerenstraat and the Breedestraat was quite different from that in the large store on the Gomezplein. The common *yu'i Korsou* often found the big store to be far too chic; they didn't really feel comfortable going inside, while the stores on the Heerenstraat and the Breedestraat appealed much more to the local population.

In 1968, the building which formerly housed the *Europa* store on the Breedestraat was purchased. In it *Spritzer + Fuhrmann* established *Renaissance*, a store for porcelain and service sets.

Ernö Spritzer did not witness this phase of development. He and Fuhrmann did not get along very well and, in part for health reasons, Ernö and his family moved to the Netherlands in 1958. When the Venezuelan bolivar plummeted in value in the 1980s and Fuhrmann had no one to succeed him, it brought an end to this famous company in 1987, which in its heyday had employed some 550 people. For the store's 50th anniversary in 1977, the Antillean postal service dedicated three special postage stamps to *Spritzer + Fuhrmann*. It was the first time a store had been given such an honor.

First-day cover with the postage stamps celebrating the 50th anniversary of Spritzer + Fuhrmann. (photo: Jeannette van Ditzhuijzen)

14 The Congregation Becomes Smaller and More Orthodox

As the years of economic prosperity were coming to an end, Shaarei Tsedek purchased a piece of land for a new synagogue. But it would take until 2006 before it was actually completed. Until then, the congregation made do with a house that they converted into a synagogue. In the meanwhile, two groups of Sephardic Jews preferred the shiel over the snoa. They thought the snoa had become too liberal.

No Money for a Rabbi

Due to the departure of several Ashkenazic families after May 1969 and again after the fall of the bolivar in 1983, the congregation gradually became smaller. As a result, there was relatively less money to pay a rabbi. According to Nachman Grynsztein, this was the reason *Shaarei Tsedek* decided to make do without a rabbi for a number of years. "It was not a good decision. Over the years, we became morally bankrupt in the area of Jewish faith, because we had no leader, like Rabbi Yeshurun who we now have. Altogether, it took much too long, I think from 1982 to 1996. Occasionally, we were blessed with a rabbi, but he always left before long. It was not permanent employment, as it is now."

Due to the absence of a rabbi, attendance at the synagogue also declined. Omer Grynsztein recalled how happy the other men were when he came into the synagogue after he had become *bar mitzvah* in the mid 1980s. 'You are number ten', he was told, which meant they had a minyan.

Since then much has changed. For a good number of years it seldom occurred that there were not enough men to form a minyan. But since the rabbi and a few other congregation members have left the island in the late 2010s (Rabbi Yeshurun is now working part-time for Shaarei Tsedek), it got more difficult to get 10 Jewish men together.

When there was no rabbi at all several members of the congregation took over the leadership in the *shiel*. Socher Kirzner, for instance, and Bill Gerstenbluth. Grynsztein: "They were the two pillars that kept us together. They were always there. I have great respect for what they did."

At services, particularly for life cycle events (*bar mitzvahs*, weddings, funerals, etc.), the rabbis of one congregation would take responsibility for performing religious duties for the other congregation when it did not have a rabbi or chazzan. Thus Aaron Peller – rabbi at *Mikvé Israel-Emanuel* from 1978 to 1994 – occasionally led services at *Shaarei Tsedek*.[155] Conversely, it sometimes happened that someone like Abraham Wiznitzer went to the *snoa* to read from the Torah when a Sephardic rabbi was absent.

When *Shaarei Tsedek* had no religious leader, Rabbi Peller and other liberal rabbis of *Mikvé Israel-Emanuel* instructed many an Ashkenazic boy in preparation for his *bar mitzvah*. In the year leading up to their religious adulthood, the boys are taught, among other things, to read from the Torah using the correct melody and the correct intonation. During their training, they are also taught so much about Judaism that, to some degree, they also understand what they are reading.

During the period that there was no Ashkenazic rabbi, the boys would sometimes receive *bar mitzvah* lessons from educated men from their own congregation. Socher Kirzner was one, while in the 1970s Ulli Steiger assumed these duties. Steiger came from Israel and was married to the Ashkenazi Shirley Gärtner. In the eyes of many, he was very respected and well-loved, in part due to his love for Judaism in general.

Whenever an Ashkenazic boy became a *bar mitzvah* in the *snoa* because *Shaarei Tsedek* had no rabbi at the time or because his parents found the ambiance of the *snoa* more beautiful and more spacious, the family then had to become members of *Mikvé Israel-Emanuel* a year in advance.

A Reform Conversion

The rabbis of *Mikvé Israel-Emanuel* were always helpful when non-Jews wanted to become Jews through conversion (called *giyyur*) and *Shaarei Tsedek* did not have a rabbi. It usually concerned a woman that wanted to marry an Ashkenazic Jew. After all, only the children of a Jewish mother are considered to be Jewish.

Despite the religious differences, most of the *Shaarei Tsedek* members see no problem with a reform conversion. The circumstances on Curaçao are simply different from what they would be in a larger congregation. But later, orthodox rabbis occasionally had difficulty with this concept. As a rule, orthodox rabbis do not accept reform conversions.

This became clear in 2011 when some members of *Shaarei Tsedek* suddenly stopped counting the male liberal converts or the female converts' sons when forming a minyan. This has divided the congregation and – if worst comes to worst – could result in a schism within the community.

The first non-Jewish woman in the Ashkenazic community was Olivia Conquet. In the 1930s, she married Herman Gärtner, but did not become Jewish immediately. She did later, probably for the sake of the children, so her daughter Shirley thought. Gärtner realized that, because of his relationship with an initially non-Jewish woman, he was regarded as a little bit of a maverick in the tightly-knit community of those days. He himself had absolutely no problem with it and simply continued to go to the synagogue.

Ori Zahavi was the first Ashkenazic Jew to become bar mitzvah in the synagogue on the Lelieweg. Next to him is Socher Kirzner and behind him, wearing glasses, is Lupu Bonaparte. (photo: private collection of Sonia Racin-Kirzner)

The next Ashkenazic Jew to marry a local woman (as far as is known) was Fajwel Becher. His wife, Ida Antoinette, became Jewish just before their wedding in 1946. The couple went to Caracas for the purpose, where she converted under the auspices of the Cuban Chief Rabbi. After that they were married. Her son Ivan recalled that his mother raised the children very religiously and with a deep faith. Perhaps she was so devoted because she had converted.

Plans and Grounds for a New Synagogue

At the beginning of 1982, a year before the devaluation of the bolivar, the Ashkenazim purchased a piece of land on the Magdalenaweg in Mahaai. They planned to build a new synagogue there. They were so convinced that it could be completed within a year that the bulletin of *Shaarei Tsedek* reported that 1982 would be the last year that the congregation would celebrate *Rosh Hashanah* and *Yom Kippur* in Scharloo's synagogue. In the years to follow, the bulletins kept silent on the subject. But who could have guessed in 1982 that the Ashkenazic Jews would run into hard times financially because of the devaluation of the bolivar?

In 1982 everything still seemed peachy keen. On 30 April of that year, the boards of *Shaarei Tsedek* and Club Union organized a barbecue brunch at the

From 1986-2006, the Ashkenazic synagogue was established in a house on the Lelieweg. (photo: Jeannette van Ditzhuijzen)

spot of 'our future Jewish Social Center' on the Magdalenaweg.[156] Despite problems with obtaining a building permit, the hope of quickly realizing a Jewish Center was kept alive. Almost two years later, on 14 December 1983, a *Fund Raising Party* was organized for the *Jewish Center*. A similar gathering was held in 1984 'at the land for the new Center at Rooi Katoochi'.[157] No one at the time could have known that the piece of land would remain undeveloped for more than 20 years.

According to Paul Ackerman, each year there would be enthusiastic discussions on a new synagogue: "At *Rosh Hashanah* people would begin making plans, by *Yom Kippur* you could envision the synagogue, but when *Simchat Torah*[158] finally came around the planning would stop; until the following year."

Still, people wanted to leave Scharloo. Partly because most of *Shaarei Tsedek's* members no longer lived in the city center. But also because many Scharloo residents (some of them Sephardic Jews) had gradually moved to the outlying districts and Scharloo was degenerating.

Thus in 1986, *Shaarei Tsedek*, instead of moving to a new synagogue on the Magdalenaweg, moved to a residence on the Lelieweg. It was conveniently located for the Ashkenazic Jews, most of whom lived in the neighborhood and so could easily walk to the synagogue if they wished.

The house had been owned by congregation members Shlom and Fruma Milstein. Fruma died at the end of 1985. Shlom had died in 1975, and the congregation was given the opportunity to purchase this house at a good price. Just like the property at Scharlooweg 39, the house was converted into a synagogue. The women sat in the middle, more or less separated from the men, who sat to the left and right. Although there was no *mechitza,* the men could barely see the women.

The idea that it was only a temporary move must have dominated most people's thoughts. No one remembered clearly, how or when exactly the Torahs were brought over from Scharloo to the Lelieweg. Obviously, nobody realized that the congregation was to hold its services and festivities here for more than 20 years. Yet everyone was happy with the arrangement.

Sephardic Jews in the Shiel

Around the same time, several Sephardic Jews began to prefer going to the Ashkenazic *shiel*. They were not Curaçao Sephardic Jews that were married to Ashkenazim – these are often members of both congregations and they make no point of visiting both synagogues alternately. They were Sephardic Jews that primarily came from the Middle East and Morocco. Sephardim that did not feel at home (anymore) at the liberal *Mikvé Israel-Emanuel*.

The Lebanese

The first group, Jews from the Middle East and the Mediterranean region, had started to immigrate to Curaçao at the start of the 20th century. William Cohen, who would later become the Consul for Israel, came from Egypt. José Cohen from Turkey and the Amón, Sarfatti and Levantou families all came from Greece. Victor Abady recalled that his grandfather left Beirut in 1898. He wanted to go to Haiti, but due to a revolution there the ship continued on to Venezuela. "In 1907 my father also went to Venezuela and his brother Jacobo followed in 1909. Because of problems he had with a nephew of the then dictator Juan Vizente Gómez, my uncle Jacobo left for Curaçao in 1920. He saw that there were many opportunities on the island and asked my father to join him. Their business was called *Casa Abady*. Later my father had his own business on the Prinsenstraat, *Casa Aron Abady*."

What these Jews from the Middle East had in common was their Sephardic origin. They were all more or less orthodox – at least, they were not liberal. This naturally meant that they initially went to the *snoa* of *Mikvé Israel*, which was still orthodox at the time. But, according to Victor Abady, the Jews from the Middle East were not treated as equals by the Portuguese Jews at the *snoa*. In social terms the older generation of *Mikvé Israel* probably saw little difference between these newcomers and the *Polakos*. For this reason, several Jews from the Mediterranean region sought their social contacts more and more among the Ashkenazic congregation and joined Club Union and/or Maccabi. The brothers Abraham and José Abady, for example, were already Maccabi members during the war. Abraham was Maccabi's treasurer and later even its president. Most Middle Eastern Jews attended the Ashkenazic Moria School (see Chapter 12), where, in 1951, Victor Abady was one of the very first students.

The more liberal *Mikvé Israel-Emanuel* became, the more this group of Jews reached out for *Shaarei Tsedek*, which is more orthodox and traditional. For a start they would become members of both synagogues. Thus, as early as 1962, S. Sarfatti and William Cohen were on the *Shaarei Tsedek* membership list. Sarfatti was also a Club Union member, just like the Abadys.

Some of these orthodox Jews now no longer live on Curaçao, or only for part of the year at most. But when they are there, some prefer attending the *Shaarei Tsedek* synagogue over that of *Mikvé Israel-Emanuel*. The brothers Victor and Maurice Abady and their children, for example, attend *Shaarei Tsedek* these days. This is because of the equal position that women have been given at *Mikvé*

Israel-Emanuel – a practice which they reject – but also because of the extremely religious women with whom their sons are married.

Victor's son Aron Abady became *shomer Shabbat* and therefore adheres to all the laws that are connected to the Sabbath (such as not working on Saturday, not using any electrical equipment and not driving a car). Aron Abady was the president of the Ashkenazic congregation in the 1990s and under his leadership the orthodox Rabbi Yeshurun was brought to Curaçao in 2000.

The Moroccans

A second group of Sephardic Jews that has preferred *Shaarei Tsedek* over the Sephardic *snoa* are the Moroccans, who started coming to Curaçao in 1986. Strictly speaking, they were not the very first Moroccans on the island. That was Fanny van der Elzen, who over the years regularly taught at the Hebrew School. She was born and raised in Morocco and later moved to Israel, where she married. Afterwards the couple came to Curaçao.

But in the 1980s, a wave of Moroccan Jews came to Curaçao. Armand Elmaleh was one of them. His stay on the island was to be temporary, or so he thought. He lived in Paris at the time and his cousin in New York needed his help in a company in Curaçao's Free Zone. Another cousin already lived on Curaçao, but he had left for Morocco for a couple of months in order to introduce his future wife to his family.

Elmaleh, Sephardic by birth, went to the snoa for the first Sabbath of his stay on Curaçao. "When I went inside, it was an enormous shock for me. Until I was 22, I had been raised in a synagogue where the women were separated from the men, where there was no organ playing and where no electrical equipment was used. And here there was an organ, people were using a microphone and – the biggest shock – the women were sitting among the men. I didn't even know such a thing existed. In Marrakesh and Casablanca, where I have lived, there were some fifty synagogues, but none of us had even heard of a *reformed synagogue*."

Via Ivan Becher, who operated a restaurant in the Free Zone, Elmaleh heard that there was another Jewish congregation on the island – an Ashkenazic one. He was somewhat skeptical about it, because in Europe it is the Ashkenazic Jews who are more progressive than the Sephardic Jews. And if the Sephardic congregation on Curaçao was already so progressive, how much more progressive would the Ashkenazim turn out to be?

"Ivan Becher picked me up and, when we got to the synagogue on the Lelieweg, I got the next big shock: the average age of the congregation was 70+, I was 23. At the time, Socher Kirzner, the old Kisilevich, Sloima Zonenschain and the Wiznitzer brothers were still alive. There were only two boys, Ori Zahavi and Omer Grynsztein, who had just done their *bar mitzvah*. There were no women at all. In those years, they never came on Friday evenings. There was no rabbi either. Bill Gerstenbluth led the service. And if he wasn't there, then Avrum Wiznitzer or Socher Kirzner took over. Those present were all talking at the same time and a service that should have been at least 30 to 45 minutes long, lasted only five to ten minutes. There was no singing, the men mumbled their prayers quickly and it was all over."

The Wiznitzer brothers: from left to right Mozes, Salomon and Abraham. (photo: private collection of Leo Wiznitzer)

Despite the shock, Elmaleh decided to go to *Shaarei Tsedek* from then on. There the service was at least not *reformed* like it was at *Mikvé Israel-Emanuel*. Besides, even though the *snoa* was Sephardic, the melodies and the manner of praying were very different from what Elmaleh had been used to in Morocco. "Although the Ashkenazim mumbled during their service, it was at least in Hebrew, not in English as it was in the *snoa*."

Because help was needed at the store, Elmaleh remained on Curaçao; he even brought more members of his family from Morocco to the island. "At the peak, we had nine Moroccan men here and together we could almost form a minyan."

Shaarei Tsedek Becomes more Orthodox

The American-Israeli Hannah, whom Elmaleh married in 1992, thought that initially the Ashkenazim probably felt intimidated by the sudden increase in the numbers of Moroccans. The Moroccan Jews, for instance, wanted only kosher food to be brought into the synagogue. They also had objections to the early hour at which the service was held on Saturdays. Hannah: "Everywhere else in the world the service begins at 10:00 or 10:30 on Saturdays. Here it was quickly rattled off between 7 and 8 o'clock. We called it the express service."

Both acknowledged that, under the influence of the Moroccan Jews, the congregation became more orthodox. In 1999, Elmaleh even stopped working on the Sabbath. Like the Ashkenazic Jews, he had initially simply continued to work on Saturday – that is until his children asked him about it. For him that was the moment he had to stop the practice and he was glad he did. Following his lead, several Ashkenazim also stopped working on the Sabbath either partially or entirely.

According to Hannah, the contacts with the Sephardic congregation are good. "We have friendly relations with them and if we are invited to a *bar mitzvah*, then we go, unless it is held on a Saturday. On the Sabbath we do not drive cars and I am not really comfortable in the *snoa*."

Most of the Moroccans have now left Curaçao. But an immigration wave like this one does indicate how the congregation can suddenly expand.

The Old Generation Makes Way for the New

Starting in the 1990s, the congregation experienced a rejuvenation. A number of men from the first generation had died and several young people who had been studying abroad returned to the island. The time was ripe for change. Omer Grynsztein, president of the congregation between 2007-2011: "With our desire for change, we were the Obamas of the 1990s. Something had to give. We had not had a rabbi for years; so we also had no religious leadership."

Starting in 1990, the 'youth' took control. First Paul Morón became president, then Isaac Grynsztein, Aron Abady, again Isaac Grynsztein and then his brother Omer. The older people in the congregation were certainly not against a 'takeover' by the younger members of the congregation, but they did have some reservations. Isaac Grynsztein: "They of course were strong personalities and found it difficult to relinquish control of the board." Socher Kirzner missed his work on the board enormously. Just like Leon Seibald he had devoted himself to the congregation for years.

Another reason for the older generation's misgivings was financial in nature. Isaac Grynsztein: "A younger board had taken control once before, but it had left the funds nearly depleted at the end. They were afraid that this would recur. It is understandable – they were the pioneers and didn't want to see things go awry again."

Rabbis Come and Go

In the 1990s, the new boards brought a succession of rabbis to Curaçao. Unfortunately, not all of them proved to be successful. The Spanish-speaking Rabbi Armon, for instance, soon disappeared from the stage again. Students of the Hebrew School recalled that he refused to wear his hearing aid when he taught classes. The consequences are easy to imagine.

After that, in 1993, came Alan Bright. Most people remember him as a charming individual that livened things up and forged the congregation into a unity. Under Bright, *Shaarei Tsedek* blossomed; the synagogue was jam-packed every Sabbath and extra chairs had to be set up. On Saturday morning, he organized a service for the children, at their level. The service was so popular that many Sephardic children attended it as well. And the contacts with *Mikvé Israel-Emanuel* were very successful under this rabbi because he was willing to give and take.

Adam Morón remembered the blowing of the *shofar* with Rabbi Bright for hospital patients, and the successful family services that Bright introduced. "People found time to attend his services." Many congregation members were saddened when this popular rabbi was fired a year later because he had worked privately for people from the congregation. He was much loved as a religious leader.

Rabbi Poupko arrived in 1996. Evidenced by the stories told about his strict stances concerning the *kashrut* (Jewish dietary laws), he was not an unequivocal success (see Chapter 10). Isaac Grynsztein had an explanation for the problems with the rabbis: "Bear in mind that we are a small congregation, so we cannot attract highly qualified people. There is also the matter of funds. Rabbis ask top dollar and our small congregation does not have that much money. I think the three rabbis mentioned were all shocked when they arrived on Curaçao. Our congregation is not exactly a stepping stone in a rabbi's career."

Finally, A New Shiel

In 2000, Rabbi Ariel Yeshurun came to Curaçao. He belonged to *Beit Amiel* and the Sephardic Center in Jerusalem, which trained young rabbis to serve as religious leaders in the Diaspora. He stayed much longer than his three predecessors. Except for *shochet* Szmukler, who led the services from 1928 to 1954, Yeshurun was, in 2011, the longest serving religious leader the Ashkenazic congregation had ever had.

Yeshurun's greatest legacy was successfully raising the money to build the congregation's own synagogue on the land purchased in 1982 on the Magdalenaweg. The plans had lain inactive for years even though there were concrete proposals for their implementation. But a lack of funds had always kept the project from getting off the ground.

Not everyone supported the building of a new synagogue. Some people thought the congregation was too small and feared there would not be enough money to maintain it. On the other hand, one of those interviewed recalled that in 1986 there was also some resistance to the move from Scharloo to the Lelieweg. That's just the way it is with change.

Yet gradually, more people became enthusiastic about the prospect of a new synagogue on the Magdalenaweg. Particularly after Herman Tauber had made the first, very generous, financial commitment. According to Yeshurun, this marked a milestone in his campaign to raise funds. With a large amount of money in the account, it was easier for him to persuade the other members of the congregation to commit themselves. "But it still wasn't easy. Few people believed in the project. It had been tried so many times before, why would it be successful this time? But I believed in the project and fought on."

Besides, long before Yeshurun's arrival, Victor Abady had deposited a considerable amount of money in a separate account as a donation for a new synagogue. "It took everyone by complete surprise. I was still going to the *snoa* at the time, but I simply thought that the Ashkenazim should have a big synagogue. Later Tauber gave much more money. He was the main sponsor."

The interior of the synagogue on the Magdalenaweg. (photo: Sinaya Wolfert)

The synagogue on the Magdalenaweg (photo: Jeannette van Ditzhuijzen)

183   THE CONGREGATION BECOMES SMALLER AND MORE ORTHODOX

On 25 June 2006, the Torahs were ceremoniously transferred from the synagogue on the Lelieweg to the synagogue on the Magdalenaweg. (photo: collection of Shaarei Tsedek)

The First Spade

Finally, enough money was raised and, on 25 January 2004, the first spade broke ground with much ceremony, accompanied by music and singing. The older congregation members, the rabbi, the president of the congregation and the sponsors were each given an opportunity to wield the spade in turn.

According to Adam Morón, who was a teenager at the time, it was a wonderful moment. "Everyone was there. More people came than attended *Rosh Hashanah* services. Particularly the older men – Traytel Oberman, Leo Shuman, Leon Seibald, Johnny Frankel and my grandfather, Bill Gerstenbluth – were all enthusiastic. They had the shovel ready as if they wanted to build the synagogue at one go. This was the realization of their lifelong dream."

On the spot where the bimah now stands, a CD-Rom was buried with photographs of the signing of the building contract at the architect's office. A blessing was also buried. Of course, speeches were given by the rabbi, by the main sponsor Herman Tauber and by Lazaro Grynsztein, the building committee president, among others. From that moment on it would take a little over two years before the round building with its glass dome was completed.

Moving the Torahs

The last service in the synagogue on the Lelieweg was held on 10 June 2006. For some this was a very emotional event. Although this synagogue had always been meant as a temporary accommodation, many congregation members had become attached to the snug space and pleasant atmosphere.

One week later, the first service was held in the new synagogue. It was a special occasion, in view of the fact that Gideon Zahavi did his *bar mitzvah* on that day. It was all the more special because his uncle, Ori Zahavi, was the very first *bar mitzvah* in the synagogue on the Lelieweg (see photo p. 176)

For the *bar mitzvah*, one Torah was brought over from the Lelieweg to the Magdalenaweg. The official procession, during which all the Torahs were carried to the new synagogue, took place on Sunday, 25 June, after the morning service on the Lelieweg, which for this occasion did not begin until 9 o'clock. The Torah scrolls were handed over to the board members and the rabbi also carried one. Adam Morón recalled that you could normally walk the distance between the two synagogues in five minutes, but the congregation members now took 45 minutes to cover the distance. "Anyone that wanted to was allowed to carry one of the Torahs for a bit." They arrived at the synagogue singing and dancing; and, according to Rabbi Yeshurun, many people had tears in their eyes.

More Women in the New Shiel

According to Omer Grynsztein, the newly built synagogue is one of the reasons why today more women attend the services. "Because of the building's round shape, the women are more involved in the service. The old *shul* was only a house, a temporary accommodation."

It is true that, in the past, many women only went to the synagogue during the High Holidays. This was also because, regularly, there was no rabbi. After the arrival of Rabbi Yeshurun, several women said they attended more often. "The rabbi does a wonderful service, his prayers are said with so much feeling. Even when I don't understand it, I simply sit and listen. Besides, it is pleasant." Others honestly admitted that they came primarily for the social contacts, particularly since the Women's Committee has started providing a common breakfast each Saturday morning after the service. Hannah Elmaleh: "The women generally come to the service a little later, around 9 o'clock, but afterwards many remain until 11 o'clock sitting at a table talking and enjoying breakfast."

A Large but Empty Synagogue?

After the joy felt about a new synagogue, reality set in. Some asked themselves whether this beautiful synagogue was not too large for a congregation that was growing smaller. In 2009, several members left the island because they thought their children would receive a better Jewish upbringing in America than they would on Curaçao. At the Hebrew School, after all, the children received no more than four hours of Jewish lessons per week, which according to some was much too little. That is why several families, including the rabbi's, decided that the wife and children would live in America, while the father would remain on the island. Whether the children will ever return to Curaçao is still an open question.

The rabbi recognized that this departure of so many was a considerable blow for the congregation. "It weakens the community, without a doubt. Still, building this large synagogue was justified. No one could have predicted the exodus of 2009. When we started the fund-raising, we had absolutely no indication that this would happen."

He pointed out the fact that the majority of the congregation's members still lived on the island.[159] "Despite the departure of several young couples that inspired the *shul*, a wonderful congregation remains to work with. And this building was a dream that was conceived years before I came to Curaçao. The fact that the congregation purchased the piece of land on the Magdalenaweg way back in 1982 attests to their strong desire to build a new synagogue."

Shaarei Tsedek's former president Isaac Grynsztein also firmly supported the decision to build a new synagogue. "At the time we had a flourishing congregation. Yes, people are now leaving the island, but things are not all that gloomy. We have had these ups and downs before, as I have heard from the older generation. And yes, we are now experiencing a 'down'."

Armand Elmaleh was more dispirited. In 2009 he said: "Come back in five years and *Shaarei Tsedek* will no longer exist; unfortunately. Unless a miracle happens. The only miracle possible would be for Jews to come here from Venezuela, due to the social and political situation there. But most of them are going to Panama because it is Spanish-speaking. I give the congregation here another five years at most. On the other hand, when I arrived in 1986 I could never have imagined that the synagogue would have lasted more than two years. And yet it happened. So you never know."

According to his wife Hannah, having its own synagogue is the only way to keep a Jewish congregation together. "Not a single Jew will come to this island if it is impossible to attend services on the High Holidays. You need a synagogue and leadership. That keeps people together."

Tradition as the Stuff that Binds

Others have pointed out that something other than the synagogue ties the Ashkenazic Jews to Curaçao: the Eastern European *Yiddishkeit*, the Jewish identity and the feeling for tradition. That is what nearly everyone received from their parents and grandparents, with whom most of them spoke Yiddish. From them they learned the Jewish customs and traditions and how to prepare Jewish food. It is probably correct to attribute the congregation's survival over all these years, even when there was no rabbi, to this *Yiddishkeit*.

Various Eastern European Jews said that their family was hardly or not religious at all and certainly not orthodox. But they were traditional. That word 'traditional' came up repeatedly in the interviews and it was stressed. "The word 'orthodox' is now attached to our synagogue, but it is only a name."[160] The Jews of Curaçao are not all that orthodox. Everyone experiences their faith as he or she interprets it", one of the interviewees expressed the general feeling. This corresponds with the stories of families that do not eat kosher, except on Passover, *Rosh Hashanah* and *Yom Kippur*. They do fast on *Yom Kippur*, they sometimes even go to the synagogue on foot that day, but they also work on the Sabbath.

A Small Congregation is Better than no Congregation

In 1970 Isaac Emmanuel, the former rabbi of the orthodox congregation *Mikvé Israel*, had grave doubts about whether the new congregation *Mikvé Israel-Emanuel* would survive. In his book about the Sephardic Jews, he gave several suggestions that might ensure that this congregation would survive on Curaçao. Amongst other things he recommended a much closer collaboration with the Ashkenazic Jews. Not only socially, but also in the field of religion.[161]

But the vast majority of those people interviewed thought that nothing would ever come of it. Even those that were members of both congregations and personally had no objection to a merger. One of them: "Unite the two? No, for this generation that's impossible. *Mikvé Israel-Emanuel* is reformed, and I respect that, but we are very traditional. It is unfortunate because we do not have enough people, nor do they. Personally I wouldn't object to it, because it is more important that we continue to exist. But knowing the people like I do, I do not think it will happen." "It is still two separate congregations", mused Shirley Gärtner. In her view this fact can be attributed to an 'old sore' – the way the Sephardim treated the immigrants from Eastern Europe after they had arrived.

Now that increasingly more young people are marrying a partner from outside the Ashkenazic-Curaçao group, the internal cohesion is weakening and the older members in particular said the congregation is no longer as tightly-knit as it used to be. Despite this, to the outside world they still form a single front. Hannah Elmaleh: "The congregation on Curaçao is your family as well. You won't find that in other Jewish congregations. Despite the discrepancies that certainly exist, within *Shaarei Tsedek* everyone looks out for everyone else."

Even those who have lived abroad for years belong to the congregation as much as the Jews that have always remained on the island. When someone from the congregation dies, all the members of the congregation know about it within a day, whether they now live in the Netherlands, America or in Israel.

"I have left Curaçao behind, but not the people who live there", declared Fanny Sprung-Weisinger from New York, attempting to describe these steadfast ties. As long as that feeling of solidarity dominates, the congregation will continue to exist. Regardless of how small it becomes and regardless of how differently the members profess their faith.

▶ ## Rabbi Ariel Yeshurun (Rehovot, Israel, 1976)

Rabbi Yeshurun.(photo: Sinaya Wolfert)

"I was 24 when I came to Curaçao in 2000, immediately after I graduated from the rabbinical seminary. I came with my wife Ruhama and a four months old baby. Originally, I wanted to stay for two years, but I am still here in 2009 and we now have three children."

"Why did I come to Curaçao? Because you can still make a difference here. We soon realized that there were many opportunities in the congregation. I immediately tried to get more people to come to the synagogue, to inspire them."

"If fewer people went to the synagogue in the past, as I have heard, it can be explained. There was not a rabbi at the time and a lack of leadership creates a decline in synagogue attendance. A rabbi should inspire people, give sermons, know the melodies, etc. In the past, the president of the board filled the leadership role. The Jews here have considerable knowledge about their faith because many of them were raised orthodox. But to be able to pass on this knowledge, that is another thing altogether. A rabbi is trained to impart knowledge and to lead the congregation."

"Originally, the Saturday service was held at 6 o'clock in the morning, and later at 7. It was held so early because it gave the men enough time to go to their stores in the city after the service. I changed it to 8. It is, after all, only reasonable that everyone should have the chance to visit the *shul*. The Sabbath is a day of rest and therefore it simply won't do to openly adapt the service times to people who are working on that day. The fact that they work is their business, but let us at least try to honor the day of rest. Everybody is now happy about the change."

"They had been talking about the new synagogue for around twenty years and it has now finally been built. I heard about the wishes of the successive boards through the years. I heard that each year they proposed the synagogue be built, but nothing ever came of it. When I proposed it, I was told that the plan was too ambitious. Yet the long-expected dream of the congregation and my personal ambitions have now finally been fulfilled."

◀

Part V

Relations Outside the Community

15 Contacts with Jews on Other Islands

Not all Eastern European Jews remained on Curaçao. After a couple of years, some traveled on to Panama, Venezuela or Colombia. A few of them finally made it to America or left after the war for the new country of Israel. Other Ashkenazim came to Curaçao as a second choice, after having first lived on Aruba or Trinidad.

Sephardic and Ashkenazic Jews on Aruba

Aruba had just as much appeal to the enterprising Eastern Europeans as Curaçao. Even though there was never such a large Ashkenazic community there as on the neighboring island, there were always lively contacts between the two islands.

In past centuries, Sephardic Jews regularly moved from Curaçao to Aruba in order to do business and to live there. Because this was only a small group, they never formed a real congregation. Between 1816 and 1832, there were between 19 and 32 Jews on Aruba;[162] for decades after that it was never more than a handful.

All this changed in the 1920s. Starting in 1927, a refinery owned by Lago was built on Aruba and, as had happened with Shell, attracted employees from outside the island. Some of them were Jews from Suriname, primarily Sephardim. At the same time, the immigration of Ashkenazic Jews from Eastern Europe took off. Some of them found jobs at the Lago refinery; others became peddlers or started dry goods stores just like on Curaçao.

Some of these Ashkenazim came via Curaçao or a third country, while others came to Aruba directly. The Romanian Aron Libman ended up on the island by accident. He had left Noua Suliţă in 1927 bound for Colombia, where he tried to set up a small business. Three years later he went back to Romania, only to return to Colombia for a second time soon. On the way, his ship moored on Aruba and Libman simply stayed there. After he had his wife and daughters brought over in 1936, it seems that his youngest daughter, Clara, really liked attending the Aruban Roman Catholic school. "I actually wanted to become a nun and went to church with friends. When my mother found out about it, she started to worry about there being too much of a Catholic influence on me. That is why we moved to Curaçao in 1938, where there was a larger Jewish congregation."

A Club, a Cemetery and a Congregation

Letters written to the government on Curaçao reveal that from April 1941 there were plans for the establishment of a Dutch-Israeli congregation on Aruba. But a couple of months later, the lawyer F. Frerker reported to the colonial government secretary that the plan for this congregation had quite recently been abandoned: "Various difficulties between the parties involved seem to have led to this decision."[163]

So no new congregation was created, though a club was: the Country Club that the Aruban Jews founded in 1942 on Aruba's Palm Beach. In view of the small numbers, this club had both Sephardic and Ashkenazic members. Like Club Union on Curaçao, the Country Club was a center for social activities such as wedding parties, *bar mitzvahs*, *Purim* festivals and activities for the youth.

After the war, the Jewish Country Club was officially recognized by the government as a center for prayer, a social center and a Jewish school. For lack of their own synagogue, according to a 1946 issue of the Monthly Magazine for Israeli Households on the Netherlands Antilles, the services for Rosh Hashanah and Yom Kippur were held at the house of Adolf Fuchs. After the Country Club was founded, the Aruban Jews had a cemetery built. Before that time they had used the old cemetery of the Jews from Curaçao that dates from approximately 1837.

It wasn't until 1956 that the Aruban Jews founded their own congregation, for which they obtained royal approval in that same year. They had a synagogue built, *Beth Israel* (House of Israel), which was consecrated in 1962 by the religious leaders of the three Curaçao congregations: Chazzan Abramovic of the Ashkenazic congregation of *Shaarei Tsedek*, Rabbi Maslin from the Temple *Emanu-El* and Rabbi Amine from *Mikvé Israel*. The Curaçao congregations also brought gifts. On behalf of *Shaarei Tsedek*, they were presented by Marco Cheis.

In Business Together on Aruba and Curaçao

The Ashkenazic merchants of Aruba and Curaçao were certainly no strangers to each other. This can be concluded from the bulletins that *Mikvé Israel* published in the 1940s, '50s and '60s on the occasion of *Rosh Hashanah*. They regularly featured advertisements with new year's greetings from the Ashkenazic Jewish stores on both Curaçao and Aruba.

One of these merchants, Adolf Fuchs, had come to Aruba in the 1930s, probably from Poland. He and the Polish Jew, Israel Gelbstein, began *THE No. 1 Store*, a store for ladies', men's and children's clothing and general merchandise. This Gelbstein was actually named Weisinger, but he had his mother's name placed in his passport, which enabled him to escape compulsory military service since her name was not registered. Initially, he lived on Curaçao where he was employed in a coffee shop. Later he purchased merchandise from the Curaçao wholesaler *Peicher & Kardonski* and took it to Aruba.

Like the Wiznitzer brothers on Curaçao, Fuchs began importing goods from Japan starting as early as the mid 1930s. "In 1939 he was on the same boat on which my husband and I sailed to Kobe", recalled Ida Hirschberg. "He also went to buy merchandise." Although Fuchs and Salomon Wiznitzer lived on different islands, at an advanced age they still made business trips together to the Far East, recalled Salomon's son 'Butchie' Wiznitzer.

Fuchs and Gelbstein initially were in business with Chaim Gottfried, a Romanian merchant that also came to Aruba via Curaçao. But after a while, he left the threesome in order to found *Casa Haime*, a wholesale business that still exists. Gelbstein was married to Chava Gerstenbluth, Isaac Gerstenbluth's sister, who had lived on Sint Maarten and later moved to New York (see the portrait in Chapter 6).

Charles Fuhrmann from the *Spritzer + Fuhrmann* store (later to be famous, see also the portrait in Chapter 13) temporarily left Curaçao for Aruba in the early 1930s in order to see whether he could earn money there. At the time, business on Curaçao was going through a rough patch. He began a store on the Nassaustraat, called *German Watchmaker*. At the 50th anniversary of *Spritzer + Fuhrmann* in 1977, he said that it was nothing more than a space that he had built in under an overhanging balcony. In the evening hours he repaired watches. During the day, he went from house to house selling cuckoo clocks.

But the sales were disappointing. He felt he could earn more money at the Lago refinery in San Nicolas. So he started a simple store there, which was

A Torah cloak in the synagogue on Aruba, donated by the children of Leon Tauber, who traveled from Poland to Curaçao around 1929. In the 1980s, he moved to Aruba. (Photo: Dr. Mario Gurevich, MD)

A SHTETL UNDER THE SUN **192**

The synagogue Beth Israel on Aruba. (photo: collection of the Beth Israel congregation)

actually a branch of Curaçao's *Spritzer + Fuhrmann*. For purchasing and for the necessary contacts, he traveled back and forth to Curaçao, but in the end he wanted to return there definitely. The Aruban branch was then first run by Spritzer's son Ernö. Later Leo Berlinski ran the business. Over time *Spritzer + Fuhrmann* had seven stores on Aruba.

After the war, the Ashkenazic merchants from Curaçao started spreading their wings to expand their businesses to Aruba. Herman and Leon Tauber's sons, for example, opened a branch store of the successful Curaçao fashion shop *Aquarius* on Aruba at the end of the 1970s. Their mother, Miriam Tauber: "They bought the newest collections of Italian and French designers in Europe, which were gaining in popularity. Their clientele consisted largely of Venezuelans, who sometimes flew to the island in private planes for a day of shopping." For them, too, the fall of the Venezuelan bolivar in 1983 marked the end of a successful business.

Youth Camp on Aruba

On personal levels as well, there were many contacts between the Jews of the two islands. Gottfried's daughter Martha, for instance, regularly traveled for a weekend to her native island Curaçao, where she visited friends and family. It was there that she met her future husband, Lucien 'Lucky' Hirschberg.

To strengthen the contacts, the first Jewish youth camp was held on Aruba from 13 to 24 August 1947. Isaac Kisilevich recalled that for the occasion about twenty members of the Maccabi youth club were allowed to sail from Curaçao to Aruba on the Dutch war ship Van Speijk. This had been arranged by Governor Kasteel. The Sephardic leader Jessurun Cardozo led the group, father Chaim Kisilevich went along as chaperone and cook, and on Aruba Chaim Gottfried was in charge of the organization. The youth stayed at the Country Club of the Aruban Jews, ten of whom took part in the camp.

Only a Small Congregation

After the war, the Jewish community expanded with the arrival of a few Dutch Jews. They were hoping to build a new life for themselves on Aruba. Jaap de Vries and Isidoor de Vries (not related), for example, who later both moved to Curaçao. Or Isidoor Kan, who fairly quickly with an Aruban partner started the company *Oduber & Kan,* now a well-known optician's store.

In 1950, out of the 50,000 Aruban inhabitants, approximately 150 were Jewish.[164] But over time the number of Jews on the island declined again. In the 1960s, many Aruban young people left to study abroad. Some of their parents moved away with them and thus the congregation became smaller. This meant that the social center at the Country Club died a quiet death. The congregation has continued to exist and in 2011 had some 70 members out of a total island population of approximately 107,500.

The 'Calypso Jews' of Trinidad[165]

Another island where many Eastern European Jews settled is Trinidad. Due to flexible immigration laws, this island received a flood of Eastern European and German Jews between 1936 and 1939. As a result, in 1939 the calypso island had some 600 Jews, nearly all refugees from Europe. Before that time, only a handful of Jewish families from Eastern Europe, primarily from Romania, lived there.

On Curaçao, the Ashkenazim for the most part were economic refugees – although their departure from Eastern Europe was also prompted by the growing anti-Semitism there. On Trinidad the Jews were primarily refugees who had escaped Nazism. In most of the countries in the region, these refugees were no longer welcome during those years, but in Trinidad a deposit of fifty British pounds was enough to gain admission. The money was returned after one year.

This is how the Vorona family from Romania came to Trinidad at the start of 1939. Liza Vorona traveled with her son Shura and her mother Rachel Faerman (see Chapter 9). Their boat ticket (see p. 108) states that the trip booked was actually from Amsterdam to Curaçao, but due to stricter admission requirements, they were no longer welcome on that island. So they then left for Trinidad, where Liza's husband lived. A couple of months later, mother Faerman decided to settle on Curaçao, where her son Joske and daughter Manea already lived. She was probably allowed to enter the island because it concerned a family reunion.

Also in 1939, a sister of the Curaçao jeweler Wilu Weisinger left Czernowitz just in time to be able to settle on Trinidad with her husband. Her brother and his family also took up their residence on Trinidad for several years, after having first lived on Curaçao.

Philip Suchar, who in 1947 was to marry Dora Cheis on Curaçao, arrived on Trinidad in 1939 from the Romanian city of Herţa with his brothers Jacob and Moses. They had actually wanted to go to Maracaibo in Venezuela, where their uncle lived who had paid for their trip. But they were not welcome there.

On 15 January 1939, Trinidad too locked its doors to foreigners. Two thousand refugees from Hamburg bound for Trinidad were refused admission. And here, too, with the outbreak of the Second World War, it was decided that all Germans, Austrians and Italians had to be interned, including the Jews from these countries (see Chapter 7). The difference was that here the Jewish families were separated from the Germans from the very start. The Jews were first kept on a small island off the coast, later on the mainland. In 1943 – later than on Bonaire and Curaçao – the Jews were freed under a number of restrictions. This meant that they had to report to the police daily, had a curfew between 8 in the evening and 6 in the morning, could not ride a bicycle or drive a car, etc. Those who came from Romania, such as the Suchar brothers, were not interned, but they did have to report in daily as foreign nationals.

Just as on Curaçao, many immigrants started out as peddlers and quickly opened small stores. In the capital Port of Spain, a synagogue and a community center were established. According to Dora Suchar-Cheis, who lived on Trinidad for 30 years, it was not a real synagogue but, as at first on Curaçao, a rented house with a bimah, from where the Torah was read. The congregation never had its own rabbi or chazzan.

A Temporary Haven

Because Trinidad was not the first choice for most Jews, they left the island as soon as possible. Over the course of time, many of them settled in Israel and Canada. The longing for a different country was very noticeable, recalled Dora

For Saul Suchar's bar mitzvah in 1966, the entire family came to Trinidad from Curaçao and Venezuela. Behind the table, from left to right: Philip Suchar (Maracaïbo), Dora Suchar-Cheis, Moses Suchar, Tila Gerstenbluth-Cheis and Bill Gerstenbluth (both from Curaçao). (photo: private collection of Dora Suchar-Cheis)

Suchar-Cheis. "The Jews often stood with one foot on the island, the other foot already on their way to a new destination."

By the end of the 1940s, only some 50 Jewish families still lived on Trinidad. When the Suchars left for Curaçao in 1977, no more than two or three were left. This was in part due to the *Black Power* movement, which was active on Trinidad at the time. Regularly, there were riots and with the prewar razzias in Europe still fresh in their minds, nearly all the remaining Jews left the island for security reasons. This was the final blow for the once so flourishing Jewish community on Trinidad.

▶ ### Helen Frankel-Ashendorf (Curaçao, 1930)

Helen Frankel-Ashendorf. (photo: Jeannette van Ditzhuijzen)

"My grandfather's surname is Weisinger, but my father is named Ashendorf, my grandmother's maiden name. That is because my grandparents were first only married under the Jewish faith. Only later did they marry under the law. My father had already been born by that time. Since my uncle Wilu is younger, his surname is Weisinger."

"My father is from Czernowitz. He came to Curaçao around 1927/1928 and therefore was one of the first Ashkenazic Jews on the island. During a trip back to Europe, he picked up my mother from Sniatyn. I was born on Curaçao, but a year later we moved to Jamaica, where my sister Martha was born. We lived on Barbados for a couple of months after that and then we went to Trinidad, where we lived for a long time."

"Trinidad had a small Jewish community after the war, smaller than the one on Curaçao. Because my father had a strong Jewish identity and wanted us to grow up in a real Jewish community, we moved to Cuba around 1947 because it had a large Jewish community. He thought it would be a better place for us to grow up in."

"On Curaçao my father was a fabric peddler. The island was not highly developed and there were just a few stores. On Jamaica and Trinidad, he also went from door to door. But on Trinidad he later had his own store and on Cuba he opened a jewelry store."

"For high school I went to Connecticut (USA). During the vacation periods,

I returned to Cuba and that's how I met my husband, Johnny Frankel. It was important to my father that I should marry a Jewish man. That was also the primary reason that we had left Trinidad, so that my sister and I could grow up in a Jewish environment and find a Jewish husband."
"From Cuba I followed my husband to Aruba. I didn't like the island. We lived in San Nicolas, while my friends and several family members lived in Oranjestad. The Jewish community on Aruba was small, perhaps twenty families altogether. San Nicolas had no synagogue back then and we didn't have a car. So we were very isolated. That's why Curaçao appealed to me more; more of my family members and friends lived there and there was a synagogue."
"I did not speak Yiddish with my parents. I didn't learn the language until sometime around 1948, when my grandfather Weisinger came to Cuba. I am crazy about Yiddish now and still speak it every time I get the chance. But there are so few people that speak it now. Those that did speak it are nearly all dead."

16 The Relationship with the Sephardim and Mikvé Israel-Emanuel

In the first few decades after the war, the Sephardic and Ashkenazic Jews had little contact with each other in social and cultural respects. The rising prominence of the younger generation gradually changed this. At general Jewish affairs – celebrating the birthday of the state of Israel, in Jewish associations, and at lectures and courses – the members of the two congregations had more frequent contacts.

Three Groups of Jews, Three Worlds

In the postwar years, the Ashkenazim were so fond of Rabbi Isaac Jessurun Cardozo of *Mikvé Israel* that some of them even called him 'our rabbi'. The membership list of 1962 even shows that he later became an honorary member of *Shaarei Tsedek*. But the good relationship with the Sephardic rabbi could not hide the fact that, after the war, there was still a large gap between the two Jewish groups. Yes, there were friendships between Curaçao's Sephardic and Ashkenazic Jews, but they were exceptions.

The fact that the two groups rarely mixed is attested to in the narrative of Ida Hirschberg. Up until her marriage, she primarily mingled with Sephardic children because there were hardly any Ashkenazic children her age on Curaçao when she arrived as a seven-year-old in 1930. This changed when she and her husband, Salomon Wiznitzer, came back to the island after the war (see also the portrait in Chapter 8). "After returning from Japan, I associated only with the Ashkenazim. I was married to an Ashkenazic man and therefore simply belonged to that group, even though they were much more Eastern European than I was. Via my husband's business and his brothers, I also had more contacts with Ashkenazic Jews. It was his world and as his wife I lived in that environment. I also made no attempt to seek contacts outside the group. It wasn't because I rejected the Sephardic Jews or they me, but after spending six years in Japan it was an easy transition to make. Perhaps it was a matter of being lazy on my part. I simply did not want to cause any trouble."

In her book *A Reason Why*, Lucca Ginsburg-Koch writes that in the years she lived on Curaçao (1948-1953) three groups of Jews lived on the island: the Ashkenazim, the Sephardim and the Dutch Jews that wanted to build a new life for themselves in the West after the war. "The strange thing was that these three groups, although all of them Jewish, did not mingle at all. Their children shared the same bench in school, but they would never invite each other to a birthday party, or any other social gsthering."[166]

According to Bruno Linder, though, the Dutch Jews did keep company with the Ashkenazim. Some of them were members of Club Union or Maccabi, for example. One interviewee remembered that, in the 1950s, the children of the downstairs neighbors, Jews from the Netherlands, always played with her children, while their Sephardic neighbors never invited them to any event. For their part they made no contacts with the Sephardim either.

It is understandable that the Jews from the Netherlands behaved differently toward the Eastern European Jews than the Sephardic Jews. The Dutch Jews had never known the Ashkenazim as the poor wretches from the 1920s and '30s. What they saw were hard-working, prosperous fellow Jews.

Despite this more equal footing between the Dutch Jews and the Ashkenazim, in the early 1950s Salo Linder did not have the courage to ask Lies Jessurun Cardozo, daughter of a Sephardic Jewish lawyer from the Netherlands, out on a date. He was afraid he would be rejected because he was an Ashkenazic Jew. That is why he asked the Jewish 'grandma Kornmehl', a good friend of his mother's, to sound out Lies' parents cautiously about how they would view any such request in the future. They proved to have absolutely no objection and in 1955 Salo and Lies were married; in the *snoa* of course.

The Polish-born Miriam Tauber-Indich experienced the relationship between the Sephardim and the Ashkenazim as a shock. "When I came to Curaçao after the war, Sephardim lived across the street, but they seemed foreign to me. I had come out of the Holocaust and this was my first experience with Jews that were strangers to each other. I simply couldn't grasp it. I greeted them, but we didn't really have any further contact. It took another 15 to 20 years before the situation improved."

In hindsight, the Sephardic Jews acknowledge this situation. At the time, they were not at all aware that, while at school they had become friends with Ashkenazic Jews, the latter rarely if ever were invited to their homes. Ron Gomes Casseres, first a member of *Temple Emanu-El* and later *Mikvé Israel-Emanuel*: "At school there was no difference. We were all Jewish students and Jewish friends. But it ended there. I cannot remember us ever going to a *bar mitzvah* of Ashkenazic friends or to a service at *Shaarei Tsedek*. We did go to Club Union to celebrate the Jewish holidays, especially *Purim*." It didn't really become clear to him what the attitudes of the two groups toward each other were until he returned to Curaçao in 1968 after his studies. "Willy Aron Josub then told me that, when he was a child and teenager, his parents preferred he not play with the Jewish children of *Mikvé Israel*." This was partly due to the fact that the first generation of Ashkenazim – and to some degree the second – hardly considered their Sephardic fellow Jews to be Jewish at all. "It wasn't because the Ashkenazim were so deeply religious themselves", said someone from the younger generation.

The celebration of Israel's independence in the early 1950s. From left to right: Lucca Koch, Lily Bonaparte, Johnny Wachtel and Rita Wiznitzer. (photo: private collection of Isaac and Lily Kisilevich-Bonaparte)

Invitatie,

Tot het bijwonen van een Feest-avond ter gelegenheid van de eerste verjaardag van Israels onafhankelijkheid, welke zal worden gehouden op Woensdag 4 Mei a.s. te 8.30 uur n.m. op het Landgoed Oerdaal, welwillend ter beschikking gesteld door de fam. Serphos.

Feest-commissie gevormd door de leden van:

Club Macabbi
Dames comité O.S.E.
Dames comité W.I.Z.O.
Mikvé Israel.
Tempel Emanu El
Club Union
Eskanazische synagoge

Kleeding Vrij.

Jewish public holidays, such as the birthday of the state of Israel, were celebrated by the three Jewish congregations together. (from the collection of the Mongui Maduro Library, Curaçao)

"For us the faith was very much about maintaining the traditions. Perhaps, for our grandparents, the idea that they were more faithful Jews was a response to the social rejection they had experienced from the Sephardim during their first years on the island. In the 1950s and '60s, my parents did not have any Sephardic friends or acquaintances. They were two completely separate worlds."

The Future Belongs to the Youth

Gradually, the two groups grew closer together – which was primarily due to the younger generation. As early as 1964, both Ashkenazic and Sephardic children attended the Hebrew School and went to the *Oneg Shabbat* gatherings organized by Rabbi Maslin and Chazzan Swerling. Swerling also set up the *B'nai B'rith* Theater Troupe in which Sephardic and Ashkenazic young people put on plays. Swerling had attended theater school in America and had had a career in acting by the time he became the chazzan on Curaçao. He combined his two fields of training by rehearsing plays with the members of both Jewish congregations. Under his directorship, they performed works by Anton Chekhov, Noel Coward, Sholem Aleichem and Samuel Behrman. The plays were performed in Club Union.

Soon thereafter, in July 1967, Swerling returned to the United States.[167] He was originally Ashkenazic, as were Rabbi Maslin and all the rabbis and chazzans at *Mikvé Israel-Emanuel* after them.

As of 1967, it was Rabbi Leo Abrami of *Mikvé Israel-Emanuel* who again brought together the youth from both congregations. He organized a vacation program for young people, for instance. Once, he and his wife took a group of Jewish children, both Ashkenazic and Sephardic, to what was then the Coral Cliff Hotel for a weekend. Religious leader Ron Silverman (*Mikvé Israel-Emanuel*) organized a camp at *Ronde Klip* for the children of the Hebrew School.

Through all these joint activities, the Jewish children of the island got to know one another better. They visited each other more often and became friends. Morris Seibald still recalled that at *Rosh Hashanah* he and his friends would go to *Mikvé Israel* during the service's intermission. "It was mainly to see our friends. We were welcome there and I did not feel like a stranger." He also remembered the discos at their house. "We had a stereo system and on Saturday all of our friends would come to my sister Suzy's room. There we played music by the Beatles, the Moody Blues and many other bands. Our friends were a mix of Sephardim and Ashkenazim. Our parents used the Club to meet each other; the youth met at home." The Ashkenazic Jew, Berny Cheis, from the same generation, always played dominos, a typical Curaçao game, with his Sephardic friends.

Many Friendships but Few Marriages with the Sephardim

Although Ashkenazic and Sephardic children were allowed to become friends back then, marriages between them were rare. For the first generations of Ashkenazim it was extremely important that their children not only found a Jewish partner, the spouse also had to be Ashkenazic. The only exception for a long time was Ernö Spritzer. As a child, he kept company almost exclusively with Sephardim because, at the time, there were simply no Ashkenazic children his age; he was ten when he came to Curaçao in 1929. In 1943 he became the first Ashkenazic Jew to marry a Sephardic partner, Ivy Capriles.

From the 1970s, an increasing number of Ashkenazic young people went abroad to study or work. As a result, many of them came back to the island with a foreign, often Jewish partner. These partners sometimes brought other customs with them. One positive side effect was that, in social terms, these spouses saw no difference between the Ashkenazic and the Sephardic Jews on Curaçao. Like the Dutch Jews on Curaçao after the war, they were unfamiliar with the two communities' prior history.

Shaarei Tsedek does not want to modernize

Although *Mikvé Israel* was orthodox before 1964, that changed after its merger with the liberal Temple *Emanu-El*. As a result, the religious chasm between the newly formed liberal congregation and the orthodox *Shaarei Tsedek* only grew wider. After the Sephardic merger, women were allowed to sit among the men and from then on women were also counted for the formation of a minyan. The initial hope of Rabbi Maslin was that the Ashkenazic congregation would join in the merger; but that proved to be in vain. It was simply not an option for *Shaarei Tsedek*.

Maslin's liberal ideas were not really welcomed anyway by some of the older guard among the Ashkenazim. After his *bar mitzvah*, Morris Seibald wanted to attend the Jewish classes that Maslin taught to teenagers. "But I wasn't allowed to go. My grandfather forbade it." Fela Seibald-Meit recalled that her uncle Traytel Oberman was also against because the liberal Maslin would teach the youth wrong ideas.

In the 1960s and '70s, Lily Kisilevich-Bonaparte and her husband Isaac liked attending the joint courses for adults. "We got along with everyone, but in our congregation there were a couple of people who were absolutely against, including my own father. But once he saw what I had learned from the courses, he changed his mind. Yes, of course the old guard was against. And this continued to be a very big problem between the two congregations."

Another reason that the members of *Shaarei Tsedek* did not feel at home at *Mikvé Israel-Emanuel* was the language that was and still is used during the services. Since the merger, the language used has principally been English and not Hebrew, which the Ashkenazim were used to hearing at their *shiel*.

Until today the religious differences have played a role. Despite a growing number of friendships, many Ashkenazim – including the younger generation – hardly ever speak with their Sephardic friends about religious matters. As one Ashkenazic woman put it: "I do not talk with my Sephardic friends about the fact that we may not read from the Torah or wear a *tallit*. It's because we do not want to put each other in an awkward position. There are enough problems as it is. My Sephardic friends respect me and I respect them. And when push comes to shove and I need them, then I am sure that they will be there for me and I for them."

Between Rosh Hashanah and Yom Kippur, the members of Shaarei Tsedek and Mikvé Israel-Emanuel commemorate the dead together. To the left is Chazzan Avery Tracht of Mikvé Israel, to the right is Rabbi Ariel Yeshurun of Shaarei Tsedek. (photo: Jeannette van Ditzhuijzen)

Ashkenazim in the Snoa

Not all Ashkenazim were against a merger with the Sephardic congregation. Some of them already attended the *snoa* regularly. Following his *bar mitzvah* in 1945, Isaac Kisilevich occasionally served as the tenth man in the *snoa*. "At the end of the Sabbath on Saturday evening they held a small service there. Since my father's business on the Madurostraat was near the *snoa*, they could easily call on me. I also sang in their choir."

Starting in the 1960s, a few Ashkenazim became members of both *Shaarei Tsedek* and *Mikvé Israel-Emanuel*. Initially, the Ashkenazic Dutchman Jochanan Taytelbaum, who arrived from Jamaica during the war, went with his parents to the *snoa* only. It wasn't until after he married the Ashkenazi Lea Groisman, that he joined *Shaarei Tsedek*. Taytelbaum became president there. Later, he and his wife attended the *snoa* again. From 1979 to 1984, he even was the first non-Sephardic president of *Mikvé Israel-Emanuel*. "Since then I have been an *Ashkephardi*." In an earlier stage Herman Gärtner had been a board member at *Mikvé Israel-Emanuel* for several years and Morris Gandelman sat on the board from 1984.

Conversely, *Shaarei Tsedek* had a Sephardic president for the first time in 1990: Paul Morón, who is married to Taicy Gerstenbluth, an Ashkenazi. The Sephardic Jew Aron Abady also served as the president of the Ashkenazic congregation.

But Taytelbaum, Gärtner, Gandelman and other Ashkenazim that became members of the *snoa* were exceptions. The majority of the Ashkenazim stuck to their own congregation. They could not accept a merger with the Sephardim, although from the bulletin of *Shaarei Tsedek* in 1976 it seems that an overwhelming majority was in favor of closer ties with the other congregation. Yet nothing came of it.

The Women Unite: the OSE and the WIZO

In one area, though, there were contacts between the Sephardim and the Ashkenazim very early on – in the women's associations. In 1946, Sonia Kisilevich founded a branch of the OSE, *Œuvre de Secours aux Enfants*, a French organization that during the war saved hundreds of Jewish children from Vichy France. At its founding in Russia in 1912, the organization was still called OZE, *Obshchetsvo Zdravookhraneniya Yevreyiev*. It was intended to provide help to needy Jews. In the time of the Holocaust, the organization mainly concerned itself with children left behind after their parents had been transported to the concentration camps. After the war, it provided medical and social assistance to children. The Curaçao OSE had more Ashkenazic than Sephardic women among its members.

The OSE and Maccabi often jointly organized evenings featuring a film or a lecture. The proceeds were donated to the OSE. The OSE also sent food packages and clothing to Israel. For this purpose, Bertha Schmidt, the driving force behind the organization on Curaçao, collected clothing from Jewish families twice a year. Aruba also had an OSE.

Two years later, on 5 April 1948, the Jewish women of Curaçao united in a local branch of the WIZO, the Women's International Zionist Organization.[168] This volunteers' organization is dedicated to promoting the welfare of women in Israel and the Diaspora. According to Jane Gomes Casseres in her book *Generation to Generation*, it was the only association in those years where Sephardic and Ashkenazic women met socially.[169]

According to those interviewed, the Sephardic and Ashkenazic women indeed worked together harmoniously within the WIZO and women from both Jewish groups were equally active in raising money for Israel. In 1963 they raised 6,750 Antillean guilders for the *Children's Vocational Training* in Israel.

Shortly after the Six-Day War in 1967, Norma Moreno (a Sephardic woman that was active for the WIZO for 22 years) and others arranged for Golda Meir, who later became Israel's Prime Minister, to come to Curaçao. According to people who were present, the meeting with Meir at Club Union was a big event. Meir spoke to everyone there and she thanked the community for the money that the WIZO had raised for Israeli soldiers. During the Yom Kippur War of 1973 the WIZO again raised money for Israel.

Emily David-Fruchter recalled that Mary Sterental, who for years was active for the WIZO, always competed with her fellow Ashkenazi Bertha Schmidt of the OSE. After Ms Schmidt died in the early 1970s, the OSE faded away.[170]

Joint Dedication to a Good Cause

Although the three congregations generally operated entirely separately, during the war they worked together in the Jewish Aid Committee (see Chapter 7). Furthermore, the Monthly Magazine for Israeli Households on the Netherlands Antilles had been in existence since 1940. It was issued by *Mikvé Israel*, but – seeing the attention given to the activities of Club Union and Maccabi – it was clearly meant to be read by the Ashkenazic Jews as well. This is also apparent from the names of Ashkenazic children that regularly appeared in the magazine's youth column. They would be mentioned for things such as winning a prize for the monthly puzzle.

There were more activities for which the Sephardic congregation opened itself to the Ashkenazim. During the war, in 1942, a Jewish study club *Or Chadash* (New Light) was founded. According to a report in the monthly newsletter of *Mikvé Israel* for April/May 1943, Ashkenazic Jews were also members of this club: on the occasion of *Purim* Fanya Milstein, an Ashkenazi, gave a recitation in Hebrew and the brothers Felix and Bruno Linder played the violin. Due to the blackout measures that were in force during the war, the club evenings had to be cancelled regularly.

After the war, the Holocaust was commemorated by all Curaçao Jews together. On 17 April 1955, such a remembrance gathering took place in Club

In every Jewish home there were two savings boxes : one for the Curaçao child and the other for Keren Kayemet L'Israel (Jewish National Fund). (photo: Jeannette van Ditzhuijzen)

Union. Rabbi Schächter sang the *El Malei Rachamim*, a prayer for the Holocaust victims. The founding of the State of Israel in 1948 also brought the two communities together. From that moment on, the Ashkenazim and the Sephardim have celebrated Israel's independence together every five years.

The collection taken for the Jewish National Fund (*Keren Kayemet L'Israel* in Hebrew) was a joint effort, even though the board of the Curaçao *Keren Kayemet* Committee at the end of the 1940s was primarily made up of Ashkenazim. The committee brought together money for trees that were to be planted in Israel. This money was raised with the help of oblong blue savings boxes that could be found in every Jewish home on Curaçao. In the Monthly Magazine for Israeli Households the amounts raised each month were reported down to the last cent, along with the names of the generous givers. People also donated one or more trees on the occasion of weddings, *bar mitzvahs*, Father's Day or Mother's Day. The *Keren Kayemet* boxes were also to be found in all Jewish stores, both Sephardic and Ashkenazic. One of the people interviewed recalled that in the 1970s the BBYO youth used to pick up these boxes so that they could be emptied.

Joint donations were also made. The guests at the wedding of Mali Seibald and A. Gruzecki, for instance, in 1955 donated 58 trees as a group. In May 1954, at the celebration of Israel's independence, a tea service donated by *Spritzer + Fuhrmann* was auctioned off at a meeting with hundreds of people present. With the proceeds, seventy trees were purchased.

The adults also saw each other at joint gatherings. In June 1954 a small club for speakers of modern Hebrew was started. They met twice a month in Club Union, not only to learn Hebrew, but also to hear lectures and readings, followed by discussions.[171]

Outside this club, discussion evenings and lectures were also held for members of all three congregations. In March 1961, for example, the American Rabbi Simon Noveck gave a series of lectures on Curaçao. He worked in the education program for adults of the American *B'nai B'rith* organization.

Getting to Know Each Other via B'nai B'rith

A year later this organization set up a branch on Curaçao. Its foundation took place on 26 July, the day on which Alonso de Ojeda 'discovered' Curaçao in 1499. *B'nai B'rith* (Hebrew for 'Sons of the Covenant') is the oldest Jewish service club in the world. It was set up in 1843 in New York with the objectives of defending human rights, organizing education for adults and youngsters, helping hospitals and philanthropic institutions and, of course, promoting the welfare of Israel.

At the club's founding in Hotel Curaçao Intercontinentaal in 1962, a total of 32 men became members of *B'nai B'rith*. They came from all three congregations. It wasn't until 1976 that women were allowed to be members. In that year, eight women joined, including the Ashkenazim Ida Becher and Karny Vorona.

On Curaçao, *B'nai B'rith* focused on adult education, charity work and the promotion of art and culture.[172] The organization, for instance, sponsored the

The founding of B'nai B'rith on 26 July 1962, at which all three congregations were represented. (photo: private collection of Frieda Pais-Fruchter)

aforementioned plays that Chazzan Norman Swerling produced. *B'nai B'rith* also donated a thousand books on Jewish heritage to the library in 1989.[173]

For the adults, *B'nai B'rith* organized classes, movie nights and lectures on subjects such as Israel, Jewish communities in South America or political issues. These were held at the Hebrew School. Gala dinners put on for a good cause were also part of *B'nai B'rith* activities.

Frank Delvalle of the Sephardic congregation was one of the founders of *B'nai B'rith*. At the meetings, he got to know the Ashkenazic Jews better and he became friends with them. He also spoke more often with Eastern European Jews via Rabbi Maslin's adult education classes. Because he thought it was his duty as a Jew to set an example, he became a Club Union member. He wanted the Jews to act as a joint community, for the benefit of both the local population and Israel.

B'nai B'rith still exists today.

Taking in Cuban Jews[174]

The reception of Jewish refugees from Cuba at the end of 1965 was also a matter that involved both the Sephardim and the Ashkenazim. This concerned 11 families (42 people) that had escaped the communist Castro regime; so it was not a matter of religious persecution. The original plan was for the Cubans to travel on to their final destination within three months. Nearly all of them wanted to go to the United States to be reunited with relatives. But as of 1 December 1965, this unfortunately was no longer possible. After that date, only people with specific knowledge or skills were admitted to the US from Latin America. Most of the Cuban Jews that had come to Curaçao were merchants and storekeepers without any specific education. Israel was not an option for most of them because of its entirely different environment. With respect to their language and culture, a South American country was a much more logical choice.

These refugees were received under the auspices of *B'nai B'rith*, while the HIAS (Hebrew Immigrant Aid Society) paid for the majority of the costs involved in taking them in. Local businesses also attributed their share. After a stay in the Park Hotel at a greatly reduced rate, the Cubans were able to move into Shell staff accommodations. The Central Jewish Committee, set up especially for the occasion, consisted of members from both Jewish congregations. The religious leaders of *Shaarei Tsedek* and *Mikvé Israel-Emanuel* also showed concern for the refugees.

The committee organized trips to the beach and even birthday parties for the children. It also made sure that each Cuban family had someone from the Jewish community to ensure that they could find their way on the island. For years, Lily Kisilevich-Bonaparte kept in touch with 'her' Cuban family, which finally traveled on to Panama.

The social gap that originally existed between the two communities is no longer there. Today Sephardic and Ashkenazic children have the same opportunities, study at the same universities and are each other's friends. Yet some Ashkenazic Jews, even young ones, still find themselves thinking in terms of 'us' and 'them'; regardless of the good friendships they have forged with members of *Mikvé Israel-Emanuel*. And some Ashkenazim still do not feel welcome in the *snoa*, or at least they do not feel at ease there.

▶ ## Sheila Seibald-Delvalle (Curaçao, 1954)

"I grew up in a Sephardic Jewish family and we were members of *Mikvé Israel*, which was the orthodox congregation until 1964. My parents would not allow me to go to the Temple of the liberal congregation and I still remember very clearly that I went there for the first time when I was eleven. I went with friends of my parents. I was particularly surprised that it did not look like a church, as I had expected. But this does show that there were differences within the Sephardic community as well, just as between the Ashkenazic and Sephardic congregations."

"Our neighbors were Ashkenazim and as a child I had several Ashkenazic friends, both boys and girls. Because my mother had lived on the island for only a short time during her childhood, when she returned she did not have the prejudices against the Ashkenazic Jews that most Sephardim harbor."

"Through the Hebrew School, the young people of both congregations came more and more in contact with each other. Together with the Ashkenazic girls we had confirmation, and at school we really learned a lot about the substance of Judaism from Rabbi Maslin of the Temple. Joint activities were organized, which meant that occasionally I went to *Shaarei*

Sheila Seibald

Tsedek. But I also went there because I had Ashkenazic friends."

"After the merger of the two Sephardic congregations in 1964, I got used to seeing men and women sitting together and to women being counted to form a minyan. When I married Morris, an Ashkenazic man, in 1975, we were faced with a dilemma – which synagogue should we attend? *Rosh Hashanah* presented no problem; the Ashkenazim celebrate it on two days while we do it on one day. But for the rest of the year it was a dilemma, all the more so because both families had certain expectations of us. Rabbi Aaron Peller of *Mikvé Israel-Emanuel* then took the step of approaching my parents-in-law. He emphasized the fact that we were all Jews and asked them why they did not come to *Mikvé Israel-Emanuel* every now and then. The idea appealed to them, especially to my father-in-law, and they joined *Mikvé Israel-Emanuel*. After that, more people became members of both congregations. Sometimes it was because at a particular moment *Shaarei Tsedek* did not have a rabbi. Or because at *Mikvé Israel-Emanuel* women could participate in the service more."

"Our marriage was consecrated by Rabbi Levin of *Shaarei Tsedek* and Chazzan Slavensky of *Mikvé Israel-Emanuel*. We were given a *ketubah* (marriage contract) by Levin and one by *Mikvé Israel-Emanuel*. Our son's *brith milah* was also attended to by two rabbis. His *bar mitzvah* was held on Saturday in the *snoa*, after he had donned the *tefillin* on Thursday in *Shaarei Tsedek*.'

17   From Polakos to Curaçao Islanders?

The Polakos sought Ashkenazic Jewish marriage partners, went to their own clubs and shiel and even lived in the same neighborhood for a long time. Still, they came in contact with the Curaçao population from the start – and not only via their stores. Gradually, the Eastern European Jews fully participated in the Curaçao community, even though not everyone felt like a real Curaçaoan.

Shell and Population Growth in the 1920s

Curaçao's population has always been very mixed, but also rather segmented. That is to say, each segment of the population has its own social institutions and there is little or no interaction between these segments. Thus the two segments that traditionally made up the elite class on the island – the Sephardic Jews and the white Protestants – had few contacts with each other until well into the 20th century. At the beginning of the 20th century, a Catholic elite arose, consisting of whites and light-skinned people. Next to this elite the population consisted primarily of Roman Catholic Afro-Curaçaoans.

The composition of the population changed after Shell had opened a refinery on the island in 1918 (see Chapter 4). The refinery urgently needed personnel and recruited migrant laborers; primarily from the Caribbean Region (the Windward Islands, the British West Indies, Venezuela and Suriname). Shell kept these nationalities segregated by housing them in separate sheds and barracks. This created a Suriname village, a Venezuelan camp, etc. This segregation policy was abolished after the Second World War, but for quite some time the different population groups continued to live in the same neighborhood, which is now called Suffisant and is located far outside Punda and Otrobanda.

Thus, in a short span of time, the local population was confronted with several groups of foreigners. Each group spoke its own language, had its own customs and established its own clubs. As a result, and due to segregated living, initially there was no integration between the newcomers and the old inhabitants of the island. In that respect, the *Polakos* had an advantage: after arriving on Curaçao in the 1920s and '30s, most of them found a room, floor, house or boardinghouse in Punda, Otrobanda or in Pietermaai. So they lived among the local population. They also had a lot of contacts with Curaçaoans in other ways: working as peddlers, they called on their houses on a daily basis and later the local population shopped in their Punda and Otrobanda stores.

More Groups of Economic Immigrants

During those years, Dutch people also settled on the island: Shell senior managers and civil servants that came to reinforce the government apparatus. In addition to all of these new island inhabitants, Curaçao was also home to immigrant merchants, some of whom arrived before the Ashkenazim. Like the Eastern European Jews, they benefited from the increased prosperity that the refinery generated.

At the start of the 20th century for instance, before the arrival of Shell, immigrants had come to Curaçao from Syria and Lebanon. On the island they were referred to as 'Arabs' or 'Turkos'. Like the Ashkenazic Jews, these immigrants arrived penniless, but quickly climbed the economic ladder through hard work. The East Indians were another group, not recruited by Shell either, that moved to the island (see Chapter 13).

A third group, the Chinese, came to Curaçao at the start of the 20th century, some of them for jobs at Shell. They came mostly from surrounding islands. Others came on the off chance they could find work. Gradually they started their own stores, often selling food. The Chinese also had laundries and (takeaway) restaurants.

In the second half of the 20th century, a fourth group of immigrants became active in trade: the Portuguese. Most of them were from Madeira and they were originally brought to Curaçao by Shell. After their dismissal in the 1950s, some remained on the island. In the 1960s, a range of food stores and supermarkets were acquired by these Portuguese.

So the *Polakos* were by no means the only immigrants in the 1930s that tried to make a place for themselves under the Curaçao sun. In some areas they quickly found a connection with the locals, while in other fields they preferred to follow their own path.

Work as a Means of Integrating

The fact that the Ashkenazim opened their stores on the Sabbath from the very start shows that they were willing to adapt to the society in which they had ended up. Actually, they had no choice – Saturday was the most important day of the week in terms of sales. The stores were frequented by all strata of the Curaçao population and they often employed local personnel. Through these employees, the Ashkenazim gradually built up social contacts with the Afro-Curaçao population. Sometimes, members of staff would invite their employers for occasions such as the First Communion. In turn, some Ashkenazim invited the salesgirls to Jewish festivals. In a few cases, even children went to each other's birthday parties.

The relationships between personnel and storeowners were sometimes so good that some employees gave their children Jewish names. Thus Erwin Koense named his first son David. "In honor of my employer, Herman Gärtner." During those years, Koense attended many a *bar mitzvah* and *brith milah* and felt as though the Gärtners had adopted him as a member of the family. Before *La Aurora*, Koense worked at *Tauber Hermanos*. "I lived in San Juan at the time, on the western side of the island, and I regularly took the Tauber children fishing in my father's boat."

Some Ashkenazim understood that a good social network was essential for a businessman and they made sure they got in touch with the right people. Gilbert Wawoe named Bernardo Metsch (1911-1978) and Charles Fuhrmann (1906-1989) as examples. "Metsch clearly understood that you needed a social network. When you entered his store, there were always people from the Curaçao community, drinking a coffee. Civil servants or politicians. He also did charity work; not only for his own group but also for the local community, with whom he kept in close touch. Thus, he was also able to achieve things for his own Jewish community."

According to Wawoe, Charles Fuhrmann had a similar social network and, like Metsch, he quite regularly invited non-Jews to Jewish festivities. "Unlike the white Dutchmen in those years, who did not so readily engage with the locals. The gap between the white transients and the black islanders was larger than that between the *Polakos* and the blacks."

Both Jochanan Taytelbaum and Shura Vorona were active in the Curaçao Chamber of Commerce, but generally speaking the Ashkenazic merchants did not play a visible role in the association. A small number of Ashkenazim, though, was involved in the storekeepers' association of Otrobanda (the *Sosiedat di Komershantenan di Otrobanda*): Leon Seibald, Isaac Kisilevich and Isaac Grynsztein, for example. In the 1990s Yak Baroud took over the chair of the association from Leon Seibald. "In the 1980s, I was still attending school in Lebanon and I only came to Curaçao during vacations. Seibald would then always take me along to a local eatery. I found the *Polakos* to be very integrated into the island's society and that inspired me to integrate as they had done."

Living in the Same Neighborhood

It wasn't long before the Eastern European Jews' businesses were doing so well that they were able to trade in their simple houses in the city for larger quarters in the outlying districts of Willemstad. The districts of Mahaai and Van Engelen, in particular, were popular. So many Ashkenazim lived on one street in Van Engelen – the Boy Ecuryweg – that the Jews jokingly referred to it as the 'Jewish ghetto'.

According to Willy Aron Josub, his family was the first to move to the Boy

The Boy Ecuryweg. (photo: Jeannette van Ditzhuijzen)

Ecuryweg. "My father owned several lots and resold the plots of land next door I think, to the Brandes and Weisinger families. I know for sure that the house on the corner, where we lived, was built in 1942."

In addition to the aforementioned families, the U-shaped street was also where the Ackerman, Meit, Oberman, Silberstein, Crivosei, Vorona and many other families lived. Until well into the 1960s, it was a real 'Jewish street'. Esty da Costa-Frankel's grandparents (Ashendorf) and several uncles and aunts also lived on the Boy Ecuryweg. "You could go from house to house or simply climb over the fence. It was really a wonderful street. The only non-Jew that I can remember living there was police officer Gieling. I was friends with his daughter." A number of Ashkenazic Jews also lived on the adjacent Van Engelenweg. In this neighborhood, everyone knew everybody else, all the children played together and the neighbors helped each other. Marie Brandes recalled that the food for her wedding and that of her sister was cooked by neighbors and acquaintances and then brought to the Club. "The entire street lent a hand. To them you were family."

The Wiznitzers were one of the few families that had no inclination to move to the outlying districts. Until sometime in the 1970s, they lived in the chic district of Scharloo, where during the war Abraham Wiznitzer had two houses built. One was shared by his brothers Moishe and Salomon and their families and his uncle Shmiel. He himself lived on the top floor of the other house. In 1954, Abraham made room on his floor for Rabbi Schächter and his family. Salomon's son

'Butchie' remembered how the rabbi, who also served as a *shochet*, used to wrap himself up in a white garment to slaughter the chickens for the Jewish High Holidays in the garden between the two houses.

The only people that lived in an entirely different part of Curaçao, i.e. east of the city center, were the furniture dealers Selig, Salomon and Moishe Seibald. They had their houses, workplace and warehouse on the somewhat eccentrically located Caracasbaaiweg, across from one another.

Today, the Ashkenazic Jews still live in the beautiful outlying districts of Willemstad, only now more spread out over the island and among other Curaçaoans.

Children Go to (White) Public Schools

Curaçao has no Jewish daytime education. After they had arrived on the island, the Ashkenazim could choose to send their children to public or Roman Catholic schools. Like the Sephardic Jews, they preferred the public schools: initially the Hendrik School (for boys) and the Wilhelmina School (for girls), both located in Punda. Later, after the Ashkenazim had left Punda and Otrobanda, most of the children attended the public Johan van Walbeeck School in Mahaai.

For high school, the Jewish parents also preferred public schools for their children. Like the Sephardim, most Eastern European Jews attended the A.M.S., i.e. the *Algemene Middelbare School* or General Secondary School, established in 1941 and later renamed Peter Stuyvesant College. The Radulphus College and the Maria Immaculata Lyceum, both Roman Catholic institutions, were simply not considered.

At school the Jewish children therefore came in contact with the local population, though seldom with native Afro-Curaçaoans. This was not only because these were predominantly Roman Catholic and attended other schools, but also because until the 1970s whites and blacks rarely kept each other's company. From the start, though, there were friendships with white Curaçaoans. Curaçao historian James Schrils recalled that he played with Ashkenazic children, even at their homes. Gitta Meit, who arrived on the island after the war when she was nine, mentioned Curaçao school friends (white and black) who came home with her. "The relationship with Curaçao's population was always good. We went to each other's birthday parties, but our respective parents did not keep company with one another. Also, our parents did not speak the local language yet."

These days many Ashkenazic children attend the international school. Here the prevailing language, English, presents no barrier when one of the parents comes from South America or the United States. But the children, have less contact with the local population because this school is elite and fairly expensive.

For their higher education, the Ashkenazim prefer to go to the USA, in contrast to most other Curaçaoans, who go to the Netherlands to study. The Eastern European Jews were oriented towards America from the very start and they often had family and/or friends living there who had been able to emigrate to the

United States in the 1920s. Initially, many of them enrolled in practical study programs such as business administration, which would come in handy when they took over their parents' companies. But some of the generation born since the 1950s headed in an entirely different direction: medicine, pharmacology, law, chemistry or psychology. Bruno Linder and Piet Meit were trailblazers: they left for America to enroll in higher education as early as the 1940s.

Preferably a Partner from One's Own Set

Integrating in Curaçao society by looking for a marriage partner in the local population was not an option for the Eastern European Jews. They preferred marriage partners from the Jewish populations in South America, Israel, North America and (initially) Eastern Europe.

Lily Kisilevich said that, as a child in the 1950s, you knew only too well that you were expected to marry another Jew. "The same was true for most Jews on Curaçao. I still remember a girl that used to hang around with non-Jewish boys – she was beaten by her mother with a belt. Another girl was punished by being grounded for a long time. Our group always went to the movies on Friday evening, where we would of course meet boys; Jewish boys."

Another woman interviewed said she did not feel pressured to come home with a Jewish boy. "But I knew that I simply could not come home with a non-Jewish boy. Is that pressure?" In the 1970s, one Jewish woman who was dating a non-Jewish boy, was sent to Israel by her mother. There she met and married a Jewish man, with whom she had two children. She has since divorced, but she does not blame her mother.

According to the generation that grew up in the 1960s and '70s, it was (and is) very difficult to find a Jewish partner on Curaçao. One of them said: "It is difficult enough to find someone nice; the fact that he or she also has to be Jewish makes it all the more difficult. Many people in Miami, where there is a large Jewish community, are looking for Jewish spouses and even there it is not easy."

Another woman said that the Jewish community on Curaçao in the 1960s was so small (300 to 400 Ashkenazim out of approximately 135,000 inhabitants) that she had known all the Jewish boys since they were very young and therefore saw them mainly as brothers. She had an agreement with one of the Ashkenazic boys that she knew well. He would pick her up and take her back home at night. In the meantime, they would separately have their own evenings out; sometimes even keeping company with non-Jews. Her parents would certainly not have approved. For example, when her sister's non-Jewish friends came by, they were made to wait for her out at the front gate.

In the 1980s and '90s, several Ashkenazim looked for a marriage partner in Caracas, which had a large Jewish community. It was not uncommon for them to indeed come back home with a Jewish partner. On the other hand, marriages with non-Jewish partners are not as uncommon these days as they were back then, even though most parents would still prefer their son or daughter to marry a Jew. One Jewish boy who was asked how important it was for him to marry a

Jewish girl answered: "Actually, it is not that important, but marrying a Jewish girl would make life a lot easier. So for that reason alone it is important."

Traditional ideas still live on today, as is revealed by a quote from Hannah Elmaleh, one of the women that left for America with her children in 2009. "I do not want my children to grow up in a congregation in which mixed marriages are acceptable. There have to be limits. I want my children to have a certain kind of life and I do not want the traditions that my family passed on to me to be forgotten. I am also afraid of a slippery slope: if you accept one thing, you eventually end up accepting the other."

Speaking Dutch, Papiamento and Other Languages

The ability to speak and read the new country's language is always the prominent means for newcomers to (be able to) get in touch with the local population and find their way around in the new society. The Eastern European Jews seem to have mastered the island's languages, Dutch and Papiamento, quite quickly. At the same time, the first generation of Ashkenazim held on to Yiddish for a long

Out on the town in the car in the 1930s. At far left, dressed in white: Bernardo Metsch. Seated, from left to right: Samuel Brandes, Sonja Kisilevich, Liza Becher, Isaac Kisilevich, Otilia Kisilevich and Fajwel Becher. At the wheel is Abram Ackerman with Molka Weisinger behind him. Behind the unknown child: Fanya Becher, next to her is Berta Becher. Standing: Chaim Kisilevich. (photo: private collection of Fanya Gandelman-Becher)

time. It was, after all, the language they spoke at home with their children. But the children quickly learned both Dutch and Papiamento at school. Sloima Zonenschain, who was seven when he arrived on the island, spoke 'Papiamento like a Curaçaoan', according to a *yu'i Korsou*.

Outside the family, during Maccabi meetings for instance, the young people initially spoke mostly Dutch. Thus, the club newsletter *Shomer Hanóar* was published in Dutch. Only the club song was in Hebrew.[175] In the 1960s, in contrast, the *Polakos* primarily spoke English among themselves in the schoolyard, as a former student of Peter Stuyvesant College remembered. With the other students they spoke Dutch and/or Papiamento.

Because of the stores that several newcomers started in the 1930s, the first generation of Ashkenazim quickly learned to speak Papiamento as well. This contrasted with the East Indians, most of whom have continued to speak English, even when they deal with local customers. Among themselves, the older Ashkenazim spoke Yiddish, particularly if they did not want others to understand what they were saying. But they spoke it so often that, over the course of time, many Curaçao shop assistants also learned to speak and/or understand Yiddish.

For official letters to the government or an organization, the first generation did not always master Dutch sufficiently well. Gilbert Wawoe, former Shell director and State Councilor, remembered that he sometimes helped Bernardo Metsch and other Ashkenazic Jews writing official letters.

Spending Leisure Time with Curaçaoans

Because of the many detailed memories of Club Union and Maccabi, it very much seems as though the Ashkenazim primarily spent their free time in each other's company. Yet, apparently there were also many contacts with the local population. Fanya Gandelman recalled that her family and the Ackerman family owned a car as early as the 1930s. They and the Kisilevich family would drive nearly every Sunday to the Santa Cruz estate on the west side of Curaçao. "My father had a friend that lived there and we would spend the entire day at the estate. We took hammocks along, had picnics and swam in the bay. At the end of the day, we were allowed to fill the car with the mangos that lay under the hundreds of mango trees."

The owner of the Santa Cruz plantation at the time was August George Statius Muller, popularly known as 'shon Eti'. He was a member of the white Protestant elite and was, at one time, Chairman of the Colonial Council. According to his nephew, the Curaçao pianist and composer Wim Statius Muller, only family and good friends were admitted to the bay and the garden in those days. So apparently the Becher, Kisilevich and Ackerman families had made good contacts beyond their own Jewish circles in a short span of time – all three men arrived on Curaçao before or in 1930.

As early as the 1940s, several *Polakos* joined the 'Rimboezwervers' (Jungle Roamers) a scouting club not associated with any church, that was started by scout master Marinus van der Maarel. It was attended primarily by white and light-skinned Curaçaoans; Afro-Curaçaoans went to the Roman Catholic scouting club.

In the 1950s, several Ashkenazim were members of the Piscadera Bay Club. Piscadera Bay lies on the island's southern coast to the west of Willemstad. Here the Dutch and white Curaçaoans swam in those years. Though the club was initially meant for Shell employees only, other islanders could also join.

From what 'Butchie' Wiznitzer remembered, it seems that the Ashkenazim did sit together in groups once they had arrived at the Piscadera Bay Club: "The club played an important role in our lives. Many families were members and came together there on Sunday morning. Our parents sat under the large manchineel tree on the north side, while we swam in the protected coves and dived into the bay from the diving board or a wooden raft. During vacations and on days off, my friends and I also often went there to swim and play tennis."

Sports Outside One's Own Clubs

In the area of sports, Ashkenazic young people may have been active within Maccabi only, this Jewish sports club fully participated in the island competition. The young people played volleyball, for example, against the sports clubs *Kwiek* and *Van Engelen*, of which primarily white islanders were members. A former member of one of these clubs recalled that the Maccabi volleyball team was 'very good'. "We were amateurs and did little more than get the ball over the net."

Maccabi's acivities in the island's sport life are for example apparent from their participation in sports club parades. For both Princess Christina's birth (still named Marijke at the time) on 18 February 1947 and Queen Juliana's visit in 1955, the Jewish youth club put in appearances. At other Royal festivities, the youth club was always represented as well.[176]

Elias Linder, who was crazy about sports, attended the soccer matches of the Curaçao Football Association 'Volharding' back in the 1930s to cheer on the players with other soccer fans. He supported this soccer club financially as well and forewent everything else on Sunday afternoons to watch the matches. His son Bruno: "He found this just as important as going to the synagogue on Saturday morning."

The *Polakos* also participated in the Curaçao table tennis championships. Both Isuhar Meit and Sloima Zonenschain were island champions at various times. Isuhar Meit was also a tennis champion. In the 1970s, bowling became popular and the Ashkenazim went to the Watapana Bowling Alley, a non-Jewish club.

Long before Maccabi was founded in 1942, two Ashkenazic Jews joined the Chess Association 'Curaçao'. This club had been in existence since 1934 and Jacobo Fruchter was one of its first members. Charles Fuhrmann became a member in 1938. Later on, chess players could also join Maccabi or Club Union, but for a few excellent players such as Sloima Zonenschain and Morris Gandelman, those clubs represented too little challenge. Zonenschain joined the Chess Association 'Curaçao' in 1942 and remained a member for the rest of his life.

Maccabi members during the parade celebrating Princess Christina's birth in 1947. (photo: private collection of Esther Gal-Jessurun Cardozo)

Maccabi members pay tribute to the House of Orange on behalf of the State of Israel. (photo: private collection of Esther Gal-Jessurun Cardozo)

According to this page from the cashbook of the Chess Association 'Curaçao', in 1953 at least nine Ashkenazim were members. (from the archives of the Chess Association 'Curaçao')

Members of the Chess Association 'Curaçao' in 1953. Third from the right is Sloima Zonenschain. To the left behind him: Jaap de Vries and far left is Samuel Fruchter. (photo: private collection of Frieda Pais-Fruchter)

During an interview held on the anniversary of his 50th year of membership in 1992, he said that he and Morris Gandelman had known one another from Noua Suliţă and secretly played chess together in 1937 during the religious lessons they received at the Hendrik School. Gandelman was also a member of the Curaçao Chess Association for a long time, as were several other Ashkenazic Jews.

Not only did the Ashkenazim go to 'non-Jewish' clubs, gentiles also went to the Club to play sports. At the end of the 1960s, Erwin Koense worked at *La Aurora,* owned by Herman Gärtner, and he remembered that he often went to the Club in Scharloo to play volleyball. "I also sometimes went to the synagogue."

Club Union and Maccabi no longer exist, and even as early as the 1960s the Ashkenazim have joined the Curaçao Sports Club, the Curaçao Yachting Club and other general (sports) associations.

Contacts via Art and Culture

In the field of music, too, there were contacts with the local population, particularly through several star players in this field. The brothers Felix, Bruno and Salo Linder, for example, played the violin in the Curaçao Philharmonic Orchestra, founded in 1939 by Rudolph Boskaljon. According to J. van de Walle, a journalist on Curaçao at the time, this orchestra, made up entirely of amateurs, played a significant role on the island.[177] The famous Curaçao pianist Edgar Palm mentions Felix and Bruno Linder in his book '*Muziek en musici van de Nederlandse Antillen*' as being very talented.[178]

Pianist Wim Statius Muller and Felix Linder perform at Club Union in 1948. To Felix' left is his sister Ana. To Statius Muller's right: Lucca Koch. (photo: private collection of Marcia Linder-Geiger)

The brothers also associated with the young pianist Wim Statius Muller, and, at the end of the 1940s, went to his house regularly to play music. These sessions resulted in performances at Maccabi, where Statius Muller played solo as well. Once, he also accompanied a Yiddish acting couple on the piano. They visited Curaçao around 1948 and sang Yiddish songs for the Club members.

Statius Muller recalled that he and Felix Linder added luster to the official opening of a new section of the Sailor's Home of the Norwegian protestant minister Hindal by playing the violin and the piano. "Governor Piet Kasteel, who inaugurated the building, was Roman Catholic, the violinist was Jewish and the pianist was Protestant."

Felix Linder was later appointed concertmaster of the Philharmonic Orchestra and for more than ten years was the second violinist in the Curaçao String Quartet, founded in 1964 by violin teacher Eric Gorsira.

```
                    voor de
            MUZIKALE MIDDAG
              te geven door
                    V.C.C.
            (vrouwen organisatie Curacao)
              op Dinsdag 6 April 1943
         in de gymnastiekzaal van de A.M.S.
            te Willemstad Curacao N.W.I.

    Medewerkenden:  Mevr. Ph.J.A. Ioslinga-Stoové
                    Mevr. R. Maal-Hamer
                    Mevr. R. Maduro-Moron
                    Mevr. N. Tange-Patten
                    Mevr. B. Erkelens-Fresco
                    Mej.  C. de Vos-Burchart
                    Hr.   Felix Linder
                    Hr.   Bruno Linder

    De totale opbrengst dezer uitvoering komt
    ten goede aan:

          DE MILITAIREN OF CURACAO

                    Aanvang ; 3 u.30 n.m.
```

From the very start, the Ashkenazic Linder brothers performed with Curaçao musicians. During the war, they helped raise money in this way to support the troops. (from the collection of the Mongui Maduro Library, Curaçao)

Cautious Participation in Local Politics

Feeling at home in a society and committing yourself to it can be brought about by actively participating in (local) politics. Yet in the beginning, the Eastern European Jews had absolutely no time for or interest in politics. All of their attention at the time was focused on building up a better life for their families. Besides, they had not yet become Dutch citizens and therefore had no voting rights.

But over time, their interest increased and they started supporting certain political parties financially, especially the Democratic Party (DP) and the National People's Party, later called the *Partido Nashonal di Pueblo* (PNP). As one businessman put it: "If things are going well for the island, things are going well for us."

On the other hand, someone like Salomon Wiznitzer thought it imprudent as a businessman to get involved in politics. His son: "So when a politician came by asking for donations for the party, the Wiznitzers gave equal, modest amounts to each party that knocked on the door."

To some extent, the PNP may have been popular among the Ashkenazim because of William Rufus Plantz. This PNP politician, who hailed from the

Windward Islands, was known as a strong advocate of naturalization for the Ashkenazic Jews after the war. Plantz was Minister of Finance from 1951 to 1954.

Apart from financial support, the Ashkenazim kept politics in the background. This was probably due to a fear of sticking their necks out too far. It was something that Eastern European Jews preferred not to do. The discrimination, the pogroms and the persecution they had suffered before and during the Second World War were still too fresh in their minds. Frieda Fruchter, who came to Curaçao after the war: "As a child I was always taught to keep myself in the background. Not to flaunt my religion or anything else. I can still clearly remember how afraid my mother was of anyone wearing a uniform. When she was strolling down the Breedestraat in Punda and a couple of sailors were to walk in her direction, neatly dressed in white uniforms, my mother would automatically cross the street. The Sephardic Jews had no such fear."

Fajwel Becher (1922-1978) was one of the few Ashkenazim that did get involved in politics. Although he was not on the list of DP candidates, he always joined the electoral parades. His son Ivan was a member of *Hubentut Democratico*, the youth section of the DP, for two years. Behind the scenes, Traytel Oberman was also active in the DP.

Up to the present day, the Eastern European Jews are not very active in local politics.

Active Commitment to Society

During the Second World War, many Ashkenazim voiced their concerns about the developments in the Netherlands. First and foremost, the Ashkenazim were and are grateful to the Netherlands and the Dutch Royal Family for the opportunity they were given to build a new life on Curaçao. So they were just as shocked as all other islanders by the German invasion of the Netherlands on 10 May 1940. When collections came round for the Dutch war victims, they gave generously. Like everyone else, the Ashkenazic women helped knitting shawls for the RAF and for the Dutch that were freezing in the cold some 9,000 kilometers away.

The *Polakos* were also active in the civil militia. This voluntary corps focused on supervising the blackout, keeping watch over the bays and performing policing duties. Many people remembered that their fathers or brothers had joined this volunteer force during the war.

Furthermore, several Eastern European Jews joined the Masonic lodge *Igualdad* in the 1950s, while other Ashkenazim were and still are members of service clubs such as the Rotary Club. It was through these organizations that they performed charity work.

Still, those interviewed outside Ashkenazic circles generally thought that the *Polakos* were not socially involved enough. Some acknowledged the fact that several Ashkenazic Jews have been active in organizations such as the Red Cross or the Princess Wilhelmina Fund. But due to the modest number of Eastern European Jews that still live on Curaçao, this involvement goes largely unnoticed.

At a more personal level, the Jewish storekeepers would always help their staff in times of need. Erwin Koense remembered Herman Gärtner as a socially conscious man that did much for the poor, sometimes via social welfare organizations. "He donated money, but he didn't go around boasting about it."

Accepted as Fellow Citizens

The love of the Ashkenazim for the Netherlands was not unrequited. Their participation in the parade organized on the occasion of Princess Juliana's visit to the island in 1944 was only possible because the political elite had offered them a place in the parade. And that was because they were now accepted as a (new) section of the population.

Eleven years later, on the occasion of Queen Juliana and Prince Bernhard's visit in 1955, the Ashkenazic congregation served as hosts for the royal couple together with the board of the Sephardic congregation. Because the president of *Shaarei Tsedek* was not on the island at the time, the honor of addressing the queen on behalf of the congregation fell to the second vice-president Joske Faerman, who was not a man that loved stepping into the limelight. His daughter remembered that he thanked the queen in his best English for the fact that the Netherlands had 'tolerated' the Jews on Curaçao. But Queen Juliana corrected him: the English word tolerated had a bit of a negative tint to it, she told Faerman. The Netherlands had "accepted the Ashkenazic Jews as fellow citizens", and in her eyes that was something entirely different.

During the royal visit of 1965, Queen Juliana invited the president of *Shaarei Tsedek*, Socher Kirzner at the time, to a reception. Although the reception was held on an important Jewish holiday (his son seemed to remember it was *Yom Kippur,* no less), Kirzner attended the reception anyway. To his great surprise, the queen not only knew who he was, she even asked him why he was not at the *shul*. In her opinion he should not have sacrificed that important day for her.

The Ashkenazim have experienced little or no anti-Semitism on Curaçao. Even their contacts with the approximately one thousand Muslims on Curaçao are good. As far back as the 1930s, Muslims and Ashkenazim have done business together. Some of those interviewed did mention a few negative points, though. The fact that, in the past, white Protestants called them *Polako stinki* (stinking *Polakos*), for example. But it was no different for the Sephardic Jews, recalled Lio Capriles from his own youth. As a child he was sometimes called 'stinking Jew'.[179] Others remembered that at the Roman Catholic schools it was said that the Jews murdered Jesus and the story went round that when Jews die they grow a tail and two horns.

Apart from these negative experiences, the Ashkenazim were and still are accepted on Curaçao as full fellow citizens.

A Jew First and then a Curaçaoan?

Through their work and participation in education, local associations and other social institutions, the *Polakos* were gradually incorporated into Curaçao society. Of course, this participation was not and still is not equally strong in every area. In the areas of education and sports, there were more contacts between the Ashkenazim and the local population than there were in politics. After all, from the beginning, the Ashkenazim attended the existing schools on Curaçao. Their numbers were simply too small to establish their own schools for daytime education.

The fact that they initially all lived in the same neighborhood and that their social lives largely revolved around Club Union is understandable. They had arrived on a strange island and this is how they sought support and comfort with each other. Even the Dutch people that came to work at Shell initially hardly ever mixed with the rest of the population. They lived in gated communities built by Shell (Emmastad and Julianadorp) and just like the Ashkenazim they had their own clubs.

But gradually, the Ashkenazim found their place in Curaçao society, though they were sometimes 'forced' into certain situations by business interests – such as keeping their stores open on the Sabbath and the financial support given to political parties. They also operated outside their own Jewish social network. Any of them that excelled in a certain area (chess, music, sports) soon tried to join Curaçao associations.

It was only when they were seeking a marriage partner that the majority of the Ashkenazim focused on their own group. They still do. It is understandable, because marriages concern religion, an essential part of Jewish culture. As Lily Kisilevich put it: "If you share the same background, things are much easier." The Curaçao Sephardim also sought their marriage partners within their own circles, by the way, until well into the 20th century.

As to the languages that they speak: English, Papiamento, Spanish and Dutch are commonly used at home and at work; the same languages the other population groups of Curaçao speak. Yiddish is still spoken only by a very limited number of Jews.

Despite their social interactions, the Ashkenazim remain *Polakos* to the average islander. Just as each Curaçaoan knows exactly who is Lebanese and who is Portuguese. This is because Curaçao still has a segmented society. The use of the word *Polako* says nothing about the extent to which the Ashkenazim are accepted. They are a part of society, yet at the same time they have a different history from the Afro-Curaçaoans.

Conversely, not all Ashkenazim feel like they are Curaçaoans. For some of them, the economic opportunities on the island were more important than the social benefits. This is obvious from the departure of many Ashkenazim for America or Israel after 1969 and 1983, when the economic tide turned. The ties with Curaçao were apparently not strong enough for the departing Ashkenazim to decide to stay on the island, come what may.

And still today, several Ashkenazim identify themselves first as Jews and only then as Curaçaoans. As one of them put it: "The Sephardic Jews identify themselves first as *yu'i Korsou* and only secondly as Jews. Yet, when it comes right down to it, the Curaçaoans do not accept me as *yu'i Korsou*. So I do not consider myself a Curaçaoan either."

▶ ## Bruno Linder (Sniatyn, 1924)

Bruno Linder (photo Jeannette van Ditzhuijzen)

"In Poland, our father played *klezmer* music on the violin so we, his four children, naturally all played the violin. Soon after we arrived on Curaçao in 1933, my eldest brother Felix took music lessons from Miss Wagenaar, a Dutch woman. Later I also took lessons with her. Across from Miss Wagenaar's lived the German Consul, Carl Fensohn[180], who was a good musician. Because we played the violin, he took an interest in us and Felix and I visited him at least once a week; he lived in a beautiful house in Otrobanda."

"Of course we knew what was going on in Germany at the time. But my father thought that Hitler would disappear from the stage after a couple of years. That is why I am a little hesitant to tell the following: in 1938 a German warship entered the harbor and a big party was held for the German crew in Fensohn's house. The consul had asked Felix and me to play for the Germans at the party and after that the crew invited us back to the ship for a tour. That's how Germans and Jews treated each other on Curaçao at that time."

"In the 1930s, Felix and I played in the I.D.O. (*In de Olie*), a palm-court orchestra set up by Shell employees. At the time, we were about 15 and 13 years old, respectively. This orchestra performed regularly at *Club Asiento*, the club of senior Shell personnel. Our audience there consisted mainly of white Dutchmen and we played mostly classical European music. Herr Fensohn also regularly came to the performances in a chauffeur-driven car. On those occasions Felix and I often rode with him."

"After the I.D.O. disbanded, Felix, my other brother Salomon and I played in the Curaçao Philharmonic Orchestra. We performed for a white and light-skinned Curaçao audience. During the war we also regularly went to the home of the Palm family to play music with pianist Edgar Palm. Like us, the Palms lived in Otrobanda."

"Naturally I had many Jewish friends because you saw them in the synagogue and at the Club. But I also had many Curaçao friends. I knew them from school and we went to each other's houses. And of course we also had contacts with the people that came into the store. Because every other day, Felix and I had to help out at the store." ◀

Epilogue

Moishe Seibald, the first Eastern European Jew to settle on Curaçao, could never have dreamed that one day his grandson would graduate from Harvard Law School. Because Moishe had barely had the chance to go to school during the First World War and left Poland at the age of 16, he probably had little more than an elementary school education. From hardly being educated at all to graduating from one of the world's most prestigious universities: a bigger contrast between the first and the third generations of Ashkenazim is hard to imagine.

The economic development of the Eastern European Jews on Curaçao progressed rapidly. They came to the island with only the clothes they had on their backs, three-quarters of a century later most of them have worked their way up to being prosperous citizens of Curaçao society. Hard work, frugality, considerable ambition and a healthy dose of luck (the establishment of the Shell refinery and later consumer tourism) contributed to this success. Trade is still an important means of earning a living for the Ashkenazim, even though Eastern European Jews are increasingly choosing different professions these days. It is remarkable that these professionals tend to live outside the island of Curaçao.

In the early days, it was undoubtedly difficult for the Sephardim to see how their hegemony in trade gradually crumbled away after the arrival of the Eastern European newcomers. On the other hand, it must have been hard for the Ashkenazim to realize that, after ten to fifteen years of economic success, upward social mobility remained out of reach. According to former bank director Lio Capriles, this was in part due to the fact that they contributed insufficiently to society. "But it was also due to the Sephardic Jews and the white Protestants, who saw themselves as lords and masters of the island. The Ashkenazim were not raised with this status and they encountered resistance from the elite, who kept their distance. Just like us, the Sephardic Jews, who were kept at arm's length for years. Initially, we were also outcasts and it took a long time before we received recognition."

Another reason for the status normally attached to their financial success being withheld, lay in the fact that it all happened too fast. The *Polakos* had achieved economic prosperity, but the rest of the population still remembered them from their 'days of poverty' and simply did not associate an elite class with the former peddlers.

The social aloofness of the early decades that characterized the relationship with the Shephardic Jews has disappeared. A few of the elderly Ashkenazim do still perhaps harbor some resentment toward the Sephardim and some parents have passed this resentment on to their children. But the majority of the second and third generations of Ashkenazim have become friends with

Sephardic Jews – in part due to the Hebrew School. And barely an eyebrow is raised anymore about a marriage between an Ashkenazi and a Sephardi.

In the area of religion, though, the Ashkenazim maintain the Eastern European traditions, at least in so far as this is possible. Only a few of them would welcome a merger with the liberal Sephardim. Apart from the religious differences between orthodox and liberal Jews, the Eastern European *Yiddishkeit* probably plays a role here: apparently, the cultural and traditional aspects of Judaism are more important for the Ashkenazim than they are for the Sephardim. That makes it doubly difficult to bring the two groups together.

After having lived on Curaçao for more than 80 years, the Ashkenazim can still be clearly distinguished from the Sephardic Jews. Other than that, a lot of progress has been made in a couple of generations. The *Polakos* are now accepted members of Curaçao society and have achieved the things they yearned for in Poland or Romania: freedom of religion and economic prosperity.

Notes

1. Under the 'Immigration Act of 1924', the number of immigrants was restricted. The number of immigrants per nationality that was admitted was equal to 2 per cent of the number of people of that nationality that lived in the United States in 1890. Source: American State Department.
2. Until 1959, the name of the company was *N.V. Curaçaosche Petroleum Industrie Maatschappij*. For the sake of convenience, we use the name 'Shell'.
3. Told to the author by Leib's son Sloima during an interview held in December 1992.
4. Langenfeld 1999, pp. 13-20.
5. Emmanuel 1970, p. 335 and p. 337.
6. Langenfeld 1999, p. 83.
7. If a husband was a member of the liberal Temple and his wife a member of the orthodox Mikvé Israel – or vice versa – then they were still buried in the same cemetery. Langenfeld 1999, p. 95.
8. Langenfeld 1999, p. 96.
9. Van Straten 2009, p. 18.
10. Van Straten 2009, pp. 22-24.
11. Van Straten 2009, p. 59.
12. Van Straten 2009, pp. 93-94.
13. Van Straten 2009, p. 12.
14. Posthuma 2000. pp. 70-74.
15. Emmanuel 1957, pp. 261-265.
16. Hendrikse 2003. pp. 6-7.
17. Figures for 1789 from: J.C. Sontag, General Report on Curaçao and dependent islands, appendix no. 16 ARA Council of the Colonies 120. Number of Jews 1902: Van Soest 1977, p. 17. Population numbers in Curaçao after 1789: Central Bureau of Statistics Curaçao. Number of Jews in 1950: *Israëlitische Almanak*, 1950/51. 1968: Karner 1969, p. 68. 2009: figures taken from both congregations. This concerned the number of members, plus children, that lived permanently on Curaçao. Because, from the 1960s onward, several Jews were members of both congregations, the member numbers of the individual congregations cannot be combined. The total number of Jews living on Curaçao is therefore an estimate. Including the foreign members, Mikvé Israel-Emanuel has 203 members and Shaarei Tsedek 180.
18. Not all Eastern European Jews came from a small shtetl. Czernowitz, the capital of Bukovina, had a population of some 90,000 after the First World War, for example.
19. Halpern 1997, p. 14.
20. Mendelsohn 1983, p. 59.
21. Halpern 1997, p. 8.
22. Halpern 1997, p. 18.
23. The Sabbath begins on Friday evening as soon as the sun sets.
24. Lang 1968: http://www.jewishgen.org/yizkor/khorostkov/kho292.html#page321.
25. In 1923, Cuza founded an anti-Semitic political party whose symbol was a swastika (Butnaru 1992, p. 38).
26. For more information on Poland and Galicia between the two World Wars, see Mendelsohn 1983, pp. 10-83.
27. Yiddish began in Germany in the middle ages as the everyday language of the Jews. It is a mixture of German and Hebrew, but also has Slavic and Romanian words. It is written using the Hebrew alphabet. Hebrew is a Semitic language whose history goes back to before the Christian Era. It plays an important role in Judaism and almost all Jewish children are educated in Hebrew. In Israel people speak modern Hebrew.
28. According to Heller (1977, p. 228), the public gymnasia had a higher reputation.
29. Poland had such assimilated Jews, but they were a very small minority (Heller 1977, p. 188).
30. Heller 1977, pp. 51-52.
31. In this context the term *ghetto benches* was used.
32. Hausleitner and Katz 1995, p. 139; Heller 1977, p. 104.

33 According to Heller (1977, p. 101), it is estimated that 80 per cent of Polish Jews lived in poverty in the 1920s.
34 Mendelsohn 1983, p. 75.
35 For more information on Bukovina and Bessarabia in Romania between the two World Wars, see Mendelsohn 1983, pp. 170-211.
36 Sternberg 1962, p. 49.
37 Ioanid, Rado 2000: introduction at http://www.romanianjewish.org/en/In_Romania.html.
38 Hausleitner and Katz 1995, p. 61.
39 Mendelsohn 1983, p. 178 and p. 179.
40 In Czernowitz (the capital of Bukovina) the Jews made up 47.4% of the population in 1919. In 1930, Noua Suliță in Bessarabia, from where many Curaçao Jews originate, was 63.9 per cent Jewish. The Moldavian city of Herța, from where the Cheis family originates, was a quarter Jewish (Beth Hatefutsoth, The Nahum Goldmann Museum of the Jewish Diaspora).
41 Reifer 1962, pp. 1-26.
42 Butnaru 1992, p. 35.
43 In 1930, 97 per cent of the Jews in Bessarabia named Yiddish as their mother tongue. In Bukovina, 80 per cent of the Jews did the same.
44 For a more detailed description of these types: see Mendelsohn 1983, pp. 6-7.
45 Sternberg 1962, p. 30.
46 Mendelsohn (1983, p. 2) defines acculturation as adopting the external characteristics of the majority culture, such as the language. Assimilation goes further: Jews adopt the identity of the majority and are absorbed by this majority. They become Polish or Romanian.
47 In Bukovina, the Jews sent their children more often to public schools. They were initially German and later Romanian (Mendelsohn 1983, pp. 200-201).
48 This text was taken from an address given by Ernö Spritzer in November 1963.
49 Ackerman arrived in February 1929. Perhaps the reference is to the Banana Bloodbath of December 1928, in which several people were killed.
50 This is Chaskiel Katz, a brother of Janina Katz, who was to come to Curaçao with her father after the war.
51 Tonia traveled with the Gerstenbluth family in 1937. The mother, daughter and son Bill were following father Isaac Gerstenbluth (see Prologue and portrait in Chapter 6), who already lived on Sint Maarten. Tonia later married Bernardo Metsch, the owner of the *Casa Bernardo* store.
52 Römer 1979, p. 69.
53 By most of those interviewed the word *Polako* was not considered to be a derogatory term. It was viewed as derogatory if they were called *Polako stinki* or if the context was clearly negative.
54 *Surinaamsch Verslag* 1931, appendix C.
55 Taken from the *Koloniaal Verslag 1926-1930*: Annual Statistical Overview; *Surinaamsch Verslag 1931*; *Curaçaosch Verslag 1932-1935*.
56 Today this wharf is known as the *Sha i Lio Caprileskade*.
57 It wasn't until after the war that most of the Eastern European Jews became naturalized Dutch citizens.
58 According to Heller (1977, p. 197), civil marriages did not exist in Poland at the time.
59 Based on his boat ticket, Salomon's year of arrival (and probably that of Selig as well) can be established as 1930. According to the Curaçao Registry Office, they did not register with the civil authorities until later: Salomon in 1931 and Selig in 1932. Moishe registered in 1930. A civil register did not exist until 1928.
60 The 1st district is 'the city' (Willemstad), the 2nd district consists of the surrounding area: Band'ariba and Band'abou up to and including Grote Berg.
61 Hartog 1961, p. 1136.
62 *Curaçaosch Verslag* 1926 and 1931, appendix B.
63 Pais 1992, p. 8.
64 Pais 1992, p. 8.
65 Pais 1992, p. 22.

66 *Koloniaal Verslag* 1927-1930: Annual Statistical Overview.
67 *Surinaamsch Verslag* 1931, appendix P.
68 Gomes Casseres 2006, p. 64.
69 Gomes Casseres 2006, p. 53.
70 *Curaçaosch Verslag* 1934, p. 20.
71 *Curaçaosch Verslag* 1935, p. 8.
72 *Koloniaal Verslag* 1929, and *Curaçaosch Verslag* 1936.
73 Gomes Casseres 2006, p. 131.
74 From the Foreword by Professor H. Hoetink in *The Sephardics of Curaçao*, Karner (1969).
75 Langenfeld 1999, p. 56.
76 Annexes, Koloniale Raad 1932 (National Archives Curaçao).
77 Annexes, Koloniale Raad 1935/36 (National Archives Curaçao).
78 Koloniale Raad 1932 (National Archives Curaçao).
79 Letter from the Governor of Curaçao to the Minister for the Colonies, No. 315 II/67 (Documentaire informatievoorziening, Curaçao).
80 The name of Jules or Julius Penha was mentioned by several interviewees.
81 Koloniale Raad 1934-35, p.30 (National Archives Curaçao).
82 *Publicatieblad 1937*, No. 58 (National Archives Curaçao).
83 *Curaçaosch Verslag* 1938, p. 13.
84 National Archives The Hague: Ministry for the Colonies, 001940, confidential report, Inventory number 409, V21-11-1933, T-27. www.inghist.nl/Onderzoek/Projecten/RapportenCentraleInlichtingendienst1919-1940/data/.
85 Emmanuel 1970, p. 497.
86 Emmanuel 1970, p. 497.
87 Gomes Casseres 2006, p. 49.
88 According to the Jewish dietary laws, one is not permitted to eat marine animals without scales and fins.
89 On Passover the Jews commemorate the liberation of the ancient Hebrews from slavery and the exodus from Egypt. This departure from Egypt happened so quickly, there was not enough time to let dough rise. Thus the tradition on Passover to eat matzos made without yeast. In order to ensure that not even the smallest amount of bread or leavening agent remains in the house during Passover, the tableware is replaced by clean tableware which is used only for Passover.
90 Emmanuel 1970, p. 497.
91 Santine 1999, p. 419.
92 De Jong 1979, p. 468.
93 For detailed information on the internment on Bonaire and Curaçao, see especially Sint Jago (2007).
94 The internment camp on Bonaire was located beside the sea and after the war it was rebuilt into the Flamingo Beach Hotel, which still exists today.
95 Van der Horst 2004, p. 74.
96 In fact, Ashkenazic Jews and German Jews are the same. The Kywis probably did not want to be associated with the Eastern European Jews.
97 *Beurs- en Nieuwsberichten*, 7 October 1941 (Mongui Maduro Library).
98 Letter from the Attorney General to Governor Wouters, dated 12/11/1941 advising on a telegram to be sent to the Minister for the Colonies, Welter, in London (*Documentaire Informatievoorziening*, Curaçao).
99 *Curaçaosch Verslag* 1942, p. 295.
100 Da Costa Gomez has a Jewish name, but was Roman Catholic.
101 *Curaçaosch Verslag* 1944, p. 135.
102 *Beurs- en Nieuwsberichten*, 7 October 1952: report on the examination of Governor Wouters.
103 *Beurs-en Nieuwsberichten*, 16 October 1952: letter from former Governor Wouters, dated 23 June 1951, to the Board of Inquiry Concerning the Refugee Problem (Mongui Maduro Library).
104 De Jong, 1979, part 9, p. 29.
105 Van der Horst 2004, p. 110.
106 Emmanuel 1970, p. 500.

107 Emmanuel 1957, p. 478.
108 *Maandblad voor Israelitische Huisgezinnen op de Nederlandse Antillen*, September 1945 (Mongui Maduro Library).
109 Van der Horst 2004, p. 113.
110 http://www.bevrijdinginterculureel.nl/eng/antillen.html
111 *Curaçaosch Verslag* 1945, Statistical Overview.
112 *Curaçaosch Verslag* 1943, p. 25; Van Soest 1977, p. 471.
113 Gibbes e.a. 1999, p. 166.
114 *Maandblad voor Israelitische Huisgezinnen op de Nederlandse Antillen*, September 1945 (Mongui Maduro Library).
115 *Curaçaosch Verslag* 1943, p. 18.
116 Van Soest, 1977, p. 482.
117 *Maandblad voor Israelitische Huisgezinnen op de Nederlandse Antillen*, January/March 1943 (Mongui Maduro Library).
118 During *Oneg Shabbat* the children are told exciting stories, they have discussions, sing Sabbath songs or make music in another manner. Delicious snacks and drinks are also an integral part of it. The afternoon is concluded with the *havdalah*. This ceremony marks the end of the Sabbath for which four blessings are spoken: over the wine, over sweet condiments – to hold onto the sweet taste of the Sabbath – over the light of the braided havdalah candle – in the hope that the light will continue to shine in the week to come – and finally, a blessing for God, who has separated the light from the darkness, the six workdays from the Sabbath.
119 *Maandblad voor Israelitische Huisgezinnen op de Nederlandse Antillen*, October/November 1945 (Mongui Maduro Library).
120 As told by her son Tsale Kirzner.
121 Kosher bread is bread that is baked by a Jew under the supervision of a rabbi.
122 *Mikvé Israel, Maandblad voor Israelitische Huisgezinnen op de Nederlandse Antillen*, February 1952 (Mongui Maduro Library).
123 Emmanuel, 1970, p. 497.
124 *Beurs- en Nieuwsberichten*, 18 February 1959 (Mongui Maduro Library).
125 Marriage ceremonies are performed under a *chuppah*, a canopy that symbolizes the new house the newlyweds will set up.
126 Hartog, 1961, p. 856.
127 The Antilles and Suriname became autonomous countries within the Kingdom of the Netherlands in 1950. This was officially established in 1954 via the Statute for the Kingdom of the Netherlands.
128 During the Feast of Tabernacles (Sukkot) the Jews commemorate the 40 years of wandering in the desert. They lived in huts out in the open during these years. During Sukkot, Jews eat in self-made huts (pl. *sukkot*, s. *sukkah*) made of branches.
129 Emmanuel, 1970, p. 492.
130 *Mikvé Israel, Maandblad voor Israelitische Huisgezinnen op de Nederlandse Antillen*, September 1941 (Mongui Maduro Library).
131 At Purim the Jews commemorate the escape of the Jewish people from extermination in the 5th century BC. Queen Esther played a crucial role in this escape. Purim is a jolly festival that resembles Mardi Gras because of its costumes.
132 For more information about the Hebrew School, see Gomes Casseres, 2003, pp. 75-82.
133 The Römer School is a public elementary school.
134 *Tu B'Shevat* is the festival of the new year of trees that is celebrated in January/February.
135 Hassidism is an ultra orthodox movement within Judaism.
136 Gomes Casseres, 2003, p. 81.
137 *Mikvé Israel, Maandblad voor Israelitische huisgezinnen op de Nederlandse Antillen*, July/August 1954 (Mongui Maduro Library).
138 De la Try Ellis, 1946, p. 48 and p. 57, statement IV.
139 Letter from the Attorney General to the Governor, d.d. 5 November 1945 (Documentaire Informatievoorziening, Curaçao).
140 Letter from the Chamber of Commerce to the Governor, d.d. 6 June 1944 (Documentaire Informatievoorziening, Curaçao).
141 De la Try Ellis, 1946, p. 59, staat VI.

142 Gomes Casseres, 1991, p. 84.
143 Hartog, 1961, pp. 1032-1033.
144 Ginsburg, 2003, p. 87.
145 Gibbes et al, 1999, pp. 198-199.
146 Haan, 1998, p. 22.
147 Karner, 1969, p. 68 and Grossman 1977, quoted from Abraham-Van der Mark 2000, p. 268.
148 Gomes Casseres, 2003, p. 72.
149 Gibbes et al, 1999, pp. 198-199.
150 Oostindie (red.), 1999, pp. 118-119.
151 Gomes Casseres, 1991, p. 84.
152 Gomes Casseres, 1991, p. 69.
153 Gomes Casseres, 1991, p. 73.
154 Haan 1998, p. 52.
155 Gomes Casseres, 2003, p. 67.
156 From a letter sent by Shaarei Tsedek to the members of the Jewish congregations on Curaçao (Mongui Maduro Library).
157 From the bulletins of Shaarei Tsedek (Mongui Maduro Library).
158 Between Rosh Hashanah and Simchat Torah lies a period of only a few weeks.
159 In 2009 Shaarei Tsedek had 134 members, of which approximately 103 lived on Curaçao.
160 To the right of the synagogue entrance are written the words: Shaarei Tsedek Ashkenazic Orthodox Jewish Community; the other side of the entrance says: The Herman and Miriam Tauber Jewish Center.
161 Emmanuel, 1970, pp. 516-517.
162 Emmanuel, 1970, p. 530.
163 Letter from F. Frerkens to the Colonial Administration Secretary for Curaçao, dated 20 June 1941 (Documentaire Informatievoorziening, Curaçao).
164 *Israëlitische Almanak*, 1950/51 (Mongui Maduro Library).
165 For information on the Jews of Trinidad, see Jufe et al (1998).
166 Ginsburg, 2003, p. 89.
167 Gomes Casseres, 2003, p. 29 and p. 38.
168 *Mikvé Israel, Maandblad voor Israelitische Huisgezinnen op de Nederlandse Antillen*, April 1948 (Mongui Maduro Library).
169 Gomes Casseres, 2003, p. 74.
170 Gomes Casseres, 2003, p. 188, note 17.
171 *Mikvé Israel, Maandblad voor Israelitische Huisgezinnen op de Nederlandse Antillen*, July/August 1954 (Mongui Maduro Library).
172 For information about B'nai B'rith, see Gomes Casseres, 2003, pp. 71-74.
173 *Amigoe* newspaper, 5 September 1989 (Mongui Maduro Library).
174 This information comes from Gomes Casseres 2003, pp. 33-37 and the *Beurs- en Nieuwsberichten*, 25 January 1966 (Mongui Maduro Library).
175 *Mikvé Israel – Maandblad voor Israelitische Huisgezinnen op de Nederlandse Antillen*, January/February 1947.
176 *Oranje en de Zes Caraïbische Parelen 1948*, p. 120.
177 Van de Walle, 1974, p. 92.
178 Palm, 1978, p. 9.
179 Told to the author in an interview for the *Trouw* newspaper, January 2000.
180 Fensohn originally represented Austria, but after that country had been annexed by Hitler in 1938, he was also seen as the German representative on the island.

Jewish definitions:

Aron Kodesh	– Torah Ark, a cabinet containing the Torah scrolls in the synagogue.
Bar mitzvah	– religious adulthood of boys at the age of thirteen years and one day.
Bat mitzvah	– religious adulthood of girls at the age of twelve years and one day.
Brith milah	– circumcision of boys eight days after their birth.
Challah	– braided bread that is eaten on Sabbath eve.
Chazzan	– religious leader of Jewish services.
Cheder	– private school with a rabbi.
Chevra kadisha	– sacred society of men or women that ensures rituals surrounding death and burial are observed.
Chuppah	– a canopy under which the Jewish marriage ceremony is held. It symbolizes the new house that the married couple will form.
Hachsharah	– education meant for the pioneers (*chalutzim*) who wanted to emigrate to Israel to work in a kibbutz.
Hagadah	– the story attached to Passover (Pesach) about the enslavement and subsequent liberation of the ancient Israelites.
Hamantashen	– three-cornered pastry that is usually filled with prunes and nuts and traditionally eaten during Purim.
Hanukkah	– Festival of lights in commemoration of the rededication of the Holy Temple of Jerusalem in 164 BC.
Havdalah	– the ceremony marking the end of the Sabbath and at which four blessings are recited.
Kol Nidrei	– the prayer with which the Yom Kippur service begins; also the name of the same service.
Menora	– seven-branch candelabrum
Minyan	– a quorum of (at least) ten Jewish men who are thirteen years or older, which is necessary in order to hold an official Jewish service.
Mohel	– person authorized to perform a circumcision.
Moreh	– Jewish teacher
Oneg Shabbat	– an informal gathering for young people that is usually held on Saturday afternoon.
Pesach	– or Passover, commemorating the ancient Israelites' liberation from slavery and the exodus from Egypt.
Purim	– the holiday on which the Jews celebrate the deliverance of the Jewish people from destruction in the 5th century before Christ.
Rosh Hashanah	– Jewish New Year
Seder	– the first evening of Pesach which is coupled with certain traditions and rituals.
Shabbes goy	– a non-Jew (gentile) that performs work that Jews are not allowed to perform on the Sabbath.
Shlogn kapores/ Kaparot	– Transferring one's own sins to a live chicken on the day before Yom Kippur.
Shochet	– ritual slaughterer.
Shofar	– ram's horn which is blown during Rosh Hashanah and Yom Kippur services
Shomer Shabbat	– someone that is shomer Shabbat observes all the rules surrounding the Sabbath.
Sukkot	– Feast of Tabernacles. The Jews commemorate the 40 years the ancient Israelites spent wandering in the wilderness while living in primitive shelters.
Tefillin	– Prayer straps. Black leather straps worn on the left arm and head during morning prayer (except on the Sabbath and during holidays). Each strap has a small cubic box which contains scrolls of parchment inscribed with verses from the Torah.
Tu B'Shevat	– the new year's feast of the trees.
Treife	– non-kosher food.

Yom Kippur	– Day of Atonement. This is the day on which people express remorse for their wrong actions against both their fellow humans and against God.
Yahrzeit	– on the anniversary of someone's death each year at least ten men come together to keep the memory of the deceased alive and to say prayers.

Sources:

Persons that have provided information about the Ashkenazic community
(T = by telephone; E = via e-mail)

Aron Abady (E)
Victor Abady
Paul Ackerman
Ida Aminoff-Hirschberg
Willy Aron Josub
Donald Bakhuis
Yak Baroud
Janchi Beaujon (E)
Ivan Becher
Judith Becher
Doulatram Boolchand
Marie Brandes
Aart G. Broek
Lio Capriles
Sonia Causanschi-Zonenschain (T)
Berny Cheis
Karen Cheis
Esty and Ernest Da Costa-Frankel
Marjorie da Costa Gomez-Brandao
Orlando Cuales
Ena Dankmeijer-Maduro
Jan Willem Ellis (T)
Armand and Hannah Elmaleh
Clara Faerman-Libman (T)
Lupe Felicia (T)
Johnny and Helen Frankel-Ashendorf
Emily David-Fruchter
Nora Fuhrman-Faerman
Fanya Gandelman-Becher
Chaim Jacob Geiger
Frieda Geller-Faerman
Claire Fixman-Seibald
Esther Gal-Jessurun Cardozo (E/T)
Shirley Gärtner
Bill and Tila Gerstenbluth-Cheis
Izzy Gerstenbluth
Lucca Ginsburg-Koch (E)
Ron Gomes Casseres (E)
Clara Goudsmit-Meit
Isaac Grynsztein
Nachman Grynsztein
Omer Grynsztein
Norbert Hendrikse
Isaac and Lily Kisilevich-Bonaparte
Tsale Kirzner
Erwin Koense
Diane Liebeskind-Linder
Bruno Linder
David Linder (E)
Felix and Marcia Linder-Geiger
Lies Linder-Jessurun Cardozo
Elsita Luckman
René Maduro (T)

Janina de Marchena-Katz
Gitta Meit-Fruchter
Michelle Metsch
Adam Morón
Annette Morón
Paul and Taicy Morón-Gerstenbluth
Dolly Paiken-Becher (E)
Frieda Pais-Fruchter
Sonia Racin-Kirzner
Alex Roose
Jaime Saleh
Mirjam Schipper-Moffie (E)
James Schrils (T)
Marijke Schweitz
Benny Seibald
Fela and Leon Seibald-Meit
Liza Seibald-Becher
Morris and Sheila Seibald-Delvalle
Sharon Seibald
Yvonne Serphos-de Castro (T)
Ralph Spritzer
Fanny Sprung-Weisinger (T)
Wim Statius Muller
Dora Suchar-Cheis
Herman and Miriam Tauber-Indich
Jochanan Taytelbaum (E)
David de Vries (E)
Gilbert Wawoe (T)
Leo Wiznitzer (E)
Mark Wiznitzer (E)
Michelle Wiznitzer (E)
Rira Wiznitzer (E)
Ariel Yeshurun
Rosita Zonenschain-Linker

Bibliography

Abraham-Van der Mark, Eva (2000), The Ashkenazi Jews of Curaçao: A Trading Minority, *Nieuwe West-Indische Gids*, vol. 74, nos. 3 & 4, 257-280.

Benjamin, Alan F. (2002). *Jews of the Dutch Caribbean: Exploring ethnic identity on Curaçao*. London: Routledge.

Boskaljon, R. (1958). *Honderd Jaar Muziekleven op Curaçao*. Assen: Van Gorcum & comp. Can be found at: http://books.caribseek.com/Curacao/Honderd_Jaar_Muziekleven_op_Curacao/

Bruggen Bouwen (2004). Eindrapport Tijdelijke Commissie Onderzoek Integratiebeleid (Final Report of Temporary Committee to Study Integration Policy). The Hague: SDU uitgevers, pp. 63-68.

Coomans-Eustatia, Maritza et al (1998). *Breekbare Banden, Feiten en visies over Aruba, Bonaire en Curaçao na de Vrede van Münster 1648-1998*, Bloemendaal: Stichting Libri Antilliani.

Curaçaosche Verslagen (Curaçaoan Reports),1932-1947.

Ditzhuijzen, Jeannette van (2003). *Oog op Aruba Bonaire Curaçao – Geschiedenis, cultuur en natuur van de ABC-Eilanden*. Rijswijk: Uitgeverij Elmar.

Emmanuel, Isaac S. & Suzanne A. (1957). *Precious Stones of the Jews of Curaçao, Curaçaoan Jewry 1656-1957*. New York: Bloch Publishing Company.

Emmanuel, Isaac S. & Suzanne A. (1970). *History of the Jews of the Netherlands Antilles, volume I*, Assen: Royal Van Gorcum.

Evers, Lou (2005). *Jodendom voor beginners*, Amsterdam: De Boekerij.

Jufe, Lorna, Arthur Siegler & Zeno Strasberg (1998). *Calypso Shtetl*, Toronto.

Gibbes, F.E., N.C. Römer-Kenepa & M.A. Scriwanek (1999). *De Bewoners van Curaçao, vijf eeuwen lief en leed 1499-1999*. Curaçao: Stichting Curaçao 1499-1999.

Ginsburg, Lucca (2003). *A Reason Why*. Israel: Bibliobooks.

Gomes Casseres, Charles (1991). *History of Tourism, Tourism Awareness Programme for the Industry*, pp. 67-84, Curaçao.

Gomes Casseres, Charles (2004). *Punda Punda*. Curaçao: Uitgeverij Amigoe.

Gomes Casseres, Jane (2003). *Generation to Generation*, Curaçao.

Haan, Edo (1998). *Antilliaanse instituties: de economische ontwikkeling van de Nederlandse Antillen en Aruba, 1969-1995*, Capelle a/d IJssel: Labyrinth Publication. Can be found at: http://books.google.nl/books?id=dVYkd7O8VeAC&pg=PP1&dq=%22edo+haan%22&sig=ACfU3U3gvTXLMoEjZI1j6CqfoYTQ8XqZrw#PPP1,M1.

Halpern, Sam. (1997). *Darkness and Hope*. New York: Shengold Books.

Hartog, dr. Joh. (1961). *Curaçao. Van Kolonie tot Autonomie (volume II)*, Oranjestad: D.J. de Wit.

Hausleitner, Mariana & Monika Katz (Hrsg.) (1995). *Juden und Antisemitismus im östlichen Europa*. Wiesbaden: Harrassowitz Verlag.

Heller, Celia S. (1977). *On the Edge of Destruction*. New York: Columbia University Press.

Hendrikse, Norbert (2003). *Een Snoek op reis*. Curaçao: Omni Media.

Horst, Liesbeth van der (2004). *Wereldoorlog in de West – Suriname, de Nederlandse Antillen en Aruba 1940-1945*. Hilversum: Publisher Lost.

Jong, dr. L. de (1979). *Het Koninkrijk der Nederlanden in de Tweede Wereldoorlog, volume 9*. The Hague: Staatsuitgeverij.

Karner, Frances P. (1969). *The Sephardics of Curaçao*. Assen: Van Gorcum & comp.

Koloniale Verslagen,1925-1930.

Lang, Morton R. (1968). Summation and Overview of Pre WW1 Chorostkow Until WW2. :In: Shtokfish. D. (Ed), *Chorostkow Book volume 2*, Tel Aviv. Can be found at: http://www.jewishgen.org/yizkor/khorostkov/Khorostkov.html#TOC

Langenfeld, Els en Henk Langenfeld (1999). *Tussen Dood en Recht – De Tempel: van begraafplaats tot Openbaar Ministerie*. Curaçao: Stichting Curaçao Style.

Lansen, Oscar E. (1999). Victims of Circumstance: Jewish Enemy Nationals in the Dutch West Indies 1938–1947. In: *Holocaust and Genocide Studies* V13 N3: pp. 437-458.

Lichtblau, Albert & Michael John (1996). Jewries in Galicia and Bukovina. In: Lemberg & Czernowitz, *Two Divergent Examples of Jewish Communities in the Far East of the Austro-Hungary Monarchy*. Can be found at: http://www.ibiblio.org/yiddish/Tshernovits/Lichtblau/lichtblau.html.

The May days of Curaçao. The full and unaltered report of the Commission set up to study the background and causes of the riots that took place on 30 May 1969 on Curaçao (1970). A publication of the Algemeen Culturele Maandblad *RUKU*.

Mendelsohn, Ezra (1983). *The Jews of East Central Europe between the World Wars*. Bloomington: Indiana University Press.

Oostindie, Gert (red.) (1999). Curaçao 30 May 1969. Stories about the revolt, Amsterdam: Amsterdam University Press.

Oranje en de Zes Caraïbische Parelen (The House of Orange and the Six Caribbean Pearls). *Official commemorative book published on the occasion of the golden jubilee of the reign of Her Majesty Queen Wilhelmina, Helena, Pauline, Maria 1898-31 August 1948* (1948). Amsterdam: Printer and Publisher H. de Bussy.

Pais-Fruchter, Frieda (1992). *Consumentenkrediet op Curaçao* (doctoral dissertation), Curaçao: Faculty of Law for the Netherlands Antilles.

Palm, Edgar (1978). *Muziek en Musici van de Nederlandse Antillen*, Curaçao.
Can be found at: http://books.caribseek.com/Curacao/Muziek_en_Musici_Nederlandse_Antillen/

Palm, J.Ph. de (red.) (1985). *Encyclopedie van de Nederlandse Antillen*. Zutphen: De Walburg Pers.

Posthuma, Roelof (2000). *Zij zullen mij tot een volk zijn, de historie van het jodendom*. Kampen: De Groot Goudriaan.

Pruneti Winkel, P. (1987). *Scharloo, a nineteenth century quarter of Willemstad* Florence: Edizioni Poligrafico Fiorentino.

Reifer, dr. Manfred s.a. (1962). History of the Jews in Bukovina (1919-1944). In: Hugo Gold (Ed.), *History of the Jews in Bukovina (1919-1944), volume II*, Tel Aviv. Can be found at: http://www.jewishgen.org/yizkor/bukowinabook/Bukowina.html#TOC2.

Römer, dr. René A. (1979). *Een volk op weg, un pueblo na kaminda*. A sociological historical study of the Curaçaoan society. Zutphen: De Walburg Pers.

Rupert, Linda (1999). *Roots of our Future, a commercial history of Curaçao*. Curaçao: Curaçao Chamber of Commerce & Industry. Can be found at: http://books.caribseek.com/Curacao/Commercial_History_of_Curacao

Santine, Luis (1999). Sociale Clubs – "Omgevallen Monumenten". In: Henny Coomans e.a. (Red.) *Veranderend Curaçao*. Bloemendaal: Stichting Libri Antilliani.

Sint Jago, drs. Junnes E. (2007). *Wuiven vanaf de Waranda, de interneringskampen op Bonaire en Curaçao tijdens WO-II*. Published in house.

Soest, dr. Jaap van (1977). *Olie als Water, de Curaçaose economie van de twintigste eeuw*. Zutphen: De Walburg Pers.

Spritzer, Ernö (1963). *Levensbericht van Ernö Spritzer*, held for the Rotary Club Wassenaar in 1963.

Sternberg, prof. dr. Hermann (1962). *Zur Geschichte der Juden in Czernowitz*. Tel Aviv: Lidor Press.

Straten, Jits van (2009). *De herkomst van de Asjkenazische joden: de controverse opgelost*. Bennekom: published in house.

Surinaamsch Verslag (Suriname Report), 1931.

Try Ellis, dr. W.Ch. de la, et al (1946). Report of the Commission set up under Colonial Administration order of 10 October 1945, no. 7981, to research and study the political views and wishes held in the City District Curaçao, for the preparation of the National Government Conference, The Hague, 1946.

Vries, Isidoor de (1995). *De vreemde waarheid, herinneringen van een joodse jongen 1921-1948*. Apeldoorn: De Ramshorst.

Walle, J. van de (1974). *Beneden de Wind, herinneringen aan Curaçao*, Amsterdam: Querido. Can be found at: http://www.dbnl.org/tekst/wall006bene01_01/

Furthermore: all bulletins of the three Jewish congregations on the island, including the *Maandblad voor Israelitische Huisgezinnen op de Nederlandse Antillen* from 1940 onward and the *Israëlitische Almanak, Yearbook for the Jewish Communities on Curaçao and Aruba*, published by the Joods Hulp Comité after the war. These are all available to read in the Mongui Maduro Library at the Rooi Catootje estate.

Index

30 May 1969, 163-167

A

Abady, Abraham, 178
Abady, Aron, 152, 179. 181, 204
Abady, Aron Abraham, 82
Abady, Jacobo, 178
Abady, José 100, 126, 178
Abady, Laurie, 154
Abady, Maurice, 178
Abady, Victor, 178, 182
Abrami, Leo, 201
Abramovic, Chaim, 148-150, 191
Acherman, Dunia (Bonaparte), 52, 59
Ackerman, Abram, 34, 38-39, 50, 232
Ackerman family, 217
Ackerman, Paul, 65, 139-140, 177
Ackerman (store), 39,
Adlerstein, David, 81,
AGY, 155
Altnaj, Tonia (Metsch), 40, 101, 104, 232
Altnaj/Altneu, Mozes, 11, 13, 40, 44, 63,
Amine, Rabbi, 191
Antoinette, Ida (Becher), 129, 176, 206
Aquarius, 193
Armon, Rabbi, 181
Aron Josub, Lina, 125
Aron Josub, Willy, 55, 107-108, 128-129, 199, 212
Aron Josub, Zalman, 48, 55, 67, 107
Aron Josub-Faerman, Manea, 48-49, 106-109
Aruba, 143, 169, 190-194
Aurora, La, 84, 166, 212, 221
Ashendorf, Fridel, 49-50
Ashendorf, Helen (Frankel), 115, 196-197
Ashendorf-Streifler, Klara, 49-50

B

Baroud, Yak, 212
BBYO, 122, 155
Becher, Fajwel, 129, 176, 224
Becher, Fanya (Gandelman), 43, 66, 86, 95, 99, 217
Becher, Gershon, 41, 43, 58, 96, 99,
Becher, Ivan, 148-150, 155, 176, 179, 224
Becher, Larry, 128
Becher, Liza (Seibald), 123, 165
Becher-Antoinette, Ida, 129, 176, 206
Becher-Bialostocky, Berta, 41
Benesch, Julius, 86, 140
Bentley, Philip, 151

Berlinski, Leo, 193
Bessarabia, 24, 29-34, 232
Beth Israel (A), 191
B'nai B'rith, 206-207, 208
Bonaparte, Lily (Kisilevich), 51-52, 59, 124-125, 151, 169, 202, 208, 215, 226
Bonaparte, Lupu, 59
Bonaparte, Mark, 128
Bonaparte-Acherman, Dunia, 59
Boy Ecuryweg, 212-213
Brandao, Marjorie (da Costa Gomez), 69
Brandes, Marie, 33, 67, 82, 104, 213
Brandes, Margit, 67
Brandes, Samuel, 34, 67, 81
Brandes-Crivosei, Nettie, 50, 65, 67
Bright, Alan, 181-182
Bruder, Max, 41
Buena Ventura, La, 78
Bukovina, 12, 24, 29-34, 232

C

Capriles, Ivy (Spritzer), 201
Capriles, Lio, 66, 163, 225, 228
Capriles, Sha, 66, 163
Casa Abady, 178
Casa Aron Abady, 178
Casa Bernardo, 84, 232
Casa Bill, 169
Casa Brandes, 67
Casa Cohen, 55, 62
Casa Haime (A), 192
Casa José, 166
Casa Keis, 44, 48, 65, 79, 84
Casa Leon, 165
Casa Los Dos Amigos, 166
Casa Marco, 48, 84, 104
Casa Moderna, 129
Casa Salomon, 129, 166
Casa Seibald, 165
Castro, Max de, 88
Castro, Yvonne de, 88
Castro-Kywi, Elvira de, 88
Causanschi, Nioma, 98, 123
Causanschi-Zonenschain, Sonia, 98
cemeteries:
    Beth Haim, 15, 19, 78
    Berg Altena, 16, 19, 46, 78
    Aruba, 191
Cheis, Berny, 149, 201
Cheis, Dora (Suchar), 11, 22, 31, 34, 47, 65, 78, 79, 93, 94, 97, 130-131, 137, 194-196
Cheis, Hersch, 11, 47, 66
Cheis, Karen, 138, 139

Cheis, Marco, 104, 119, 170, 191
Cheis, Rosa, 130-131
Cheis, Tila (Gerstenbluth), 69, 79, 84, 131, 170
Cheis-Aklipa, Ana, 79
Centraal Joods Comite (Central Jewish Comittee), 208
Chérie, 169
Chic Americano, El, 63
Chisinau, 33
Chorostków, 11, 20-22
Chumaceiro, Rita, 155
Club Union, 9, 81-82, 97-98, 116-123, 178, 199, 206, 207, 218, 221,
Codreanu, Corneliu, 33
Cohen, José, 178
Cohen, William, 55, 178
Cohen Henriquez, Haim, 72
Confianza, La, 64, 129, 159
Conquet, Olivia, 175
Continental, El, 62, 159
Costa Gomez, Moisés da, 90, 233
Costa Gomez-Brandao, Marjorie da, 69
Costa-Frankel, Esty da, 50, 142, 154, 213
Crivosei, Saul, 67
Cuales, Teofilio, 123
Cuban Jews, 207-208
Cuza, Alexander, 22, 31, 32, 34
Curiel, Elias, 72
Czernowitz, 12, 23, 33, 51, 98, 231, 232

D

David-Fruchter, Emily, 109, 205
David's (winkel), 166
Delvalle, Benjamin, 79
Delvalle, Frank, 207
Delvalle, Sheila (Seibald), 208-209
Delvalle, Sol, 79

E

East Indians, 64, 170-171, 211, 217
Economia, La, 84
Ellis, Jan Willem, 167
Elmaleh, Armand, 179-180, 186
Elmaleh, Hannah, 180-181, 185, 186, 187, 216
Elzen, Fanny van der, 151, 179
Emmanuel, Isaac, 75, 78, 81, 145, 187
Esquina, La, 107
Estrella, La, 63, 159

F

Faerman, Esther (Katz), 106-109
Faerman, family, 106-109
Faerman, Fanny (Fruchter), 106-109, 224
Faerman, Frieda (Geller), 43, 57, 107, 139
Faerman, Josif/Joske, 23, 43, 48, 55, 57, 67, 81, 106-109, 130, 225
Faerman, Liza (Vorona), 106-109 194
Faerman, Manea (Aron Josub), 48-49, 106-109
Faerman, Rachel, 106-109, 194
Faerman, Tauba (Sztam), 106-109
Faerman-Libman, Clara, 31, 130, 190
Fama, La, 64
Feintuch, Yossi, 152
Fensohn, Carl, 227, 235
Fischer, Fred, 86
Fitterman, Menachim, 151
Fixman-Seibald, Claire, 116, 138
Flondor, Jancu, 30
Frankel, Esty (Da Costa), 50, 142, 154, 213
Frankel, Johnny, 113-115, 184, 197
Frankel-Ashendorf, Helen, 115, 196-197
Frimmerman, Samuel, 119
Fruchter, Emily (David), 109, 205
Fruchter, Esty, 128
Fruchter, Frieda (Pais), 33, 106-107, 224
Fruchter, Gitta (Meit), 33, 106, 161, 169, 214
Fruchter, Jacobo, 62, 98, 159, 218
Fruchter, Max, 62, 159
Fruchter, Samuel, 106
Fruchter-Faerman, Fanny, 106-109
Fuchs, Adolf, 191-192
Fuhrmann, Charles, 58, 109, 135, 171-173, 192, 212, 218
Fuhrmann-Spritzer, Frida, 171

G

Galicia, 12, 24-29
Gal-Jessurun Cardozo, Esther, 98
Gandelman, Ana, 65, 78
Gandelman, Haim, 55, 65, 78
Gandelman, Marco, 92
Gandelman, Morris, 203, 218, 221,
Gandelman-Becher, Fanya, 43, 66, 86, 95, 99, 217
Gärtner, Henri, 125
Gärtner, Herman, 84, 109, 119, 143, 166, 175, 203, 212, 221, 225
Gärtner, Robert, 125
Gärtner, Shirley, 175, 187
Geiger, Chaim Jacob, 50, 94, 98, 130
Geiger, Marcia (Linder), 50, 55
Geiger, Moishe, 47, 55
Geiger, Rachmiel, 159

Geiger-Zuckerman, Mina, 45, 50
Gelber, Jacob, 143
Gelbstein, Israel, 191-192
Geller-Faerman, Frieda, 43, 57, 107, 139
German Watchmaker, 192
Gerstenbluth, Chava, 192
Gerstenbluth, Isaac, 11, 27, 34, 83-84, 232
Gerstenbluth, Izzy, 154
Gerstenbluth, Jacob Gabriel ('Bill'), 20, 22, 25, 27, 83-84, 139, 143, 169, 170, 174, 179, 185, 232
Gerstenbluth, Taicy (Morón), 204
Gerstenbluth-Cheis, Tila, 69, 79, 84, 131, 170
Ghitman, Saul, 41, 119
Ginsburg-Koch, Lucca (Rachel), 105-106, 123, 138-139, 161, 198-199
Globo, El, 79, 166
Goga, Octavian, 32
Gomes Casseres, Charles, 65, 166
Gomes Casseres, Jane, 204
Gomes Casseres, Ron, 199
Gorsira, Eric, 222
Gottfried, Chaim, 192, 193
Gottfried, Martha (Hirschberg), 193
Goudeket, Maurits, 134
Goudsmit, Artie, 98
Goudsmit-Meit, Clara, 123-124
Grynsztein, Aba, 126
Grynsztein, Esther, 125
Grynsztein, Isaac, 181, 182, 186, 212
Grynsztein, Lazaro, 184
Grynsztein, Meyer, 128
Grynsztein, Nachman, 27, 61, 73-74, 82, 116, 126, 152, 168, 174
Grynsztein, Omer, 174, 179, 181, 185
Grynsztein (store), 61, 79, 138
Grynsztein, Yitzak, 61
Groisman, Jan, 63, 81, 133,
Groisman, Lea (Taytelbaum), 203
Gruzecki-Seibald, A and M, 206

H

Haber, Adolf, 63, 125, 159
Haber, Rachilde en Saartje, 95
Hachsharah, 125-128, 235
Halpern, Sam, 21, 112-113
Hebrew School (Jewish school), 150-154 (see also Moria School)
Hector Henriquez B, 166
Herza, 11, 22, 232
Hias (Hebrew Immigrant Aid Society), 104, 208
Hirschberg family, 43, 100-102
Hirschberg, Ida (Aminoff), 76-77, 100-102, 104, 116, 192, 198

Hirschberg, Lucien ('Lucky'), 193
Hirschberg, Max, 81
Hirschberg, Victoire (Karter), 100
Hirschberg-Gottfried, Martha, 193
Hirschberg-Schwarzburd, Frieda, 66

I

Internment on Bonaire, 86-88, 89-90, 233
Internment on Curaçao, 88-90
Internment on Trinidad, 194

J

Jessurun Cardozo, David, 109, 131, 134, 140, 146
Jessurun Cardozo, Esther (Gal), 98
Jessurun Cardozo, Isaac, 78, 89, 99, 109, 125, 130-131, 146, 148, 193, 198
Jessurun Cardozo, Lies (Linder), 135, 139-140, 161, 164-165, 168, 199
Jewish Aid Committee (Joods Hulp Comité), 91, 104, 205
Jewish Country Club (A), 95, 97, 191, 193, 194
Jewish Joint Distribution Committee (JJDC), 89, 91
Jewish School/Hebrew School, 150-154 (see also Moria School)
José Faerman (store), 55
Josub, see Aron Josub

K

Kan, Isidoor, 194
Kasteel, Piet, 90, 91, 96, 193, 222
Katz, Adolf, 106-107
Katz, Bumek, 112-113
Katz, Chaskiel, 232
Katz, Jehuda, 105, 113
Katz, Janina (De Marchena), 20, 21-22, 25, 28, 105, 112-113
Katz-Faerman, Esther, 106-109
Kirzner, Socher, 119-120, 143, 163, 170, 174-175, 179, 181, 225
Kirzner, Tsale, 119-120, 128, 134-135, 138, 141, 148, 151, 155, 163, 164, 168, 170
Kirzner-Schusterman, Fania, 110-111, 119-120, 148
Kisilevich, Chaim, 57, 62, 78, 123, 179, 193
Kisilevich family, 217
Kisilevich, Isaac, 78, 86, 120, 123, 126, 141, 165, 193, 202, 203, 212
Kisilevich, Sonia, 65, 104, 123, 204

Kisilevich-Bonaparte, Lily, 51-52, 59, 124-125, 151, 169, 202, 208, 215, 226
Koch, Lucca (Rachel), 105-106, 123, 138-139, 161, 198-199
Koense, Erwin, 212, 221, 225
Kywi, Elvira (De Castro), 88
Kywi, Max en Erni, 88, 233

L

Lago refinery (A), 190, 192
Lebanese, 57, 164, 178-179, 211
Lerner, Ezra, 29, 47, 53-54
Levin, Martin, 135, 151, 208
Libman, Aron, 41, 78, 190
Libman, Clara (Faerman), 31, 130, 190
Libman-Jufe, Beila, 41, 65, 78
Lindauer, Andy, 128
Linder, Bruno, 59, 65, 78, 79, 137, 145, 199, 205, 215, 218, 221, 227
Linder, Elias, 24, 40, 59, 66, 78, 138, 161, 218
Linder, family, 81
Linder Felix, 65, 145, 205, 221-222, 227
Linder, Salomon, 140, 161, 164-165, 168, 199, 221, 227
Linder-Geiger, Marcia, 50, 55
Linder-Jessurun Cardozo, Lies, 135, 139-140, 161, 164-165, 168, 199
Linder (store), 161, 164
Linder's soda fountain/refreskeria, 65, 161
Louvre, El, 166

M

Maccabi, 98-100, 123-125, 178, 193, 199, 217, 218, 222
Maduro, Amador, 171
Maduro, Salomon, 90
Maduro & Curiel's Bank, 16, 66, 163, 166
Marchena, Armando de, 105
Marchena, Atilio de, 48, 62, 66, 131
Marchena-Katz, Janina de, 20, 21-22, 25, 28, 105, 112-113
Maslin, Simeon, 16, 150, 154, 155, 191, 201, 202, 208
Meit, Clara (Goudsmit), 123-124
Meit, Fela (Seibald), 123-124, 134, 202
Meit, Isuhar, 119, 218
Meit, Mozes Jr., 55
Meit, Pinhos/Piet, 98, 161, 215
Meit, Sunye, 125, 166
Meit-Acherman, Lea, 52
Meit-Fruchter, Gitta, 33, 106, 161, 169, 214
Metsch, Bernardo, 84, 109, 212, 217, 232
Metsch family, 135, 138

Metsch, René ('Rennie'), 128
Metsch-Altnaj, Tonia, 40, 101, 104, 232
Milstein, Fanya, 205
Milstein, Shlom, 81, 177
Milstein-Rosenfeld, Fruma, 177
Modernista, La, 166
Moffie, Jopie, 128
Moffie, Mirjam (Schipper), 154
Moreno, Norma, 204
Moria School, 119, 145-148, 152
Moroccan Jews, 179-181
Morón, Adam, 122. 152, 181-182, 184-185
Morón, Annette, 120, 121, 155-156
Morón, Paul, 120, 153, 181, 204
Morón-Gerstenbluth, Taicy, 204

N

New Store, the, 55
New York Store, 63, 159
Noua Suliță, 12, 98, 232

O

Oberman, Traytel, 135, 184, 202, 224
Oduber & Kan, 194
Oranjewinkel, 159
Oriental Store, 63
OSE, 104, 204-205

P

Pais-Fruchter, Frieda, 33, 106-107, 224
Peicher & Kardonski, 41, 191
Peller, Aaron, 175, 209
Penha, Julius, 72
Piłsudski, Józef, 27
Pimsler, Samuel, 63, 81, 159
Poupko, Rabbi, 121-122, 152, 182

R

Rabinovich, Josef, 135
Refreskeria Linder/soda fountain, 65, 161
Relojeria Alemana, 171
Refinery (Shell), 11, 54, 57, 62, 94, 161, 164, 169, 210-211, 226, 230
Renaissance, 173
Riks, Benjamin, 116
Rivièra, La, 166
Roitman, Carlos, 116

S

Sarfatti, S., 178
Schächter, Nathan, 78, 128, 133, 134, 148, 206, 213-214
Schächter, Rozika, 128
Schipper-Moffie, Mirjam, 154
Schmidt, Bertha, 149, 204-205
Schnog, Alfred, Erika en Leo, 88
Schrils, James, 214
Seibald, Basea, 53
Seibald, Benny, 139, 144, 166
Seibald, Claire (Fixman), 116, 138
Seibald family, 53, 77, 135, 136, 138, 144
Seibald Jozef ('Dikke'), 109, 165
Seibald, Leon, 25, 28, 39-40, 54, 78, 99, 109, 134, 153, 165, 181, 184, 212
Seibald, Mali (Gruzecki), 206
Seibald, Moishe, 11, 13, 45, 53-54, 56, 109, 144, 166, 213, 228, 232,
Seibald, Morris, 148-149, 201, 202, 209
Seibald, Salomon/Sloime, 38, 54, 81, 166, 213, 232
Seibald, Selig, 40, 54, 68, 78, 213, 232
Seibald, Sharon, 136
Seibald, Suzy, 201
Seibald-Becher, Liza, 123, 165
Seibald-Delvalle, Sheila, 208-209
Seibald-Landskroner, Rachel, 109
Seibald-Meit, Fela, 123-124, 134, 202
Shell, 11, 54, 57, 62, 94, 161, 164, 169, 210-211, 226, 230
Schusterman, Leib/Shuman, Leo, 111, 184
Silberstein, Pesa, 95
Silbiger family, 91
Silverman, Ron, 201
Sitzer, Isaak, 128-129
Slavensky, Pavel, 151, 209
Slobbe, Bartholomeus van, 71
Smit, Ben, 92
Sniatyn, 12, 59
Spritzer, Ernö, 23, 34-36, 50-51, 98, 171-173, 193, 201
Spritzer, Frida (Fuhrmann), 171
Spritzer, Ralph, 23
Spritzer, Wolf, 34-36, 50-51, 58, 65, 171
Spritzer-Capriles, Ivy, 201
Spritzer, Rachel (Weisz), 171
Spritzer + Fuhrmann, 157, 164, 166, 167, 171-173, 193, 206
Sprung-Weisinger, Fanny, 66, 79, 120, 187
Statius Muller, shon 'Eti', 217
Statius Muller, Wim, 217, 222
Steiger, Ulli, 175
Sterental brothers, 65
Sterental, Mary, 205

Suchar, Jacob en Moses, 194
Suchar, Philip, 130, 194
Suchar-Cheis, Dora, 11, 22, 31, 34, 47, 65, 78, 79, 93, 94, 97, 130-131, 137, 194-195
Swerling, Norman, 151, 154, 201
Synagogues:
   Mikvé Israel/snoa, 9, 75
   Tempel Emanu-El, 9, 16
Shaarei Tsedek:
   Bargestraat, 9, 77-78, 130, 131
   Scharloo, 9, 120, 131-134, 177
   Lelieweg, 177, 185
   Magdalenaweg, 176-177, 182-185
Szmukler, Gersz, 67, 77, 79, 96, 133, 182
Szmukler-Hamer, Sarah, 78
Sztam, Zelik, 107
Sztam-Faerman, Tauba, 106-109

T

Tauber family, 56, 59, 135, 136, 138
Tauber, Herman, 40, 48, 54, 62, 68, 96, 109, 161, 167, 182, 184, 193, 212
Tauber Hermanos, 57, 96, 161, 164, 166-167, 212
Tauber, Leon, 40, 57, 59, 62, 64, 96, 161, 167, 193
Tauber, Paulette, 128
Tauber-Indich, Miriam, 109-110, 193, 199
Taytelbaum family, 91-92
Taytelbaum, Jochanan, 203, 212
Taytelbaum-Groisman, Lea, 203
Tayvah, Rabbi, 152
Tayvah, Paola, 156
THE No. 1 Store, 191
Torah Island, 154
Transnistria, 106
Trinidad, 194-196
Truzman, moreh, 151

V

Violetta, La, 51
Vorona, Isaac, 107, 194
Vorona, Karny, 206
Vorona, Shura, 194, 212
Vorona-Faerman, Liza, 106-109, 194
Vorona's, 166
Vreugdenhil, 166
Vries, Isidoor de, 194
Vries, Jaap de, 194

W

Wawoe, Gilbert, 212, 217
Weinstein, Fannie, 128
Weisinger, Fanny (Sprung), 66, 79, 120, 187
Weisinger, Wilu, 34, 105, 194, 196
Weisz, Rachel (Spritzer), 171
Welter, Charles, 89
Wiznitzer, Abraham/Avrum, 23, 109, 129, 143, 175, 179, 213
Wiznitzer Brothers, 23, 64, 80, 159, 179
Wiznitzer, family, 137-138
Wiznitzer, Mark ('Butchie'), 119, 128-129, 141, 191, 213, 218, 223
Wiznitzer, Moishe, 135, 213
Wiznitzer, Rita, 125
Wiznitzer, Salomon, 101-102, 129, 141, 191, 198, 213, 223
Wiznitzer, Shmiel, 213
WIZO, 204-205
Wouters, Gielliam, 86, 88-91
Wolf, Salko de, 128
Wuhl, Hanah, 111

Y

Yeshurun, Ariel, 79, 152, 153-154, 174, 179, 182, 185, 186, 188
Yohai, Isaac, 92

Z

Zadoks family, 91
Zahavi, Gideon, 185
Zahavi, Ori, 179, 185
Zelkovicz, Hirsh, 150, 151
Zigzag, 165, 169
Zonenschain, Leib, 11, 13, 34, 138
Zonenschain, Sloima, 179, 217, 218, 221
Zonenschain, Sonia (Causanschi), 98
Zonenschain-Linker, Rosita, 34
Zuckerman, Mina (Geiger), 45

A Shtetl under the Sun, the Ashkenazic Community of Curaçao
Jeannette van Ditzhuijzen

Jeannette van Ditzhuijzen lived on Curaçao from 1990 to 1994, where she worked for the local newspaper *Amigoe*. Since then she has returned to the island regularly to write about Curaçao for Dutch newspapers and magazines. She has also written several books on Curaçao and the other islands. Van Ditzhuijzen lives in Almelo and works as a freelance journalist.

KIT Publishers
Mauritskade 63
Postbus 95001
1090 HA Amsterdam
E-mail: publishers@kit.nl
www.kitpublishers.nl

© 2011 KIT Publishers – Amsterdam/Jeannette van Ditzhuijzen

This book was brought about with support from the Jewish Historical Museum, Amsterdam (*Joods Historisch Museum*, www.jhm.nl) and the Fund for Special Journalistic Projects (*Fonds voor Bijzondere Journalistieke Projecten*, www.fondsbjp.nl).

The English language version of this book was produced with financial support from the Prince Bernhard Cultural Fund for the Netherlands Antilles and Aruba (*Prins Bernhard Cultuurfonds Nederlandse Antillen en Aruba*).

Several private individuals have also made financial contributions:
Berny & Lily Cheis and family
Karen Cheis and family
Bill(†) & Tila Gerstenbluth
Izzy & Sandra Gerstenbluth and family
Prof. dr. Lorraine M. Uhlaner & Tsale Kirzner, in honor of his parents Socher and Fania Kirzner and his uncle Leo Shuman
Janina de Marchena-Katz
Paul & Taicy Morón and family
Mark Wiznitzer, in honor of his parents Salomon Wiznitzer and Ida Hirschberg

With a special thanks to: Mongui Maduro Library Curaçao

Editing: Ingrid Smeets, Inkwell Texts & Translations, Nijmegen
Translation: Paul Towles, drs. Frans de Graaff and Rebecca Harlan, MA
Cover photographs: Jeannette van Ditzhuijzen (front cover) and Esther Gal-Jessurun Cardozo (back cover).
Cover design and inside design: Nel Punt, Weesp
Lithography and production: Hightrade, Zwolle

No part of this publication may be reproduced and/or transmitted by means of print, photocopying, microfilm or by any other means without the prior written permission of the publisher.

ISBN 978 94 6022 157 6
NUR 514/716